Help Me to Help My Child

Help Me to Help My Child

A SOURCEBOOK FOR PARENTS
OF LEARNING DISABLED CHILDREN

Jill Bloom

With a Foreword by
David K. Urion, M.D.

Director, Learning Disabilities Program
Children's Hospital, Boston

Little, Brown and Company
BOSTON   TORONTO   LONDON

FIRST EDITION

LIBRARY OF CONGRESS
CATALOGING-IN-PUBLICATION DATA

BLOOM, JILL.
    HELP ME TO HELP MY CHILD : A SOURCEBOOK FOR
PARENTS OF LEARNING DISABLED CHILDREN / JILL BLOOM.
        P.   CM.
    INCLUDES BIBLIOGRAPHICAL REFERENCES.
    ISBN 0-316-09981-3
    1. LEARNING DISABLED CHILDREN — EDUCATION —
UNITED STATES.
    2. EDUCATION — UNITED STATES — PARENT PARTIC-
IPATION.   I. TITLE.
    LC4705.B59   1990
    649'.15 — DC20   89-12854
                                                        CIP

        10 9 8 7 6 5 4 3 2

                MV–PA

        Text design by Joyce C. Weston

        Published simultaneously in Canada
        by Little, Brown & Company (Canada) Limited

    PRINTED IN THE UNITED STATES OF AMERICA

To all the Leanas of the world,
but most especially
to my Leana, the one and only

The author would like to acknowledge gratefully the support of the following people:

Mary Briggs, who provided expertise, assistance, support, and invaluable talent as a teacher;

Lois Carra, who offered thoughtful suggestions and pertinent information about testing and the psychological aspects of LD;

Susan Protter, whose insight and savvy in the publishing business were instrumental in getting this project off the ground;

Kit Ward and her staff, whose enthusiasm and direction were essential to its completion;

the many LD kids and their families who shared their thoughts and ideas with me;

my family, who supported my efforts in researching and writing this book and who provided living proof that it *can* be done.

CONTENTS

Foreword by David K. Urion, M.D.   xi

Introduction   3

Chapter 1: What *Are* Learning Disabilities?   13

Chapter 2: How Do We Find the LD Child?   35

Chapter 3: Where Do Learning Disabilities Come From?   67

Chapter 4: How Do We Find Out?   93

Chapter 5: How Do We Make It Happen?   133

Chapter 6: Meanwhile . . . What Happens When School Gets Out?   162

Chapter 7: Teaching Survival Strategies   180

Chapter 8: What Can We Do about LD?   202

Chapter 9: What Does the Future Hold?   234

Appendix A: National and Local Resources   251

Appendix B: The ANSER System   275

Appendix C: Guides and Directories   293

Glossary of Useful Terms   295

Bibliography   300

Index   306

FOREWORD

Most professionals dealing with children who exhibit those neuro-behavioral disorders we call "learning disabilities" will recognize themselves in the following parable:

During the second Vatican Council, there was a convocation of the monastic orders. It was decided that an evening service would be held to celebrate this wonderful event in a spirit of friendship. During the vespers, the lights went out quite suddenly. For the Benedictines present, this posed no trouble. They had been cele-brating the service unchanged for hundreds of years, and each knew the words by heart. The Franciscans thought for a moment, and then prayed to Sister Moon, that she might send a beam of light down on their missals so that they might read. The Domin-icans remembered that the blessed St. Thomas Aquinas had ar-gued that there were four proper and proportional causes of light; by correct and specific analogy, they attempted to deduce the causes of unlight, and thereby solve their problem. The Jesuit present went to the basement and changed the fuse.

The Learning Disabilities Clinic at Children's Hospital, Boston, serves hundreds of families who seek help for their children's learning problems. For all the professional dedication of our staff, parents too often find our advice Benedictine, our examinations of their children somewhat Dominican. And the vast majority of published material for families could be kindly considered Franciscan.

Finally, someone has changed the fuse. Jill Bloom has done us all a marvelous service in writing this splendid book. It is practi-cal, well-researched, and contemporary. Where controversy ex-ists, she addresses it and represents all sides quite evenly. As the parent of a learning disabled child, Ms. Bloom understands the complexities of such subtle but far-reaching disorders and gently takes all of us who are perplexed through the processes of evaluation, diagnosis, implementation, remediation, rehabilitation, and life beyond.

For those of us who deal daily with parents, children, and schools, this book will serve as a rational, well-organized resource, full of useful information and sources of further information. Most important, for all those families who have been struggling on behalf of their children, it will comfort the afflicted, and help them afflict the comfortable.

DAVID K. URION, M.D.
Director, Learning Disabilities Program
Children's Hospital, Boston

Help Me to Help My Child

Introduction

HERE is how it usually goes: early on, everything seems fine. The child is beautiful, bright, and deliciously unpredictable. Then, slowly it becomes clear that there is a problem. Nothing major, of course, nothing cataclysmic, but something worrisome, all the same. Little things light up like warning flares, extinguished almost before they're registered by the cheery normalcy of the child, and by our own refusal to recognize the nature of the light.

Only with hindsight are we able to piece together all the facts and realize that what we now see clearly has been there all along. There is no blame. It's just that the individual signs were so mutable, so insignificant in and of themselves. How could we possibly have known they would add up to this?

It doesn't always happen this way. There are other scenarios, but they are often heartbreakingly similar in terms of the effect they have on us. In the beginning, the feeling of being duped is overwhelming. In some ways, coming to terms with that feeling takes the longest time of all.

For the children, of course, it is more than just a feeling. School is the worst part. That bright, beautiful, delicious child is, for some reason, unable to function as well as the others in class. It doesn't matter what the particular problem is — an inexplicable and persistent lag in reading skills or a crippling inability to attend to learning basic academic functions — the feelings those problems create are still the same.

For the child: confusion, insecurity, anger, and fear. For us: the same, along with a healthy dollop of guilt and helplessness.

"Your child has a learning disability."

"Your child is dyslexic."

"Your child may have minimal brain dysfunction, or an attention deficiency disorder, or a central nervous system disorder."

"Your child is perceptually handicapped."

"We don't know what's wrong with your child, but clearly there's *something* wrong."

It doesn't much matter what the words are. The feelings they create and the havoc they raise in our lives are still the same, for us and for our children. And the immediate question that arises — and must remain painfully unanswered in so many cases — is: why? Why me, why my child?

An Untestimonial

I really wanted to avoid starting this book with a testimonial — you know, the kind you read in so many self-help books: "My child had this, and I did this, and this was the result." The implication of those books, whether written by parents or by professionals — that if *you* do the same thing, *your* child will get the same results — has always made me uncomfortable.

But Leana's story was the driving influence behind the writing of this book, and, if I promise not to draw any universal conclusions from it, I think it will help you to hear it. It will put the scenario I described above into much sharper focus.

Leana was a normal baby in every way — a bit high-strung, perhaps, and a terrible sleeper, but she talked at the "right" time and toilet-trained at the "right" time, and even learned to walk "early." We were so giddy with delight at having her that we indulged her volatility and sensitivity, attributing those traits to the high level of intelligence she so clearly possessed.

But when she was in kindergarten, a wonderful teacher gently pointed out to me that, while Leana was clearly able to keep up with her peers, she seemed to be having trouble with some basic organizational skills. Recognizing letters or numbers was very

4

hard for her, and her attempts at printing her name produced a hodgepodge of missized letters that wandered all over the page. This in itself wasn't unusual for a five-and-a-half-year-old, were it not for the fact that her grasp of concepts far exceeded her ability to execute them. In addition, she seemed to have a hard time with transitions from one activity to another, and any change in the classroom routine really threw her off balance.

In the first grade, these difficulties became more marked as her classmates began to learn how to read and write. As Leana fell further behind her peers, her behavior, her attitude, and her self-image deteriorated. She gave up trying and concentrated on being a clown instead of on attempting to decode the alphabet. An inept teacher regularly kept her in at recess for her infractions, and even sent her to the principal's office for her failure to shape up.

In the midst of our panic, Leana's father and I realized that it was time to do something. A return to kindergarten was suggested, but we thought that would only postpone the problems until the following year. Although core evaluations — comprehensive examinations of Leana's basic abilities, current skill levels, and medical and psychological profiles — were not recommended until the third grade, we agreed that an earlier assessment was in order.

The tests revealed the high intelligence we had always suspected, but also indicated an array of perceptual problems and Leana's grave doubts and anxieties about her abilities. Remedial help would be necessary to bring her skills up to grade level, and a second year of first grade was recommended to reduce the pressure of competing with kids who could do easily what came so hard to her.

It took us some time to absorb this diagnosis — a lot longer than it took Leana, who at first seemed more relieved than anything else to find that her mysterious "badness" had a name and that, with a lot of hard work, we could do something about it.

But we went through the same emotional process that you have gone through — or are going through now: the denial, the anger, the grief and guilt, and finally the acceptance. (More later about coping with our reactions as parents and people.) The stages we went through are the classic stages of mourning, and in some way, we *were* mourning the loss of the child we hoped would be: the child who breezed through life with no handicaps or traumas, who was able to conquer every goal she encountered and emerge feeling good about herself. It took us quite a while to digest the fact that some things — easy for so many of her peers — would be so hard for her. We're still trying to digest it.

And Leana is, too.

THE story ends there because this book is not intended to be a testimonial, either to Leana's victories, or to those of her teachers and therapists. After all, what has or has not worked for her might not hold true for your child. Besides, what's important is not Leana's story, but the fact that the only common denominator we have — and our children have — are those feelings of love and pain. No matter what story you have to tell, loving your child and feeling pain on his or her behalf is going to be a part of it, just as it was for me.

Good Intentions Are Not Enough

There's one other thing we all share in common, and that is the fierce determination to do whatever is necessary to improve the situation. At first the determination may be drowned in confusion or helplessness, but it's there, and it's one of the first and best forces that we can draw upon as parents.

Unfortunately, determination alone is not going to help us to help our children. No matter how much we want to help, we won't be effective unless we know what to do and how to do it. We need the *skills* to be able to advocate on their behalf, and the *knowledge* to be able to get them the kind of help that is most effective in their particular cases. Without that knowledge and those skills, the determination may be as frustrating to us as their learning disabilities must be to our children.

That is what this book is all about: the *feelings* that we and our children are experiencing when we find that there is a learning problem, the *knowledge* to help us understand those problems, and the *skills* to do something about them. It's about helping us to help our children, and about helping us *as well as* our children.

The background material in this book is extensive, but the main objective of the book is to motivate you to get out there and do what needs to be done for your child. *Help Me to Help My Child* will answer, in detail, these basic questions about learning disabilities:

What are they?
How did our children "get" them?
How can we tell they've got them?
What do the experts say about them?
How do other parents and children cope with them?
What can we do about them?
Where can we go to get help for them?
What are my legal rights regarding my child's education?

Why Another Book on LD?

What qualifies me to write this book? Certainly my experience as a parent hasn't been any guarantee of success, and I am not an expert in any portion of the vast body of knowledge that concerns itself with learning disabled children. I did not set out to write the definitive scholarly treatise on learning disabilities; that can be done far more effectively by scholars in the field, although even the scholars agree that there is no such thing as definitive when it comes to LD.

My professional curiosity, and my experience as a journalist and writer, led me to investigate this mysterious concept of "learning disability," perhaps beyond the point where it affected Leana, but I believe my skills as an involved parent and advocate were my strongest assets in writing this book. What started out as a personal quest became a professional obsession.

In my search for answers for Leana, I found answers to questions that had nothing to do with her and many questions that had no clear answers at all. By the time I sat down to write this book, I had devoted many long hours of study to the field of learning problems. I worked as a writer researching a subject in order to understand the issues, but I maintained my perspective as a parent who wanted to be able to resolve them.

As a writer I wanted to organize and clarify as much information as possible. As a parent, however, I paid particular attention to two areas: how those problems affect my child, my family, and myself, and what possibilities for treatment exist. In both areas, I looked for as many alternatives as possible, because I don't believe that any one answer works for everyone, any more than that there was one answer for Leana.

But, even with those self-imposed limitations, deciding to investigate the subject of learning disabilities was like poking a hole in a dike: after an initial, unsatisfying trickle, an incredible amount of information about LD suddenly came pouring out of the libraries and computers. Each book or journal I read cited dozens of other "must-read" sources. Each led me down other possible paths of study, all apparently indispensable to the complete understanding of the field.

The sheer bulk of the information was far too great for me to absorb, even with the time and research skills I was willing to invest. It seemed that the only way I could get a really good grasp of Leana's problem was by devoting myself to full-time study and the pursuit of a graduate degree. This was not an option for me as a working parent. More important, it wasn't in keeping with my original goal: to write a practical, hands-on guide for parents like myself. If I couldn't get a handle on the subject, how could other parents learn what they needed to know?

THERE were several problems with the material. Books available in bookstores and articles in the popular press were often written by experts who were pushing their own success stories in terms of research or treatment; many of them read like those professional testimonial "how-to's" I distrust. I already knew enough to be aware that what worked for one child did not necessarily work for another, so those uplifting stories of victory (with the implication that victory came only if one did it the author's way) were useless to me. What good was it for me to know that program A worked for Johnny and program B worked for Jane? I wanted to know about *all* the programs that could possibly work for *all* types of kids.

The research material provided in professional libraries was less self-promoting, but it presented a different problem. Most of the information was highly technical and specialized, going into great depth about specific aspects of the subject without answering the basic questions I had. I did not yet know about the ongoing controversies in the field, with eminent scholars debating everything right down to the very existence of LD. No one seemed to be able to say exactly what a learning disability was, let alone where it came from or what to do about it, a fact that I found very disheartening as a parent and as a writer. While I gained an excellent layman's grasp of the subject, the material seemed to have little practical use.

Besides, much of the information in the professional journals was contradictory, making it even more impossible to get the facts straight. Depending on the orientation of the author or the journal, learning disabilities were discussed at length by experts in the fields of education, psychology, neurology, pediatrics, sociology, statistics, and law. Sometimes the information in one field made sense if looked at from the perspective of another, and sometimes not. More often, theory A was well defended by one scholar and well demolished by another, even within a discipline. Unraveling the conflicting information seemed like a hopeless task.

As a parent, I felt that I should not be excluded from the material because of these restraints — it was not my failure to comprehend the information, but the failure of those who wrote it to make it comprehensible to *me,* a parent, and the end user, so to speak, of all those theories and hypotheses. (There are a few newsletters that focus on helping parents: *Their World,* published by the Foundation for Children with Learning Disabilities, and the Association for Children with Learning Disabilities *Newsbrief,* along with newsletters published by individual state branches.) My need for knowledge wasn't just wishful thinking, either — it was my right, by federal law, to be informed about my daughter's learning problem, and to consent to her legally mandated treatment.

I still felt, though, that my only power to help Leana lay in collecting as wide a variety of information as I possibly could. I wanted to be able to get my hands on as much information as possible, as efficiently as possible. I wanted basic background information in a variety of disciplines without having to get an advanced degree in the field. I wanted to know the meaning of the technical terms that were being thrown at me. I wanted to know why LD had happened to my child. Most of all, I wanted to know what could be done to make life better for her, and how to make sure that it *was* done.

In Search of Knowledge and Skills: The Parent as Consumer

I wrote *Help Me to Help My Child* because such a book didn't seem to exist. *Help Me to Help My Child* is a *consumer book;* as parents, it is we who are the consumers of the evaluative and therapeutic services for our children. It is a *sourcebook;* as parents, we are obligated to make the best decision possible for our children, and in order to make it, we need the widest variety of information possible. It is a *nontechnical book;* as parents, we need to have all the possibilities laid out for us in simple language. It is a *support book;* as parents, we need to be able to help our children feel better about themselves and to feel that we are not alone in our struggle to do that.

Most important, though, it is simply a practical *guidebook* to help parents get the best help for their LD children in the most efficient and effective manner.

The notion of a consumer guide on such an unwieldy topic as LD may seem simplistic, but the information in this book is not superficial. It is a digest of current available information and a source for more in-depth study materials. As parents, we are consumers of information and services, and we can no longer be cowed by the implication that we are unable to absorb all the technical intricacies of the field and thus are better off being led down whatever therapeutic path our local experts deem best for our children.

Many times, those experts are right. But it helps us to *know* that fact and not just to have to trust it. As with all consumer services, the more we know, the better off we are. We don't want or need to know it all — certainly not in the technical detail that appears in professional publications. After all, we are parents, not LD experts, and even the experts don't claim to know it all.

Results: The Bottom Line

What we do know best is our children, and we have to apply as much basic information as we can get to the specific needs of each child so that we can advocate most effectively for that child. We may not know which theory or which treatment will work best, but we can certainly weigh the options and evaluate the results as they apply to our sons and daughters. What we are interested in, more than the theories and more than the statistics, is results — results as they apply specifically to us.

Those of you who are just beginning to have suspicions that your children might have a learning problem will find clear-cut symptomatic guidelines and checklists to help you in your search for answers, as well as detailed advice on how to get more accurate and thorough evaluations.

Those of you whose children have already been diagnosed will find this book a comprehensive sourcebook of remedial techniques. It will offer clear information about the extensive legal rights of LD children, along with step-by-step guidelines for implementing those rights.

For all parents, it will provide information about a strong parent support network and the comforting sense that, by applying the technical knowledge and the advocacy skills available in these pages, we can indeed put that fierce determination to good use. We can make a difference, for ourselves and for our children.

A LITTLE knowledge is a dangerous thing. In researching this book, I went through a period of tremendous stress. There were so many possibilities, so many things I could do for Leana. What if I didn't choose the right ones, didn't explore all the possible options? Every new theory, every remediation opened up a whole new avenue of what-ifs. I was trying to digest them as a mother as well as a writer, and it was not easy.

But as I began to move past the particulars of Leana's story and into the subject of learning disabilities as it affected other parents and other children, I began to feel better about my choices. In fact, there *are* too many definitions, too many possibilities. What I learned to do (and what you will learn do to after reading this book) was to acquire as much information as possible and then apply it *critically* to my child. After all, in the final analysis, we are the only definitive experts on our own children. No one else knows them as we do, and no one else can judge their growth as we can.

Leana is *not* a candidate for certain therapies — her LD profile does *not* fit every definition of the term. I had to learn what would work for her and what wouldn't before I could feel confident about helping her, and therefore feel better about myself. Thus, although I've tried to provide a wide scope of information for you to choose from, I have tried not to make any judgments about it, except in cases where I've indicated the position of most professionals about a certain theory or treatment. In general, as you read this book, you will need to make the same critical distinctions that I did. That may seem like a difficult task, but in the end it will help both you and your child for you to be in charge and in command.

So this is not just the story of Leana — mainly because that story isn't over yet, and probably won't be for many years. It is an account of many children and many struggles, and it is written with an eye not only on reasons, but on results.

CHAPTER 1

What *Are* Learning Disabilities?

Question: "What is it like to be learning disabled?"

Answers: "Sometimes I feel so busy inside I just can't figure out what the teacher is saying. So I just stare . . . and I think, am I the only person in the world who's so dumb?"

"Life is like a gang that keeps attacking and attacking. School is like a hammer at my head all day."

"It's like you know you're not stupid, but you really are. And everybody tells you you're not stupid, but you watch the other kids do it, and you know you are."

HOW does it feel to be learning disabled? That's like asking how it feels to be blind — impossible to know the answer unless you are, and then difficult to describe to the sighted. For the learning disabled child, the question is even more complicated. She probably does not know until she starts school that she's different from the other children in any way. And then, when it becomes clear that there is a problem of some sort, the problem itself may stand in the way of her being able to describe it well to non-LD adults and peers.

It might help us, though, if we could understand a bit more about what it actually feels like to be LD. We can try to read through a prism, or write with our left (or right) hand, but those tricks deal only with one sense and don't really convey the tremendous frustration level encountered by LD kids.

Alan Ross, in *The Unrealized Potential,* suggests this test as a more adequate measure of what it must be like to be LD:

Take a three-by-five card and a pencil and stand in front of a mirror. Hold the paper against your forehead and, looking into the mirror, try to write your name on it, left to right, just as you normally would.

Hard, isn't it? The pencil feels clumsy at that angle, you're having a hard time keeping the paper straight, and you're not sure the letters are coming out as they should, because your view of them is distorted. Now, look at what you've written. The instructions, by the way, were not to write your name backward, as you probably have done in spite of yourself.

Clearly, if this were the way handwriting lessons were normally conducted, you would need a lot of training before you could write your name correctly across that piece of paper. And it probably wouldn't help if your teacher confined her instruction to comments like "Come on; it's not hard if you just *pay attention!*"

There are other analogies worth thinking about. How would you feel if you woke up in a strange city and had to find your way around by asking directions of people who spoke an unfamiliar language? How long do you think it would take you, wearing rubber gloves, to thread a fine needle? How would your boss feel if you were unable to recall verbal instructions he gave you yesterday?

How smart would you think you were if you couldn't read?

A Disclaimer

Before we talk about what learning disabilities are — and aren't — let's examine the phrase itself. First, the words *learning disability* don't really tell us a thing. In descriptive terms, they're about as useful as naming everything with a door and four walls a house. Second, even the experts can't agree on whether the disability has anything to do with learning, or whether it really is a disability. There's even a debate over whether or not such a concept as "learning disability" exists at all. (We'll talk a lot more about the great LD controversy later.) Emmett Velten and Carlene Sampson, authors of a teacher's guide on the subject, forthrightly describe LD as "just a tarted-up term referring to a child's relative lack of learning ability according to standard procedures."

The most important argument against the words, though, is the fact that they can be so pejorative, even though people don't know what they mean or can't agree on what they mean. There may be some relief in knowing that there is a reason for your child's difficulties — in giving a label to that nameless frustration and confusion. As a matter of fact, many parents report that they feel quite a bit better knowing that the problem has a name, and a history, to give it dimensions. Certainly LD kids feel better knowing that they're not dumb or retarded, as many of them feel they might be. When I first told Leana about her learning disability, I drew her a simple diagram, depicting a squiggly line which went from her perfectly good eyes to her perfectly good brain. Some people, I told her, had straight lines connecting eye and brain. A squiggly line was just as effective, except that it took a more indirect route. Leana grabbed the paper and ran next door to "explain her brain" to her best friend.

But, as we saw in the quotations at the beginning of the chapter (one of which was Leana's), knowing that you have a learning disability is no guarantee that you'll feel better about the problems it can cause. And the term doesn't help if it carries negative emotional baggage in terms of other people's perceptions. Unfortunately, in our society any label, regardless of how relatively comforting it might be to its owner, is often perceived negatively. A child who has been diagnosed as having learning problems has enough to contend with without having to deal with a handicapping label that other children might get hold of and use cruelly. This is true of any label, but especially so when the child is likely to have a fragile sense of self-esteem to begin with.

Unfortunately, we have to call it something, and, since the words *learning disability* are in such common use, it seems silly to pretend that they don't exist. What we can do, both in the interests of clarity and brevity, is just use the initials LD. They can stand for learning disability, dysfunction, or difficulty (my favorite). If it helps you or your child to use those alternate meanings, by all means go ahead and use them.

Playing the Numbers Game

It wouldn't matter so much what we were calling LD if it didn't affect so many people. But even by the most conservative accounting, an awful lot of children are involved. Like almost anything else about LD, however, no one can agree on just how large that total number really is.

Percentages may be easier to look at than raw numbers. Various studies have placed the percentage of American schoolchildren who have some form of learning disability at anywhere between 2 and 25 — and some school districts, hoping to cash in on federal funding, have reported that 100 percent of their student population is afflicted!

A lot of the discrepancy in statistics has to do with the way people define LD. If we're just talking about children with reading problems, then the percentage is relatively small (about 10 percent). If we include children with motor problems and attention problems, the number soars to 25 percent and above.

Even using the same measurement tools, such as Stanley Johnson and Robert Morasky's Learning Quotient equation (taking the child's relative age score on a series of tests, dividing it by his chronological age, and multiplying the result by 100 to get the child's learning quotient), the variation in cutoff points can result in widely varying numbers of children affected. Is a child with an LQ (learning quotient) below 90 identified as LD, or is it the child who scores below 85? Another familiar qualifier for LD concerns the degree to which a child is performing below her chronological grade level. But should we say that only children who are performing more than two years below grade level are LD? Or do we include children who are performing only a year below but who should be performing far above grade level?

There are experts who think that even the most conservative estimates are inflated — that the term *LD* has been abused by teachers and parents who are looking for an easy answer to a child's problem. And there are those who say that it has become a catchall phrase into which almost any "problem" child can be dumped. In some cases, that may be true, and it is certainly true that a learning disability is not life-threatening. But, even by those conservative estimates of 2 to 3 percent of the school-age population, LD is still by far the largest category of special-needs children in our schools today; it outnumbers by four to one all other categories combined.

The numbers may be slippery, but discounting the importance of LD, and its effect on the life of a child, is a dangerous notion, since it could lead to the shrinking of public funds for children who really do need — and can benefit from — remediation (in spite of the criminal shenanigans of some of the school systems like those who submit "100 percent" reports).

In any case, despite all the arguments over who is or is not LD, the consistency in the numbers has, in fact, been greater than the variability over the years. The most comprehensive studies — those that take into account the largest number of children over the largest geographical, socioeconomic, and ethnic areas — put the figure at about 15 percent of the American school-age population. Confirmation for this figure comes from the fact that it is equivalent to percentages found in other Western countries, such as Canada, Great Britain, France, and Denmark.

In this country alone, that works out to about eight million children. But it is not just LD children who are affected by LD. We parents know only too well what turmoil it creates in our lives and in the lives of our other children. The classmates and peers of our LD kids are affected too, as are the teachers who must work with them. The ripple-effect theory holds that the impact of having a learning disability diminishes the farther it gets from the source, but many parents and teachers would contest that premise. Even if it were true, those fifteen million children represent a large chunk of our future. The undetermined number of American adults who suffer from LD problems (some estimates run as high as eleven million) is a good example of the price we all pay when we ignore the problem. Some of those adults may have made adjustments to accommodate their LD, but many are languishing in low-level jobs because their special needs were never addressed.

Now that we have the means to identify them, we don't want that to happen to our children.

The Search for Definitions

But how do we go about identifying them without a working definition? What exactly is it that those eight million children and eleven million adults have? Researchers have been trying to answer that question for some time. In 1896, an ophthalmologist, William Pringle Morton, published an article in the *British Medical Journal* about a curious affliction he called "word blindness." He described it as a congenital inability, in spite of apparently normal intelligence, to recognize familiar words.

That's probably the last time anybody was able to define a learning disability of any kind with such simplicity. Today, the U.S. Department of Education, in defining the term *learning disability* for the Education For All Handicapped Children Act (1973, usually referred to as PL 94–142), offers the following mouthful:

> Learning disability refers to one or more significant defects in the essential learning process which may manifest itself in a discrepancy between ability and performance in one or more areas of spoken or written language, the ability to think, read, speak, write, spell or calculate, including perceptual handicaps, brain injury, dyslexia and aphasia but not learning problems that are the result of visual, auditory or motor handicaps, mental retardation, emotional disturbance, or environmental, cultural or economic handicaps.

A daunting definition, but what does it mean? It means that the Department of Education was more concerned with making clear what LD was *not* than with what it was, and with leaving itself plenty of space for open interpretation when it did make a commitment to defining LD.

Given the tangle of legal and political webwork that went into creating PL 94–142, the government had good reason to be vague. After all, its purpose was to serve the needs of children, and not to argue a scientific point of order. The official description (which has been only slightly modified in the past fifteen years) also reflects the ongoing disagreement over the exact definition of the term.

The truth is that LD as an identifiable syndrome is a fairly recent phenomenon, having developed over the past two decades from a narrow area of scientific study that had more to do with mapping areas of the brain than with the way children learn. The incredible rise in the numbers of children who are being diagnosed with it is attributable mostly to the rise in awareness of the problem, not to the number of afflicted children. Now that they have more evidence, experts may have good reason to debate such abstract words as *perceptual* and *cultural handicaps*. But, as parents, we might be better served by a more concrete explanation:

> Learning disabled children (and adults) are unable to store, process or produce information in the same way that the rest of us do, although they appear to have no physical, mental, or environmental handicaps to prevent them from doing so.

At least that's easier to manage in one breath. But it's really just as vague as PL 94-142. It's still a definition by exclusion. It tells us that there's something wrong, but it doesn't tell us what or why.

To get a better sense of the dilemma this nondefinition problem poses, imagine what it would be like if you took your sick child to the doctor, who announced that there was clearly something wrong, but she wasn't sure what it was. Anxiety would most likely be your first reaction, compounded by a strong sense of helplessness. All sorts of horrible things would go through your mind, most of them probably a lot worse than the truth.

When the pediatrician informs us that our son's or daughter's symptoms can be explained by a case of measles or chicken pox, we may be dismayed, but at least we're relieved to know that it's something definite. We knew there was something wrong, and somehow putting a name on it makes it seem a lot less frightening.

Similarly, hearing that our child is unable to produce, store, or process information doesn't tell us more than we already know. We *knew* there was something wrong with the way our child was learning — or not learning. We want to know *what* it is that's wrong, very clearly and specifically. Those generalized definitions don't go a very long way toward comforting us, because they don't help us to isolate our child's problem or identify its likely source.

To add to the problem of finding a single working definition,

many of the names and definitions for LD reflect scientists' observations that are a *result* of the learning disability, not the LD itself.
Researchers trying to unravel the mysterious ways in which we
learn can only look at the way we reflect our knowledge, not at
the way we acquire it.

Of course, there are areas in which great progress is being made
toward pinning down the exact structural causes of learning problems. Neurobiology, the study of the makeup of the brain, has
yielded some fascinating hypotheses concerning the nature of the
brain's architecture and its relationship to the way we learn (see
chapters 3 and 11). The education researchers and psychologists
base their work on observable behaviors and work backward to a
probable cause; the neurobiologists base their work on the cause
itself, and work outward to try to connect it directly to a behavior.

Unfortunately there is, as yet, no hard proof that the neurobiologists' theories are really the explanations for LD. Even the
neurobiologists admit that some of the structural differences they
find in the brains of LD people can occur in non–LD subjects as
well. So far, although the neurobiologist is working from the inside out rather than the outside in, he or she is still working in the
realm of sophisticated theory.

Another problem lies in the fact that each definition has been
created by someone with a specific approach to learning disabilities that colors his or her results. The neurologists have tried to
define LD structurally in terms of the way the brain functions.
The educators have tried to define it both structurally and behav-
iorally, in terms of the way a child acquires information and makes
use of it. The psychologists look at the way a child behaves. All
of these definitions are based on sound scientific research, and all
of them are valid.

But they don't always agree. Samuel Kirk, who, along with his
wife, Winifred, pioneered LD research in the 1960s and developed
one of the first working definitions of the term, said that there are
"two ways to define LD, depending on whether you approach it
from a causal or a behavioral result." In other words, are you looking at the structure of the disability or at the effect it creates, in
order to define it? "Labels," adds Kirk, "are satisfying to us
[professionals] but are of little concern to the child himself."

If the experts can't agree on a definition, how are we to arrive at one? Marvin Gottlieb, a developmental pediatrician and well-known researcher in the field, says that "a precise definition [of LD] is too constricting, whereas a non-specific definition tends to encompass the overwhelming majority of school-age children." In other words, says Helmer Myklebust, "tell me how many children you want to find and I'll write you a definition that will find that many."

Naming Names

Now that we know what LD isn't, and why it's so hard for the experts to come up with one definition, let's get down to the business of figuring out what it is from *our* point of view — a simple and practical concept to work with. What we want is something specific, but comprehensible — something that will help us understand more about what's wrong and why. Even more important, we want a label that will help point the way toward an effective course of treatment.

Fortunately, experts have come up with plenty of material for us to work with if it's more specific names we want. Consider, for example, the following list, offered in Sally Smith's book *No Easy Answers:*

Association Deficit
    Pathology
Attention Deficit
    Disorders
Brain-injured
Central Nervous System
    Disorder
Conceptually
    Handicapped
Congenital Alexia
Congenital
    Strephosymbolia
Diffuse Brain Damage
Dyscalculia
Dysgraphia
Dyslexia
Educationally
    Handicapped
Hyperactivity
Hyperkinetic Behavior
    Syndrome
Hypoactivity
Hypokinetic Behavior
    Syndrome
Language Disability
Language Disordered
    Child
Minimal Brain Damage

Minimal Brain
  Dysfunction
Minimal Cerebral
  Disorder
Minimal Cerebral Palsy
Multisensory Disorders
Neurological Immaturity
Neurophrenia
Neurophysiological
  Dyssynchrony
Organic Brain
  Dysfunction
Organicity

Perceptually Handicapped
Primary Reading
  Retardation
Psycholinguistic Disability
Reading Disability
Reading Disorder
Specific Dyslexia
Specific Learning
  Disabilities
Strauss Syndrome
Strephosymbolia
Waysider
Word Blindness

We wanted names, and we certainly have them now. That's the good news. The bad news is that this wealth of technical nomenclature doesn't really leave us any better off than we were with Pringle Morton's definition. What's worse, most of the names on that list are overlapping, confusing, misleading, and downright horrifying. If you've ever had one of them thrown at you by a teacher or a doctor, you know that it didn't make you feel one whit better to learn that your child had "minimal brain dysfunction" or "organicity," especially when the expert admitted to you that the definition of such a term was vague at best and hotly debated, besides.

On closer inspection, however, it turns out that most of those terms are not nearly as intimidating as they seem. In fact, most of them are just different words to express the same idea. We can see just how easy it is to topple this formidable tower of babble by applying something called "Edward Fry's do-it-yourself terminology generator." Sylvia Farnham-Diggory uses it in her book *Learning Disabilities* to point out how confusing the name game can be:

Directions: Select any word from column 1. Add any word from column 2, then any word from column 3. If you don't like the results, try again. It will mean about the same thing.

Column 1 Qualifier	Column 2 Area of Involvement	Column 3 Problem
Minimal	Brain	Dysfunction
Mild	Cerebral	Damage
Minor	Neurological	Disorder
Chronic	Neurologic	Dys-synchronization
Diffuse	Central Nervous	Handicap
Specific	System	Disability
Primary	Language	Retardation
Disorganized	Reading	Impairment
Organic	Perceptual	Pathology
Clumsy	Impulse	Syndrome
	Behavior	

Playing games like this can relieve some of the frustration we may feel, but it hasn't gotten us any closer to our conclusive definition. Now let's go back through Sally Smith's list and define a few of the more commonly heard terms used to describe specific disabilities as well as variations on the general theme.

Attention Deficit Disorder (ADD): the chronic inability to focus on pertinent stimuli for an enduring period of time

Agnosia: the loss or impairment of ability to recognize objects

Alexia: the loss or impairment of the ability to read

Anomia: the loss or impairment of the ability to remember words or names

Aphasia: the inability to evoke spoken or written language

Apraxia: the inability to reproduce written or spoken language

Auditory Perceptual Disorder: the inability to identify, organize, and interpret what is perceived by the ear

CNS (central nervous system) Disorder: a disorganization of the brain and spinal cord system, through which sensory impulses are transmitted

Cognitive Disabilities: disturbances in perception, conception, reasoning, and judging — the skills by which knowledge is acquired

Dyscalculia: disturbances in quantitative reasoning due to neurological disorders

Dysgraphia: a neurological disorder leading to the inability to transfer visual patterns to motor patterns in writing

Dyslexia: an impairment of the ability to read due to neurological dysfunction

Fine Motor Problems: a disorder in the use of hands necessary to perform precision tasks such as writing or object manipulation

Gross Motor Problems: a disorder in the use of large muscle groups used in running, jumping, hopping

Hyperactivity: increased or excessive muscular activity as a result of neurological disorder

Hyperkinesis: a restless behavior syndrome, usually connected to learning problems

Hypoactivity: reduced muscular activity for the same reason

Information Processing Disorder: an inability to organize, interpret, and store information after it has been received via the senses

Language Disability: the impairment of the learning systems involving the use of symbols to communicate

Maturational Lag: a delay in the process of becoming fully developed in character and mental capacity

Minimal Brain Dysfunction: a neurological disturbance in children of average or above-average intelligence who display no major physical, neurological, or psychological deficits

Neurological Disorder: a major or subtle dysfunction of the central nervous system

Organic Brain Syndrome: any mental disorder associated with or caused by disturbances in the function of brain tissues

Perceptually Handicapped: a disorder in the way one receives, comprehends, and organizes impressions via the senses

Specific Learning Disability: a learning problem involving a particular sensory disorder or a combination of disorders that affect the ability to absorb and organize information

Visual Perceptual Disorder: the inability to identify, organize, and interpret what is perceived by the eye

We can easily recognize our children in some of those definitions. But even if we can, we're not comforted. What good is a simple diagnosis if there isn't a simple cure? What if our child's trouble doesn't fall into the simple definitions and is instead a confusing combination of many of the above definitions?

It may be some comfort to know that only a fraction of all children diagnosed as having a learning disability have just one specific type of disorder. As a matter of fact, some experts think it's impossible for there to be an isolated case of, say, dysgraphia, without there also being signs of dyslexia. And "pure dyslexia" turns out to be not merely the inability to read, but a series of cognitive disabilities involving speech and language skills, motor incoordination, spatial and temporal confusion, difficulties in naming colors, and mixed dominance (-handedness). Since the neurological functions that control our senses and our skills are so interconnected, it is the rare child whose reading reversals aren't accompanied by a motor dysfunction, or whose memory disability isn't accompanied by an attention deficit.

In any case, the names we've defined above are often doled out to us by the experts with so many qualifiers that they are rendered useless. These people will hasten to reassure us (as if we didn't already know) that the names are confusing and overlapping and that we really don't need to worry about the technical distinctions between perceptual handicaps and cognitive disabilities, anyway.

But of course that doesn't stop us from worrying. As parents, it's not enough for us to dismiss all those words as unnecessary. Once we've begun to suspect that our child might be suffering from a learning disability, we won't rest easy until we knew exactly what that means, just as we wouldn't rest easy until we knew definitively whether it was measles or chicken pox.

Putting It in Order

Perhaps, then, a simple definition is not what we want, after all. What we might want instead is to have the concepts explained and put into some kind of order. Fortunately, this categorization has been done for us, too. Some researchers, like Daniel Hallahan, divide their definitions of LD into basic categories. In his *Introduction to LD* (written with James Kaufman), Hallahan uses four classifications: perceptual, attentional, language production, and social development disabilities. Betty Osman, in her book *Learning Disabilities,* uses a very similar system, dividing learning disabilities into three areas: language and conceptual development, perceptual skills, and behavioral manifestations. These categories are very much alike, the only exception being Hallahan's addition of the attentional disability, which Osman includes in her behavioral category.

The only difference between Osman's and Hallahan's definitions lie in *their* definitions of the words they use to describe their categories. Other researchers divide LD into categories that seem quite different: spoken language, written language, arithmetic, reasoning, and organization, for example, or verbal and nonverbal, perceptual deficits and processing deficits. Again, it's just a matter of names, and of point of view.

Larry Silver, who wrote an excellent book called *The Misunderstood Child,* defines most specific learning disabilities according to a much more detailed system. Although Silver agrees that every definition has to stand on its own because of a "lack of an agreed upon nosology [criteria for study]," his is worth including here, because it makes so much sense and doesn't rely on abstract terms that can be misunderstood or confused.

Input Disabilities: Information arrives at the brain as impulses from our eyes, ears and other senses. This process is referred to as perception: thus, when a child has problems with information coming in through one or more senses, he or she is said to have a perceptual disability. This disability can affect one or more of the following areas.

- Visual perception (what we see)
- Auditory perception (what we hear)
- Tactile perception (what we feel)

Specific reading disorders — the inability to perceive and recognize letters or groups of letters — are an example of an input disability.

Integration Disabilities: Once the information reaches the brain, it has to be understood through sequencing and abstraction skills, which are another problem area for some children. Sequencing deals with the ability to put things in their proper order; abstraction refers to the ability to infer meaning from the symbols which arrive

26

in the brain. Integration disabilities can reveal themselves in several ways.

- Visual sequencing (arranging symbols that we see)
- Auditory sequencing (arranging symbols that we hear)
- Visual abstraction (making sense of symbols that we see)
- Auditory abstraction (making sense of symbols that we hear)

Cognitive disorders — the inability to organize, interpret, and utilize sensory information — are an example of an integration disability.

Memory Disabilities: Once the information is received and integrated, it must be stored. Children with memory disabilities have trouble retaining information — sometimes even while they are concentrating on it, and sometimes after it has already been stored. In addition, the disability may affect one process of sensory input and not another, although again, it is often a combination of several. These disabilities are referred to as:

- Visual short-term memory (things we saw recently)
- Auditory short-term memory (things we heard recently)
- Visual long-term memory (things we saw a while ago)
- Auditory long-term memory (things we heard a while ago)

Spelling disorders — the inability to store and retrieve the proper sequence of letters to form a word — are an example of an integration disability.

Output Disabilities: Output refers to the ways in which information comes out of the brain — either through language (both initiative — "spontaneous" — or communicative — "demand" — language) or motor skills (sometimes with large muscle groups, known as gross motor skills, and sometimes with getting many muscle groups to work together, which are known as fine motor skills). So these specific disabilities are called:

- Spontaneous language (speech we initiate)
- Demand language (speech as a response to others)
- Gross motor skills (running, walking, jumping)
- Fine motor skills (writing, drawing)

27

> Language disorders — the inability to use symbols for communicating — are an example of an output disability.

Instead of relying on terms that need to be specifically defined, Silver groups his definitions according to their similar characteristics. His common denominator is the brain, and each category refers to a group of brain processes. Such groupings are extremely helpful. But, as with Hallahan and Osman, we need to remember that there is rarely an instance of a child who will display symptoms in only one category. We still have no way of identifying which is the primary category, if there is such a thing, or which disability might itself have created another disability.

Silver's categories are only one more way of approaching the naming game. The following chart, based on one developed by the New York Institute for Child Development, divides up the categories another way, and comes up with some equally revealing and clarifying definitions.

I. Disorders of Motor Activity
    A. **Hyperactivity:** The child is frequently restless, engaged in random activity, and erratic in behavior; the child cannot sit still.
    B. **Perseveration:** The child is unable to shift from one topic to the next. In oral reading, this child may repeat a phrase several times before he can continue.
    C. **Hypoactivity:** The child is very quiet and lethargic and causes no disturbance, but has difficulty in doing work in class.
    D. **Incoordination:** The child is physically awkward, frequently stumbles or falls, or appears to have clumsy behavior in general.

II. Disorders of Emotionality
    A. **Social Maladjustment:** The child is unable to make successful contact with the world around him; the child cannot get along with other students.
    B. **Lack of Self-Control:** The child is constantly disturbing the class, may be very disruptive and pick fights on the playground.

C. **Temper Outbursts:** The child, when the "breaking point" is reached, may yell, scream, and cry, sometimes for no apparent reason.

D. **Quick Emotional Shifts:** The child gets frustrated easily; is volatile and liable to move from pleasantness to tears in a matter of seconds, sometimes for no apparent reason.

III. Disorders of Attention

A. **Short Attention Span:** The child is attracted to every available stimulus regardless of its pertinence to the task at hand. Can be distracted by flies buzzing, other people walking by, or even the quiet person next to him. (This is also called attention deficit disorder; see chapter 2.)

B. **Excessive Attention:** The child displays abnormal fixation on unimportant details while disregarding the essentials; may give all of his attention to the page number instead of reading the printed material on the page.

IV. Disorders of Memory

A. **Poor Visual Memory:** The child is unable to revisualize letters, words, or forms. Has poor spelling habits.

B. **Poor Auditory Memory:** The child is unable to reproduce rhythm patterns, sequences of words or digits, or phrases that are presented orally.

C. **Poor Short-Term Memory:** The child, after a short period of time, is unable to remember what was learned earlier.

D. **Poor Long-Term Memory:** The child, after a long period of time, is unable to remember what was learned previously.

V. Disorders of Perception

A. **Poor Visual Memory:** The child reverses letters in reading and/or inadequately reproduces geometric forms and experiences figure/ground confusion.

B. **Poor Auditory Decoding:** The child is unable to differentiate among sounds, sound patterns, or the sounds of similar letters.

    C. **Poor Kinesthetic Decoding:** The child may have problems in directionality and in spatial orientation; difficulty in telling right from left.

VI. Disorders of Symbolism
    A. **Expressive Vocal:** The child is unable to express his thoughts verbally; shows lack of ideas for expression or command of language to express them.
    B. **Expressive Motor:** The child has difficulty with the formulation of thought required for writing ideas.
    C. **Receptive Auditory:** The child has difficulty understanding spoken symbols. Asks frequently for (or needs to be given) repeated directions or commands.
    D. **Receptive Visual:** The child, when reading silently, subvocalizes (speaks under his breath or mouths the words) in order to comprehend.

Where Silver used the brain as his common denominator, the institute's list uses the child's skills and classroom behavior as the identifying features for the categories, making this a more academically inclined list than Silver's. A third classification system, which defines LD by examining a child's behavior, can be found in chapter 2, where I'll discuss symptoms and characteristics of the LD child.

The Discrepancy Debate

By using simple definitions and organizing descriptive concepts, we've come up with a better sense of what it is that makes up a learning disability. But that's a lot to absorb, and we're left with a sense that there are too many variables for us to be able to pin down the idea of LD into a concept we can easily grasp. We need to look for a common denominator, a single word or phrase that can encompass the widest number of descriptions, definitions, and symptoms.

There is one word that many researchers seem to agree upon when they are trying to define LD: *discrepancy*. Simply put, this means the discrepancy, or variation, between what a child can do and what he or she is expected to be able to do. Age level, developmental maturity, and intelligence must be included in the equation before the discrepancy factor can be determined, of course, but it is the variation from the expected levels of achievement that provide the most clear and consistent indicator of LD.

Discrepancy can be determined in several ways, by teachers, by pediatricians, and by us, the parents. An astute doctor may notice that a child is not progressing along the usual developmental track. It might not be any one thing, such as late walking or talking, but a combination of delays that point to a difference in the way a particular child is maturing when compared to the rate at which most other children are maturing.

In school, an attentive teacher will pick up on the discrepancy between a child's verbal abilities and her written work, or between her grasp of concepts and her workbook tasks. Most children learn on a fairly even curve, while LD kids learn in fits and starts, making great leaps, only to appear to lose their new skills shortly after they've been acquired. The uneven pattern of development witnessed by the pediatrician will show up in the classroom as well, as a different cluster of uneven behaviors and skills. It is the discrepancy between a child's verbal and performance scores on standardized ability tests such as the WISC-R (see chapter 4) that offers another clue to the teacher or tester.

But it is our job as parents to notice the uneven pattern and the discrepancy between potential and achievement, because we are, in the final analysis, the most comprehensive experts on our child. We see him in every type of situation, in every kind of mood. We see how he performs in school, at home, with his peers, with us. We see how well he performs daily chores, and how well he responds to directions. We see when he is unable to manage his emotions, or overcome his clumsiness, or decode the back of the cereal box.

And we see the child's strengths, too, the clear indication that there is a discrepancy. We see his superb artwork, his unerring musical ear. We see him grasp concepts in physics beyond our comprehension and behave in a gentle and sensitive manner toward others. As Priscilla Vail, in her generous book *Smart Kids with School Problems,* describes it: "The discrepancy between a [child's] low and high skill is painful. The greater the discrepancy, the more intense the pain."

So we have the greatest variety of behaviors to judge, and we can tell when the case is not an isolated one, but a cluster of behaviors that do not ring true when we put them together. We see other children; we ask our friends and families about their children — we *know*. And we have to trust that knowledge, and get help in corroborating it.

It seems as if the concept of discrepancy — between ability and achievement, between high and low-level skills, between developmental norms and actual performance — is in fact a fairly consistent indicator of the presence of LD in a child. But what constitutes a discrepancy? How do we know what our child is capable of doing, and against what criteria do we measure his or her progress? If we and the teachers and the doctors are measuring our child's progress against that of most children, how are we to be convinced that most children's progress is normal? How can we determine what is average, and how far from average the deviation must be before it is considered worthy of intervention? Isn't the individual child's difference a strength, and not a weakness?

These are questions that have yet to be answered to our satisfaction. But the notion of discrepancy is valuable because it judges the child against her potential, not just against the norm. That means we can use the child's own abilities as a standard by which to judge the success of a given treatment, and her progress toward a fully functioning intelligence. It makes sense to us as parents because it gives us a direction in which to proceed. And the concept makes sense to those argumentative statisticians as well. When discrepancy between ability and performance is used to predict future diagnoses of LD, it turns out to be the most accurate indicator we've found so far.

Settling the Issue

Alan Ross, in his book *LD: The Unrealized Potential,* says that the term *learning disability* is just another way to explain the unexplainable. I think he means that our society, with its mania for classification, is forcing us to create a category where one might not exist. There may be, after all, other ways to explain our children's difficulties in school that have nothing to do with their academic shortcomings, their uneven developmental level, or with the variation between their ability and their skill acquisition. Howard Gardner has written a wonderful book called *Frames of Mind,* in which he examines other forms of intelligence, such as musical, creative, or interpersonal ability, and postulates that LD children are simply children with other strengths that we do not emphasize enough in our society. Other educational philosophers point out that it may not be our children who have learning disorders — perhaps it is our schools that have teaching disorders, and someday in the future, LD may be referred to as TD (teaching disability) instead!

Ross says, "LD carries the implication that the child cannot learn, not only that she has failed to learn. Even if a test proved a skill was not yet learned, how could that prove the skill was unlearnable vis-à-vis that child?

"The best we can do is say that a child fails to reflect learning under the ordinary teaching methods learned thus far."

BUT none of that is of much practical use to us now. The hard truth is, our children have to learn how to absorb, evaluate, and express information to the best of their ability in accordance with the standards we have set for others of their age. Until that changes, Johnny must learn to read, and Jenny to do math. And we have the practical task of seeing to it that they get learned, by one manner or another.

We can see that there are as many ways to name the problem as there are children who have it, and that coming up with one final definition or categorization does not get us any closer to one final answer to the problem of LD. Clearly, whoever is doing the naming is going to bring a particular focus to the task. The labels we can assign may be satisfying to us, and to the professionals who deal with our children, but they are of little help to the children themselves.

Perhaps, then, instead of trying to differentiate among the fine shadings of meaning in all those names, we should start at the other end, and look at the definitions in terms of the symptoms they produce in our children. That way, we can much more clearly see which types of disabilities apply to our child, and then determine what to do about them.

By examining and naming the symptoms, and grouping them

together in an organized fashion, we'll get a much better handle on what ails the LD child — and it won't be so frightening, since the description will be based on clearly observable behavior patterns. Once we've got the symptoms categorized — and it will most likely be a cluster of several different behaviors that we're dealing with — then we can go about looking for effective ways to handle them in a therapeutic way.

CHAPTER 2

How Do We Find the LD Child?

Question: "As a parent, what does the term **learning disability** *mean to you?"*

Answers: "I think it's a very confusing and frightening term. When we were told by our family doctor that our son had a learning disability, our hearts sank. He said that James had minimal brain damage, but he never explained what that was or how our son got it."

"It's a very troublesome term. I hate to use it . . . because I don't feel it really explains the situation. I think of a child who has a handicap, and it makes me so sad."

"Even though I've been living with this term for a good number of years, I still cannot appreciate it, nor do I fully understand it. Personally, I look at my child and say, 'No, I'm imagining this. It can't be my child.'"

35

Looking for Pigeonholes

Since there is so little consensus on what LD is, it stands to reason that it would be difficult to figure out who has an LD problem. We come up against many of the same problems when we are attempting to identify LD children that we did when we were trying to define LD. For one thing, it's often very hard to put our fingers on the information necessary to diagnose them as LD before they reach school age. LD children are usually average or above average in intelligence (otherwise there wouldn't be a large discrepancy between performance and ability), so they may appear, at first, to be within the bounds of normal behavior.

We talk with our friends about our kids, and they casually agree that their children are behaving in the same way — perhaps not as extremely, or as often, but that the type of behavior is certainly commonplace. It's only when we look at the whole picture, and see the cluster of behaviors and the range of those behaviors, that we begin to have an uneasy feeling. The discrepancy factor grows until it looms, an unnamed menace, in our minds. That's when the questions begin to crowd in, making us look more closely at our children, and at ourselves.

At what point do we, as parents, decide that our child might have a problem? Do we wait until the child has reached school age, just to be sure? Will it be too late by then? Do we take the child in for testing as early as age two or three? What damage might that do if it turns out that there is no problem? Can the experts even tell, that early? And, if there is a problem, what can we do about it?

Early intervention is clearly the best way to get help for your child. There is no possible harm in getting a child screened before she reaches school age, and the current focus of many programs is on finding LD children as early as possible. In Cambridge, Massachusetts, for example, there is a citywide outreach program that actively searches for possible at-risk children, even going to private day-care centers and homes to help parents and care-givers determine who might be in need of evaluation and remediation.

Children who are screened before school age will suffer no damage from the screening, which takes the form of games, drawing, and some friendly questions. And experts agree that not only can they spot potential problems quite often in the early intervention format, they can also get to those problems before they become compounded by school failure.

On the other hand, studies have been done that indicate that it's never too late and that the students who receive help later in their school careers can make just as much progress as those who start early. High-school students can find their progress tremendously boosted by LD tutoring, especially if they've managed to develop their own successful compensatory systems along the way. And even an older child who has a record of school failure can make remarkable strides if his educational and emotional needs are addressed with thoroughness and sensitivity.

So it doesn't matter when you begin to look, or how long you look before deciding that something needs to be done about your child. As long as you have observed long enough to determine that there is a pattern, you should feel comfortable about following through. If you have doubts about your three-year-old because he can't sit still for Sesame Street and doesn't seem to know his colors, there can be no harm in talking to your pediatrician. If your pediatrician doesn't think there's a problem and the child's lack of focus persists, find another pediatrician.

If your ten-year-old is falling farther and farther behind in school and her teachers are running out of reasons, ask for an evaluation. If you don't get a response within a reasonable period of time, ask someone in charge. These are your rights, and your child's rights, and you don't need to have amassed a huge body of evidence in order to get them acted upon.

It is you who are the best and final judge of when to start looking more closely. *Having faith in your own judgment is probably the most effective way you can help your child.* I'm going to be reminding you of that throughout this book, in addition to giving you some skills to insure that the faith will be well founded in facts. But, regardless of when it is made, that initial decision to act calls up a whole other set of dilemmas. Where do you look for help? What kind of help? How do you know if that help is the right kind?

Now is the time for pigeonholes, when we first begin to have our doubts and don't know enough about the possible answers to do anything *but* ask more questions. We want classifications, clarifications, a system by which we can organize our frightening suspicions. We look anxiously for a simple explanation, even though we don't have nearly enough facts. All the myths and rumors that we, as enlightened parents, have always dismissed rise up to haunt us. Could it be hyperactivity? Some undiagnosed illness just waiting to explode into our lives? Is our child simply not very bright?

Are we such awful parents?

The answer is probably no, but it does little good to hear that. What we need at this stage is more information. We're not ready to examine possible explanations — not until we've taken a good hard look at our child. We have to look at him systematically and symptomatically, and decide if his behavior fits into any characteristic patterns. We have to be very careful to look at all aspects of his behavior, and to draw conclusions based not on one symptom or characteristic, but on the *pattern* that we see emerge. Remember that, from a diagnostic point of view, the cluster of behaviors and their degree are far more important than the individual behaviors themselves.

Knowing this makes us a bit calmer, and we can go about assessing our child, and directing professionals to assess our child, without that paralyzing element of panic. From an emotional point of view, it's likely that the sooner we are able to intervene with help, the better off our child will be. But it would be far more damaging for the child if we were to rush to the wrong diagnostic conclusions.

Above all, it helps to remember that all children are different, even within the LD framework. There is no such thing as an average child — or a normal one, for that matter. And there is no such thing as a typical LD kid. Children are far too complex (and far too interesting) for that kind of oversimplification. Your child will have an emotional and cognitive profile as unique as his fingerprint, and the more information you can gather about it, the more precise his remediation can be.

Pinning It Down: Characteristics and Symptoms

The problem with describing symptoms is that, according to a familiar doctors' rubric, as soon as you describe 'em, everyone gets 'em. The following information should be used as a signpost that can lead us to think in a particular direction, rather than like red flags that indicate certain trouble. We'll look at the characteristics that experts most often equate with various types of LD and see if we can attribute some of them to our children. We'll also look at symptomatic behaviors most often associated with those characteristics — and learn what to look for as we observe our children at home, at school, and in social situations.

What's the difference between symptoms and characteristics? Sometimes not much. A characteristic will probably manifest itself in some form of behavioral symptom, and so the two categories will often overlap. Characteristics are more likely to be described in abstract terms, since they are usually given by the expert to the layperson: the parent. Symptoms are more observation-oriented, more pragmatic. Your pediatrician, for instance, could give you a list of characteristics to check, but you would offer your pediatrician a list of your child's symptoms to evaluate.

Characteristics tend to be more global — *some* children with learning problems exhibit *some* of these traits *some* of the time —and therefore may seem more all-inclusive. For example, hyper- and hypokinesis are commonly acknowledged characteristics of children with learning problems. But, since one means an excess and the other a deficit of body activity, it's hard to imagine one child as having both.

Symptoms tend to be more specific, more descriptive of particular behaviors. They are also age-related; the characteristic inability to identify objects correctly is not a symptom of LD at one year, but it is at three or four years of age. We can check our child against a list of characteristics, but it is by observing his behavior that we will determine whether he displays the symptoms of a learning disability.

Put simply, LD professionals have come up with lists of most of the characteristics that could describe LD children, and it's up to you (and your child's teacher or care-giver) to observe specific behaviors and match them against the experts' lists.

When you are reading this chapter, then, it's important to realize that you are looking for clues, not for a definitive diagnosis. *Only a professional evaluation can determine whether your child has a learning disability and what type of LD it is.* But, as the closest observer and acknowledged expert on your child, you are in the best position to sound the first warning and seek out that professional evaluation.

How will you determine if your child displays symptoms and characteristics of an LD problem? First of all, don't panic. LD is not a condition that requires emergency treatment. You have time to determine if your fears are grounded in fact or if they are simply the product of your own anxiety as a parent. Read the lists included in this chapter carefully, and think about your child. Do they apply some of the time? Most of the time? How many of them are familiar?

Watch your child closely while he's at home, doing routine tasks. Observe him as he interacts with your family and with his friends. Playgrounds are a great observation spot, because you can usually watch your child interact with others of his age without him paying much attention to you. Talk to his teacher or caregiver and find out what goes on when you're not around. Is he exhibiting behavior that's familiar to you, or acting much differently? How does he behave with strangers or in unexpected situations?

Nobody exhibits all of the symptoms of LD all of the time, just as no LD child has all the characteristics associated with LD. But it should become clear to you, over a period of a few months, that there is a pattern — not just one symptom, but a cluster of several (or many) of the behaviors that appear in the lists below. In order to broaden your perspective, it will also help to think back on your child's history. Did he exhibit some of the characteristics typical of many LD infants? Can you remember feeling uneasy about things that he did or did not do as a toddler?

Remember to trust your instincts and your recollections, but not to jump to any conclusions based on an isolated characteristic or a short-lived behavior pattern. Letter reversals alone do not mean your child is dyslexic, and a few weeks of the fidgets do not mean he has an attention disorder. And try to get your observations corroborated by another adult — a relative, teacher, or caregiver — to help you direct your attention to the particular kinds of behavior patterns your child exhibits. Use whatever network you have at your disposal to get help. The parents of a three-year-old in our neighborhood were concerned about their son. He seemed anxious and "overloaded" a lot of the time, and they had noticed that he didn't seem to be able to watch "Sesame Street" for more than a few minutes without getting agitated. Was this "normal"?

On the playground, the mother mentioned this to a nursery-school teacher (the child was not yet in school), who remembered another child with a similar set of reactions. She was able to direct the parent to the appropriate resources, and the child was ultimately placed in a special nursery program that was suited to his visual processing problems. The parents now credit the child's improvement to their willingness to ask questions and verify their suspicions, and wish they had done so sooner.

Once you are confident that you have observed a pattern of questionable behaviors and characteristics, you can go to your child's doctor or school with your concerns. Go armed with a list of your observations as well as questions, and go prepared to make very sure that none of them is dismissed without careful consideration. Be ready to use what you know to get the best help for your child. How to go about arranging for evaluations and interventions will be discussed in chapters 4 to 6.

A good place to start our search for the LD child is with a general list of characteristics developed by Daniel P. Hallahan, a psychologist and well-respected LD researcher. He describes five major elements that he believes are common to all LD kids. They may not apply to every child, but they are general enough to be informative even if they do raise some interesting questions.

The LD child:

1. Has academic "retardation."
2. Shows an uneven pattern of development.
3. May or may not have central nervous system dysfunction.
4. Does not owe LD to environmental disability.
5. Does not owe LD to mental retardation or emotional disturbance.

This list is certainly global enough to fit almost every LD profile — it takes into account failure to achieve in school, discrepancy between performance and ability, and possible neurological problems, and it excludes some other possible sources of those factors. But there are some problems with this list. The tendency toward "definition-by-what-it's-not" is evident. And the word *retardation* in the first item carries such heavy negative emotional baggage that we have to look beyond it to realize that Hallahan was simply referring to the lag in school grade achievement. He defines academic retardation as "the inability to demonstrate

41

knowledge of a subject at a level commensurate with intellectual ability," which is also a pretty good definition of discrepancy, which we discussed in chapter 1.

We've already seen that most LD kids are at least one year behind their peers in school. But, given the wide range of maturity levels of most youngsters, how can we measure what a child is supposed to be able to achieve at a given age? Hallahan helps us out by listing the main areas in which unevenness of learning and skill level are most likely to occur:

- oral expression: ability to express thoughts verbally
- written expression: ability to express thoughts in writing
- listening comprehension: ability to absorb information aurally
- basic reading skills: ability to decode printed symbols
- reading comprehension: ability to understand printed language
- mathematics calculation: ability to perform computations
- mathematics reasoning: ability to grasp math concepts

These subcategories cover most of the basic skills a child needs in order to get by in school, and we can excuse Hallahan for not including nonacademic skill discrepancies such as social skills and motor coordination problems, since they are not his area of focus. He does not include higher-order cognitive abilities like abstract reasoning and concept development, but they are skills that usually require the mastery of basic skills first.

Hallahan's third major category, however, is mystifyingly worded: "may or may not have central nervous system (CNS) dysfunction." It sounds as if he means that LD kids either have CNS problems or they don't, which is a bit like saying they either have heads or they don't — it's a totally inclusive category. What characteristic is he trying to pin down?

The central nervous system is made up of the brain and the spinal cord, which carries messages to it and from it. It's an extremely complicated system, made even more complex by the chemical and electrical systems that interact with it in order to make our bodies work. Dysfunctions of the CNS can manifest themselves as major handicaps such as cerebral palsy, or they can be so subtle as to go undetected by even the most particular diagnostic procedure. Major CNS problems are always accompanied by what neurologists refer to as "hard signs" of dysfunction — tics, tremors, spasticity, muscle atrophy, amnesia, convulsions, and seizures are some of the more commonly defined symptoms.

But unless a child has been medically diagnosed with conditions such as cerebral palsy or epilepsy, there is little likelihood that he will display any hard signs. It is the "soft signs" of CNS dysfunction that concern us, since they are more liable to indicate the presence of an incipient learning problem.

Soft signs are much more subtle and more difficult to detect. Some soft signs that parents might be able to notice include:

persistent right–left ambivalence: the inability to distinguish right hand or foot from left, or to indicate direction properly;

mixed dominance: ambidexterity; the ability to use either hand or foot with equal skill (or lack of skill);

visual or motor agnosia: the inability to process input from a particular sensory system; for instance, to carry the forefinger to the tip of the nose with both eyes closed;

spatial disorientation: inability to discern relative position of the body or an object in space — for instance, determining if a ball is on top of or beside a box when standing several feet away from it, or becoming excessively dizzy after spinning on a playground toy;

articulation defects: problems with speaking clearly or with producing certain sounds.

MANY researchers agree that all LD children have some neurological impairment at the root of their problem (see chapter 3), but only a very small percentage of them display hard signs, and those are usually caused by other primary problems. They are more likely to display the more subtle soft signs, and many LD children have no detectable CNS dysfunction at all. But that does not mean there is no CNS dysfunction, just that neurologists are unable to pinpoint the problem using currently available diagnostic techniques. You can get an idea of how difficult it is to detect hard evidence of subtle dysfunction if you consider that it takes at least a 50 percent change in cellular structure before a neurologist is accurately able to discern the difference; most LD problems fall far below that figure.

And the presence of these soft signs do not necessarily indicate an LD. Children with migraine headaches have soft signs and no LD, just as children with cerebral palsy have hard signs and (often) no LD. The child with an auditory processing disability, for instance, may not be able to touch the tips of his forefingers together with his eyes closed because he has not processed the directions, not because of a CNS dysfunction.

Obviously, Hallahan was hedging his bets when he said that all LD children either do or do not have CNS dysfunction. Current research has determined that they do have some degree of dysfunction, although there is still much disagreement on the nature, location, and severity of the problem. The question that arises, then, is whether CNS dysfunction *causes* abnormal behavior or whether it's the other way around. Hallahan's point is that such a distinction is largely irrelevant to the diagnosis. For our purposes, it is a good idea to be aware of those soft signs, if only to be able to rule out more serious neurological problems. CNS dysfunction, then, is not as frightening as it sounds, although we must remember that it takes a qualified neurologist to make an accurate diagnosis.

Hallahan's final two points are ones that are much debated by social advocates, who hold that cultural disadvantages and emotional disturbances are perfectly legitimate precursors to LD, and that children who suffer from them should be given the same kind and quality of extra attention as those children whose LD causes are more difficult to trace. If a Hispanic ghetto child is not doing well in school, why should we automatically assume that she is incapable of performing better, that there is no discrepancy between her abilities and her performance? Why should we blame her difficulties on her environment rather than on a learning disability?

The question of who has LD depends, to a great extent, on who is asking the question. Someone has to suspect that the child's performance does not reflect her ability. Someone has to insist on the administration of individualized testing. Someone has to call on various specialists for help in evaluation, diagnosis, and treatment. Someone has not accepted dullness or limited ability as an answer.

Given the cultural and economic realities of our society today, the chances are pretty good that that someone is white, well educated, and middle-class. Is that why such a high percentage of the

LD population is white and middle-class? Are we denying help to children who do not have that kind of advocate? LD is an academic, emotional, and cognitive issue, but it is also a social and political one, and it is up to us as parents to see that the help we get for ourselves and our children is not denied to others.

Age-appropriate Behavior

Looking at Hallahan's broad list of characteristics can give us an idea of the type of problems LD children confront, but it doesn't get very specific in terms of how those problems manifest themselves. One good way to determine that is to look at age-appropriate behavior, the kinds of behavior expected of children of a particular chronological age. The chart on pages 46–47, excerpted from one developed by researchers at the University of Tennessee, will give you a good idea of what the "normal" range of developmental expectations is for children ranging from one to six years.

That's the way it should be, according to the statistical averages. But we have to remember that there is an extremely wide range of "normal" skills levels and behaviors. Some children learn to read at age three, some at age eight, but by age ten it is impossible to differentiate between the two groups. In order to get an even closer look at characteristics of the LD child, we should look at some behaviors that indicate a deviation from the developmental norm. Researcher Louise Clarke has divided up her list (on pages 48–50) into neatly defined age categories that correspond to those of the University of Tennessee chart, although Clarke's list goes up to teenage. This makes it easy to compare what Clarke sees as characteristics of a possible LD child and the "normal" developmental sequences that are mandated by the Tennessee chart.

It's interesting that Clarke (like several other researchers) includes heredity, prenatal conditions, and possible complications of the birth process as characteristic factors, although they might more appropriately be termed causes. Still, if we're looking for risk factors, then heredity is certainly among them. Another researcher, James A. Cavanaugh, even discovered a higher incidence of dyslexia in children whose families had a pattern of graying early, making another strong argument for heredity (more about the hereditary causes in chapter 3).

Overview of the Major Sequences in Development

Age	Gross Motor	Fine Motor
40 weeks	sits alone pulls to stand	holds bottle with thumb and index finger
1 year	walks with help stands alone	has pincer grasp puts objects in cup
15 months	walks alone	has good grasp
18 months	walks well runs throws ball	turns many pages
2 years	climbs runs well	turns one page at a time
3 years	alternates feet on stairs rides tricycle	copies circle
4 years	can broad-jump throws overhand	copies square
5 years	skips can stand on one foot	copies triangle
6 years	throws ball well	copies numbers copies letters

Adaptive	Language	Personal
points	says "mama/dada"	waves turns head
holds cup serial play	says 2-3 other words obeys "no-no"	feeds self
uses crayon	names objects	indicates wants
stacks cubes scribbles	knows 10 words names body parts	feeds self well
draws a line	uses 3-word sentences follows directions uses nouns and pronouns	dresses self indicates need for toilet
builds towers/bridges	knows full name sings songs	dresses self takes turns
counts pennies draws person	uses prepositions	engages in group activities washes self laces shoes
identifies colors counts objects	names coins follows directions	asks questions
draws detailed figure knows right/left	remembers directions	knows A.M./P.M. counts to 30

1. Heredity:
   - any history of reading or language problems in family

2. Prenatal:
   - illness of mother
   - abnormal activity in utero

3. Birth:
   - prematurity
   - cesarean section
   - breech birth
   - prolonged labor
   - cord around neck and other causes of oxygen lack

4. Zero–two years:
   - jerkiness in sucking motions
   - excessive amount of drooling
   - bed-rocking and head-banging
   - poor sleeping
   - restlessness, irritability
   - poor nursing/eating
   - easily overstimulated
   - unilateral crawling (using right hand and foot together rather than opposing limbs)
   - colicky past three months
   - inability to distinguish between dissimilar sounds at six months
   - inability to speak comprehensible words by age one
   - inability to construct logical sentences by age two
   - inability to walk by twenty-two months

5. Two–five years:
   - "cluttered" speech
   - clinging to mother/separation anxiety
   - difficulty with simple block construction
   - inability to defer gratification
   - inability to follow picture-book sequences at age two
   - inability to pretend to read by looking at pages
   - inability to comprehend simple directions (first, last, top, bottom)
   - inability to verbalize emotions by age four

- lack of depth vision or coordination to play ball
- inability to master tricycle by age three
- inadequate language skills
- insufficient attention span by age five
- excessive vocal or motor activity
- inefficient motor skills
- language problems (prepositions, tenses, naming names)
- toilet training problems after age four
- difficulty with transitions and new situations

6. First grade:
   - language problems — word comprehension, meaning, artic-ulation
   - allergies
   - symptoms of tension and confusion such as nightmares and tantrums
   - not learning to read
   - not remembering basic skills taught previously
   - persistent reversals of letters, shapes, words
   - difficulty holding a pencil
   - kinetic over-/undershoot in writing (going above or not up to the line)
   - inability to discriminate among short vowel sounds
   - inability to distinguish separate syllables in a word
   - omission of endings and punctuation

7. Second–third grade:
   - all of above (without help)
   - illogical sequencing of words
   - good concepts, poor expression
   - headache, nausea, allergies (secondary symptoms)

8. Fourth grade–early teens:
   - lack of directional sense persists
   - not reading or writing to grade level, although extraordinary memory may help
   - reluctance to read
   - tires easily in school
   - able to do advanced, not simple, processes

- able to do complicated model-building from diagram, but not from written directions
- at seventh grade, testing at least 2.7 years below grade level
- magnification of adolescent problems such as aggressive behavior, withdrawal, low frustration threshold, negative attitude, low self-image, depression, anxiety, hostility, and wild mood swings

Remember that the presence of any of these characteristics does not automatically lead to a diagnosis of LD. Children who are going through a difficult period emotionally — anything from a spurt in growth to social pressures at school — often display them, and there is no reason to assume that there is an underlying LD problem because a child is having a rough time. This is particularly true of older children and adolescents.

Nevertheless, LD children are very likely to be having emotional problems as well as learning problems, for the same reasons as their non-LD peers, in addition to the burden of coping with their learning difficulties. And any indication of prolonged difficulties should be taken seriously, whether the problem is LD-related or not. If your child is displaying four or more of these behaviors over a long period of time, seek professional help regardless of the underlying cause.

Symptoms: Behaviors to Look For

We can examine the lists of characteristics and see how many of them apply to our child, but it might help to have some practical behavioral guidelines. How do these characteristics manifest themselves — how does an LD child act? It is safe to say that the kinds of behaviors listed below are demonstrated by all children at some point, just as many children display characteristics of LD children at some point. Again, it is the number of traits that your child exhibits, and the length of time over which he exhibits them, that should guide you.

There is one confusing point that bears clarification. The symptoms of LD are not necessarily the LD itself. We might call the LD child's behavior a secondary symptom of her LD, since such behavior is unquestionably the result of all the difficulty the child is having at school and at home. If the child's primary problem is a visual processing disorder, behaviors such as lack of attention, low frustration threshold, and anxiety would naturally follow. Since we are not yet at the point where we know exactly what the problem is, we must work backward from the symptoms and narrow down the possible primary causes in a professional evaluation. The behavioral symptoms must be observed before we can get to that evaluation.

The following descriptions of behaviors often associated with LD children are not age-related — any child can exhibit them, although with varying degrees of severity and sophistication. If the list seems daunting, remember that few children exhibit all of these behaviors, and never all at once, although it may seem that way to you sometimes:

aggressive or disruptive behavior: shouts out in class; hits siblings; refuses to cooperate with peers; bullies

hyperactivity: excessive motor or verbal activity; squirms in chairs; chatters aimlessly; inability to compose and control limbs or behavior on demand

hypoactivity: excessive lack of motor or verbal activity; may be perceived as shyness, dullness, laziness, fatigue; inattention

daydreaming: lacks attention to surroundings; is lost in own thoughts; "spacey"

short attention span: quickly loses interest in surroundings; is quick to change subject; is unwilling to see things through and finish projects

impulsiveness: acts without thought of consequences to self or others; interrupts; takes risks; speaks before thinking

labile emotions: broad and unpredictable mood swings; tantrums without apparent cause; excessive giddiness; easily provoked hysteria; overreaction

fragility: is easily shaken or upset; mood is easily shattered; confidence is easily destroyed

inconsistent or erratic behavior: enjoys activity one day and hates it the next; is able to complete a task one day and not the next

low frustration threshold: is easily stymied by tasks; throws crayons; crumples homework; gives up easily

disinhibition: shows lack of self-control; has lack of awareness of self in others' eyes (how friends, teachers, parents perceive him)

perseverance: persists in behavior beyond necessary limits; doesn't know when to stop a task, or is unable to stop when told; goes through repetitive behaviors

antisocial behavior: behaves rudely or inappropriately toward others; exhibits delinquency

negative attitude: is reluctant to cooperate; is unwilling to try new things

depression: has low energy and is unhappy, quiet, and withdrawn

anxiety: nervous and easily frightened, worries a lot

phobias: has fear of heights, of getting lost, of crowds, and so on

social immaturity: acts younger than others of the same age, preferring the company of younger children

drive: is hard on self, expecting perfection

poor self-image: shows lack of confidence, low self-opinion; is easily swayed by others

We can get even more particular and look at the kinds of symptomatic behaviors our LD children might exhibit in particular situations. Sally Smith, founder and director of the famous Kingsbury Laboratory School in Washington, D.C., has looked long and hard at the American educational system and what it means for LD kids. In her book *No Easy Answers,* she developed an extensive list of the typical problems that an LD child might exhibit in school. While it may duplicate some of the general behaviors described above, the list is especially useful because it's so specific.

Smith's behaviors are meant to be evaluated in a school setting, but some of them, particularly some of those traits on the lists of typical behavioral, language, and cognitive problems, will be exhibited out of school, where you are more likely to be aware of them. Because we see many of these traits as a matter of course when our children are developing, these behaviors may seem less frightening to us than the neurological characteristics we described. Obviously a two-year-old is going to be erratic, inconsistent, and unpredictable, and a four-year-old will have difficulty sticking to the main point when telling a story.

When the behaviors appear in older children, however, and

when they appear persistently and in clusters, most LD experts see them as symptomatic of learning problems. You'll be able to recognize some of these traits in your child, whether she's LD or not. Again, it's the number of behaviors and their consistency that is the key. At least five of the behaviors in any area should be observed over a period of several months before you get alarmed, and these traits should appear in the absence of other explanatory factors.

In addition to being illuminating to us as parents, Smith's lists should serve as an excellent checklist for teachers. If you feel that your child's teacher could benefit from these guidelines, or if you could benefit from having the teacher report to you, do not hesitate to pass them along.

I. General behavior: can be observed by parent or teacher in any situation.
   A. Erratic, inconsistent, unpredictable. Appears to be lazy. Good days, off days. Forgets what was learned yesterday, but, without reteaching, may remember it two days hence.
   B. Poor attention span. No sustained focus.
   C. Works very slowly. Never finishes working in an allotted time, or works carelessly, finishing in half the expected time. Feels need to hurry, without thinking.
   D. Poorly organized. Desk a mess. Always losing coat, or lunch.
   E. Late to class; lingers after class.
   F. Loses homework or hands it in late and sloppily done. Doesn't understand, or forgets, assignments.
   G. No study skills. Doesn't know how to organize work, how to plan in regard to deadlines, how to organize time.
   H. Low frustration tolerance. Gives up easily or explodes.
   I. Freezes when required to perform on demand, knows information when it is volunteered.
   J. Can't plan free time. Daydreams, acts silly, or repeats same activity over and over when given free choices.

II. Typical cognitive problems: can be observed by parent in conversation or informal learning situation (reading, art projects, interactive TV-watching) or by teacher.

A. Has difficulty sticking to main point.
B. Doesn't grasp cause-effect relationships.
C. Is rigid about concepts.
D. Has trouble with metaphors and relationships.
E. Doesn't see patterns.
F. Has poor memory.
G. Can't organize facts and concepts already absorbed, to use them in other ways.
H. Can't categorize or classify.
 I. Doesn't transfer learning over time.
J. Understands concepts too narrowly or too broadly.

III. Typical language problems: can be observed by parent or teacher on conversation.
  A. Cannot state something in an organized, cogent way. Starts in the middle of an idea. Cannot organize words properly in answer to a question.
  B. Has immature word use and ungrammatical phrasing.
  C. Has trouble following long directions.
  D. Doesn't enjoy being read to, but enjoys looking at pictures in books.
  E. Becomes distracted in class when instruction is presented orally. Learns from watching, not listening.
  F. Is very literal. Misses inferences, subtleties, innuendo.
  G. Has poor sense of humor. Doesn't understand jokes, puns, sarcasm.
  H. Has trouble with abstract words. Defines words by their concrete attributes or functions.
  I. Can't deal with multiple meanings of words; very rigid.
  J. Can't tell a story in sequence or summary. Recounts highly detailed and isolated facts.
  K. Under pressure, forgets names of things he knows and has to describe them.

IV. Typical reading problems: can be observed by teacher or by parent of five- or six-year-old child.
  A. Confuses *b* and *d,* or *p* and *g.*
  B. Confuses order of letters in words.
  C. Doesn't look carefully at details of a word and guesses from first letter.

54

   D. Loses his place on a page when reading, in the middle or at the end of a line.

   E. Can't remember common words taught from one day to the next. Most frequently forgets abstract words.

   F. Has no systematic way to decode, or figure out, a word he doesn't know.★

   G. Reads without expression and ignores punctuation. Has little awareness of the ideas expressed by writer.

   H. Reads very slowly and tires easily.

   I. Omits, substitutes, or adds words to a sentence.

   J. Reads word-by-word.

V. Typical spelling problems: can be observed by teacher or by parent helping with homework.

   A. Writes *b* for *d,* and vice versa.

   B. Transposes order of the letters.

   C. Doesn't hear sequence of sounds in a word and writes only isolated parts of it (*amil* for *animal*).

   D. Has no memory for common words not regularly spelled.

   E. Does not hear fine differences in words.

   F. Has trouble with consonants.

   G. Leaves out vowels.

   H. Writes messily.

   I. Omits capitals and punctuation.

VI. Typical writing problems: can be observed by teacher or by parent.

   A. Holds pencil awkwardly and tires easily when writing.

   B. Can't write without lined paper. Spaces letters poorly.

   C. Writes letters backward, upside down, incompletely.

   D. Mixes lower-case letters with capitals.

   E. Writes letter above and below line.

   F. Writes large because of poor control and size-relationship perception.

★Note: Reading *decodes* symbols of sound into meaning. Listening decodes sounds into meaning. Writing, on the other hand, puts meaning into symbols, which is called *encoding*. *Decoding* and *encoding* are two good words to know if you're going to be dealing with professional reading specialists.

G. Writes very small and holds pencil too tightly.
H. Writes slowly. Tries to form each letter perfectly.
I. Can't remember how to form letters.
J. Erases often.

More Statistics: Profile of an LD Kid

Let's take a brief statistical tour, and get an overview of the "typical" LD child — having already agreed that there is no such animal. In 1971, a California researcher, Freya Owen, and her colleagues compiled a statistical picture of the statistically average LD child, based on extensive psychometric tests (that is, tests that measure various psychological data in relation to the group being tested). Her results are still valid nearly twenty years later, according to the latest figures released by the U.S. Department of Education Office for Special Education. There is one big difference, though. In 1972, the total number of children in the United States with LD problems was estimated at about 600,000 (remember, this was before national legislation that attempted to define the problem). In 1987, that number stood at 1,877,030.

That figure represents 47 percent of all special needs children in the country, and 6 percent of the entire U.S. student body between the ages of six and seventeen. But, since those statistics only account for children of those ages who are currently receiving services through public schools, experts agree the actual percentage of LD kids is near 12. Seventy-one percent of them are boys (down only slightly from Owen's figure), and 67 percent are between the ages of eight and eleven.

Although the charge has been made that LD is a racially discriminatory syndrome, the racial distribution of LD closely reflects the racial distribution of the student population: 71 percent of the LD population is white, as compared to 70 percent of the overall student body. Sixty-seven percent of all LD students are educated with the help of resource rooms, where they get help in weak areas before returning to their regular classes. Twenty-two percent spend their school days in special classes, and 15 percent spend their entire days in regular classrooms. Less than 2 percent are educated in expensive separate facilities, ranging from special day schools to residential hospital settings.

But, since Freya Owen's profile still holds true, we can look back to it to give us a much more detailed picture of that non-existent "average LD child." (The profile is included in Sylvia Farnham-Diggory's 1978 book, *Learning Disabilities: A Psychological Perspective*.)

Owen's subjects were children designated by the state as "educationally handicapped" (the term in vogue at the time), and she measured them, using school achievement and adjustment tests, IQ tests, drawing and handwriting ability, neurological development, and family data. She also tested the siblings of the group, as well as a control group of non-LD children and their siblings. The socioeconomic backgrounds of all the children were similar. Parents were interviewed and tested as well.

Based on the results of the tests, an interesting demographic picture emerged of the "typical" LD child. Most obvious was the gender breakdown: 80 percent of the LD children were boys. While some experts dispute this figure, most agree that the 4:1 ratio is accurate. But what does it mean? There are several theories. One is that males are simply slower to develop than female children, and therefore are more likely to be diagnosed as having learning disabilities. The problem with this theory, of course, lies in determining whether these male children are simply slower to mature, or really are candidates for an LD diagnosis.

A widely held theory is that male children are more genetically vulnerable to the neurological disorders (or differences) that might be the cause of learning disabilities. This would account for the wide discrepancy between girls and boys even after we have factored out the slow-to-mature factor. But another research approach holds that it is the females, while still embryos, who are weaker. Unable to survive the development in utero of certain hormones, probably testosterones, which are suspected of being the culprit of neurological impairment, more female fetuses spontaneously abort; thus fewer females are born with the propensity for learning disabilities. (More on this theory in chapter 3.)

Still, Owen's statistics clearly support the 4:1 ratio. They also break down the chronological pattern (still valid today) as follows:

4 percent of them were six-year-olds.
10 percent of them were seven-year-olds.

67 percent of the LD children were in the eight-to-eleven-year-old range.

18 percent were twelve to sixteen years old.

Why the huge bulge in the middle of this demographic picture? Again, there are several explanations. It's likely that fewer children are diagnosed as having LD in the first and second grades because teachers are unable to distinguish the truly LD children from the less mature non-LD children (probably boys, given the gender statistics we just examined). It isn't until those patterns persist through the second and third grades that warning flags go up in school (another good reason to be vigilant at home). So most children aren't suspected of having a problem until then, and they aren't evaluated until the third, fourth, and fifth grades. That accounts for the dramatically higher percentage of LD-identified kids in the eight-to-eleven-year-old range.

But why the drop-off in numbers after elementary school? Once the LD kids are identified, shouldn't that percentage remain the same? Not if the LD kids move into less taxing academic programs, where their disabilities no longer inhibit them from performing up to the (lower-level) norm. These children *appear* not to need continued remediation, when in fact it may just be that the schools' expectations of what they are capable of doing has dropped.

It's also true that, with so few LD specialists available at the high-school level in American schools, many children who were identified as LD in elementary school simply fall through the cracks in high school, and "disappear" statistically. This is true in private schools, too, since the states must by law keep track of children who require special education regardless of whether they attend public, private, or parochial schools. What is *not* true, according to Sylvia Farnham-Diggory, is that LD is less frequent in high-school kids, or that it is cured by the time they reach their teens.

Statistically, LD children tend to come from well-educated homes: 63 percent of the LD kids' fathers in Owen's sample had some years of college, 21 percent had graduate-level educations (mothers' educations were inexplicably not examined). These figures are high from a national standpoint, but not extraordinary for the community in which the study was based (a middle- to upper-middle-class neighborhood in southern California). Racial and ethnic breakdowns are not made in this study, but other studies indicate that LD is predominantly a white experience. The reasons for this are obvious: it is the white, middle-class child who is most likely to be in an environment where he can be identified as having problems at school or at home, and it is most likely that those problems will not be attributed to economic, social, or physical deprivation. (We'll discuss that subject in chapter 9.)

The statistical LD kid scores as well as her non-LD friends on the WISC, a standardized test that is considered to be the basic psychometric instrument for measuring intelligence. (LD kids averaged 107 on the full score (a combination of verbal and performance scores, while non-LD kids averaged 109.) But, while the LD kid had performance scores that were much higher than her verbal scores (an indication of the discrepancy between ability and action that we mentioned as a real common denominator for all LD kids), the non-LD test taker showed no such variation. It's also interesting to note that the performance scores for the LD kids were *higher* than those of the non-LD kids — but of course the verbal scores were much lower, which accounts for the similarity in the full scores.

In school, the LD kid is at least two grades behind her chronological peers in reading, and a year and a half behind in spelling. The grade lag becomes worse with age. At home, LD kids tend to have siblings with learning problems, and their parents tended to have had lower grades when they were in school than the parents of non-LD kids.

Owen's study painted in some other statistical details. The LD child (and her siblings) performed lower than the non-LD child on a variety of perceptual tests, not because of a disability in perceiving, but because of a disability in organizing what was perceived. Speech problems were more often diagnosed for LD kids than for non-LD kids, but Owen speculated that speech difficulties may have derived from attentional difficulties — children were unable to speak clearly because they were unable to integrate the speech they heard. Neurological and medical examinations were also inconclusive.

What does all this mean? "As studied by these methods," writes

Farnham-Diggory, "LD children are shown to be in the 8–11 year-old range, predominantly male, of middle-class background with relatively well-educated parents. Their IQ is normal but their reading, spelling and drawing abilities run at least 2 years behind those of 'normal' children the same age. They may have speech problems and other indications of neurological dysfunction. Their school adjustment has been troubled. Their families have been affected by the stress of dealing with them, but one cannot attribute family problems to the LD child alone.

"Depending upon the assessment criteria," she concludes flatly, "from 2 to 40 percent of the school children in this country are believed to fit this general description."

Owen's statistical picture tells us something about the American LD child, but what about LD elsewhere? It's interesting to note that Western countries like Canada, Denmark, England, and Germany report about the same percentage of LD kids in their school-age populations. But in Japan, LD is virtually unknown.

There are a few good theories to explain this. Japan has a much more rigid social and educational system, and nonconforming children are much less easily tolerated there than in our country. Children are exposed to academic standards at an early age, and those who cannot measure up are often simply swept along with the crowd all the way up to the university level. There's another intriguing explanation, however. The Japanese language is very precise and pictorial, and there is not as much room for syntactic error or reversals. For all its complexity, the language may actually be easier to learn. There are also genetic factors to consider, since research has shown (see chapter 3) that a tendency to LD is often inherited.

Attention Deficit Disorders: A Special Case

In our descriptions of the symptoms and characteristics of LD kids, the words *poor attention* or *short attention span* appeared several times, as did words like *hyperactivity* and *hyperkinesis*. Before we go on to examine the causes of LD in the next chapter, we should spend a little more time looking at a particular subset of the LD field. It's called attention deficit disorder, and, since it's receiving a lot of attention from educators and doctors lately, the concept needs further explanation.

The term *attention deficit disorder* (ADD) is fairly new, but the syndrome it describes is not. We used to call it hyperactivity, although current research has shown that hyperactivity is a subset of ADD, and that children with ADD may not exhibit any hyperactive symptoms. The current terminology identifies a child as having ADD either with or without hyperactivity.

The connection between LD and ADD is complex. Children with LD problems are at a much greater risk than the general population for having ADD, and, nearly without exception, all ADD children have learning problems (although if the ADD is treated, the learning problems may be resolved more easily — more about that in chapter 8).

According to Larry Silver's excellent pamphlet on the subject, *ADD* is a term used to describe a group of children who have many problems with control. Dr. Mel Levine, professor at the University of North Carolina School of Medicine, director of the Clinical Center for the Study of Development and Learning there, and perhaps the foremost scholar in the field of ADD, is more specific: "ADD arises from malfunctions of neurobehavioral control systems that regulate learning and adaptation."

It's a large group — nearly one million children were diagnosed as having the problem in 1986. According to Russ Barkley, a Worcester, Massachusetts, researcher, the ratio of male to female ADD children is 6:1. Dr. Levine feels that ADD children can be found in all social and income groups: "The inner city clinics find a majority of cases in lower socio-economic groups, while the private psychiatrists find a higher incidence among high-end families. In fact, ADD occurs at all levels, although it may look different at different levels. Certainly the complications, such as conduct problems and delinquency, are greater in children from poor environments."

ADD children exhibit a wide variety of symptoms. How can we tell if our child is at risk? In general, the ADD infant will exhibit lots of motion, eating and sleeping problems, and excess stimulus sensitivity (he will reject intense interactions, even with parents, and will be easily aroused and/or distracted). As a toddler, he may be impulsive, attention-seeking, and unable to control his social behavior. School-age ADD kids are unable to focus on their academic tasks, and exhibit increasing social inappropriateness. Children may be diagnosed as early as three or four, although Dr.

Levine feels that extreme caution must be used at this age, since it is easy to mistake developmental characteristics for ADD.

Other LD children may exhibit the same symptoms, and some non-LD children may exhibit similar ones. As with all other symptoms, it is the number and severity that would lead to an accurate diagnosis.

The American Psychiatric Association's *Diagnostic and Statistical Manual for Mental Disorders* (third edition, revised) gives a list of criteria on which the APA bases a diagnosis of ADD with or without hyperactivity. The list stresses the varying degrees of these symptoms and adds that they may be present in other disorders or in the absence of any neurological disorder at all. In addition, it points out that there are age-specific features of the disorder; for instance, gross motor overactivity is a common symptom for pre-schoolers (although DSM-III R acknowledges that the disorder is frequently not recognized until the child enters school), while excessive fidgeting is common in school-age children and social impulsiveness common in adolescents. Given those caveats, the list is still a good guideline for parents to use:

A. A disturbance of at least six months during which eight of the following are present:
   1. often fidgets with hands or feet or squirms in seat
   2. has difficulty remaining seated when required to do so
   3. is easily distracted by extraneous stimuli
   4. has difficulty awaiting turns in games or group situations
   5. often blurts out answers to questions before they have been completed
   6. has difficulty following through on instructions from others (e.g., often fails to finish chores)
   7. has difficulty sustaining attention in tasks or play activities
   8. often shifts from one uncompleted activity to another
   9. has difficulty playing quietly
   10. often talks excessively
   11. often interrupts or intrudes on others
   12. often does not seem to listen to what is being said to him or her
   13. often loses things necessary for tasks or activities at home or at school

14. often engages in physically dangerous activities without considering possible consequences
B. Onset before age eight
C. Does not meet the criteria for a pervasive developmental disorder

It's perfectly natural that ADD is considered a subset of LD problems, since ADD kids have such difficulty learning. But there is very little chance that the actual ADD is not accompanied by some other type of LD problem, regardless of whether it's a result of the ADD or in addition to it. Levine says that virtually all children with ADD also have learning problems, and adds that it is often difficult to distinguish the two clinically. "It's silly to try and separate the two, because ADD acts like a magnet for a variety of problems such as memory, language and math skills. When schools try to make a mutually exclusive diagnosis they may be doing the child a disservice. We have to stop asking 'which one is it?' and concentrate on what we can do in each area that presents a problem."

With that in mind, it will help to characterize the particular attributes of an ADD child. The most important one, of course, is the inability to control behavior, and Dr. Levine has isolated nine separate systems that are affected by this lack. They're helpful because we can understand how broad the effects of ADD can be on a child's development.

1. **Lack of focal control:** inability to select the distinctive features of potentially informative stimuli (to see the outline of a house hidden in a picture or to know what to look at when confronted with a page of print)
2. **Lack of sensory control:** distractibility due to failure to inhibit one sense modality in order to focus on another (hearing intrusive noise while trying to listen to the teacher)
3. **Lack of associative control:** inability to control free associative thinking, making the child easily prone to "daydreaming"
4. **Lack of appetite control:** inability to delay physical or emotional gratification
5. **Lack of social control:** inability to filter out peers in order to concentrate on tasks, and to regulate social interactions

6. **Lack of motor control:** inefficient or non–goal-directed activity, whether by under- or overactivity (excessive squirming, pencil-tapping, or erasures); poor motivation
7. **Lack of behavioral control:** inability to regulate conscious behavior or foresee consequences of actions
8. **Lack of communicative control:** verbal disinhibition; saying the wrong thing at the wrong time
9. **Lack of affective control:** inability to control emotional range, resulting in wide mood swings (emotional lability)

While a list of these symptoms is helpful, we don't really need to be able to distinguish between the kinds of symptoms our children seem to be presenting and the particular nature of the problem. As parents, our job is to initiate the process by which professionals can arrive at a proper diagnosis, regardless of the specific nature of the problem. Any child with a suspected LD problem should be tested for possible ADD, and any child suspected of having attentional disorders should automatically be evaluated to establish the nature of her LD.

Dr. Levine has come up with a fascinating tool for establishing the behavioral criterion of ADD (see Appendix B). Since Levine plays down the separation between the two, his system, known as ANSER (Aggregate Neurobehavioral Student Health and Educational Review), is valuable for LD as well. The ANSER system has components for parents, teachers, and children, and is divided into age groups. Essentially, it is a long checklist of possible health problems, functional problems, family history, and development, and specific behaviors associated with attention. Each category can be responded to in varying degree — a little, a lot, or not at all. Some diagnosticians complain that it is unwieldy, but I think it's worth having, because it really helps parents think more clearly about their child. Even if you don't get the results evaluated, it helps you arrive at a much clearer picture of your child.

The Good News

It may seem by now that there is nothing good about the LD child. If every parent in America were to read this book tonight and apply the preceding guidelines to his or her child, there would

be mas   iild in America would be
conside
    But t   look at. We'll spend more
time la   f our LD kids, but now
might l   ositive symptomology. It
is essen   characteristics and symptoms a   en we search for possible
signs o   we focus only on the negatives,
not on   are very much a part of
our chi   good usually outweighs
the bad   vay at times.
    Prisc   *art Kids with School Prob-
lems,* pc   some terrific characteristics that
set ther   their on-LD peers. Look for
signs of   g particularly low about
your LI   list are mine):

* rapid   erability
* aware   itened perception
* energy   gent thinking
* curios   vity
* concen   used intelligence
* exceptional memory   • musicality
* empathy

It's also important to remember that, even among the LD population, every child is unique, and no two will exhibit the exact
same combination of traits in the same degree. This leaves us with
a problem. If every single child has a different set of symptoms
for LD, how are we going to know if our child's particular set
places her at risk? The problem lies not with the definition or the
description of symptoms, but with the basic premise that learning
disabilities need to be precisely defined before they can be treated.

Barbara Keogh, in her keynote address to the annual conference
held by the Division for Learning Disabilities of the Council for
Exceptional Children, has developed a very sensible approach to
the problem of identification. She feels that there are different reasons for classification. If the definition is intended to identify so
that services can be provided, then it can be broad. If it's for research purposes, perhaps it should be more narrow. "The devel-

opment of a useful classification system is a long-range goal. Meanwhile, pupils with problems in school need to be identified, and they will differ markedly in their attributes. This 'mixed bag' of pupils, however, does not negate the concept of LD or the need for services."

Keogh makes it very clear that, despite continued research into the field, identification remains a thorny and unresolved issue. "Symptoms," she says, ". . . will vary in chronicity [time of appearance], salience [intensity] and number. Rather than try to force these attributes into a single definition, we must acknowledge that they represent different types of LD. The identification of individuals as learning disabled is not a binary decision — it is not as simple as 'you are or you are not.'"

Now that we've made some headway on defining the term *LD* and identifying the child who may need it, it's time to move on. The experts have spent so much time debating the issues of definition and identification that even they are beginning to question the wisdom of spending so much time and energy in a pursuit that may have no end. Better, perhaps, to look at underlying causes for possible clues to prevent LD, and, more important, at remediation for helping the children who are suffering from it today.

be mass hysteria tomorrow and every child in America would be considered at risk for LD.

But there is a bright side of the coin to look at. We'll spend more time later on discussing the strengths of our LD kids, but now might be the perfect time for a dose of positive symptomology. It is essential to remember that the lists of characteristics and symptoms are only part of the picture — when we search for possible signs of a problem in our child, we focus only on the negatives, not on the host of wonderful things that are very much a part of our child's personality. On balance, the good usually outweighs the bad, although it may not seem that way at times.

Priscilla Vail, in her excellent book *Smart Kids with School Problems,* points out that LD kids have some terrific characteristics that set them apart — and above — their non-LD peers. Look for signs of the following when you're feeling particularly low about your LD kid (the last three items on the list are mine):

- rapid grasp of concepts
- awareness of patterns
- energy
- curiosity
- concentration
- exceptional memory
- empathy
- vulnerability
- heightened perception
- divergent thinking
- creativity
- focused intelligence
- musicality

It's also important to remember that, even among the LD population, every child is unique, and no two will exhibit the exact same combination of traits in the same degree. This leaves us with a problem. If every single child has a different set of symptoms for LD, how are we going to know if our child's particular set places her at risk? The problem lies not with the definition or the description of symptoms, but with the basic premise that learning disabilities need to be precisely defined before they can be treated.

Barbara Keogh, in her keynote address to the annual conference held by the Division for Learning Disabilities of the Council for Exceptional Children, has developed a very sensible approach to the problem of identification. She feels that there are different reasons for classification. If the definition is intended to identify so that services can be provided, then it can be broad. If it's for research purposes, perhaps it should be more narrow. "The development of a useful classification system is a long-range goal. Meanwhile, pupils with problems in school need to be identified, and they will differ markedly in their attributes. This 'mixed bag' of pupils, however, does not negate the concept of LD or the need for services."

Keogh makes it very clear that, despite continued research into the field, identification remains a thorny and unresolved issue. "Symptoms," she says, ". . . will vary in chronicity [time of appearance], salience [intensity] and number. Rather than try to force these attributes into a single definition, we must acknowledge that they represent different types of LD. The identification of individuals as learning disabled is not a binary decision — it is not as simple as 'you are or you are not.' "

Now that we've made some headway on defining the term *LD* and identifying the child who may need it, it's time to move on. The experts have spent so much time debating the issues of definition and identification that even they are beginning to question the wisdom of spending so much time and energy in a pursuit that may have no end. Better, perhaps, to look at underlying causes for possible clues to prevent LD, and, more important, at remediation for helping the children who are suffering from it today.

CHAPTER 3

Where Do Learning Disabilities Come From?

Question: "What was it like when you first found out you had a learning disability?"

Answers: "I was fine in kindergarten, and then I walked into first grade and sat down, and BOOM! It was as if everything went gray."

"When I first saw that other kids could read, I thought God must be mad at me, or something. I knew I was as smart as they were, but I thought I wasn't really."

"I was glad to find out I wasn't retarded."

WE'VE already realized that there are no simple answers to our questions about the nature and characteristics of learning disabilities. Definition by exclusion seems to be the rule rather than the exception in LD research. And surely we cannot progress in those areas of inquiry without conducting a thorough examination of what causes LD to happen in the first place.

But it's not surprising that remedial techniques lag behind laboratory research. In all areas of science, experimentation produces data long before techniques can be introduced to clinical use. Such data have to be thoroughly tested and then carefully developed into a viable therapeutic program before the technique can begin the arduous filtering-down process that eventually results in its appearance in a classroom situation. A laborious process, indeed.

Nevertheless, it helps us to know that great inroads are being made into the possible causes of learning disabilities. Even if they are not yet reflected in our children's classrooms or therapy programs, those gains are cause for hope and optimism. There may, after all, be some real answers.

But, while we wait, there's no reason why we can't examine the most up-to-date theories about the origins of LD and see if any of them make sense to us, for our children. And quite a few experimental therapies resulting from this new research (or therapies *considered* to be experimental by the medical and educational establishments) are available to the parent who is willing to seek them out, and perhaps to endure a certain degree of skepticism.

It's our right as parents to choose whatever we believe will work for our child, and to choose it as soon as we can. Of course, we must recognize that the schools have a great deal of expertise in the matter, and we should be willing to work with them. But, faced with the continuing difficulties that our children encounter at home and in school, we ought not to have to wait until reluctant establishments give their belated go-ahead.

Of course, we run the risk that the "new" approach may be disproved, not approved, after careful and cautious evaluation. So, along with the right, we have an obligation: to gather as great a variety of information as possible before we go ahead with any remedial system, whether it is the tried-and-true curriculum chosen by our child's school or the unconventional procedure we chose ourselves. But first, before we can agree with the theory about the diagnosis, or the process of remediation, we need to know if the theory about the cause makes sense to us. If we believe that our child's stomachache is caused by an unspoken fear of school rather than a real illness, we're not going to treat it with medication. Again, we have to trust our strong instincts as parents and our thorough knowledge of our children.

The study of causes is called *etiology*, and when we look at the etiology of LD, many questions arise. Where do learning disabilities come from? How do researchers go about determining possible causes? How can we determine what caused them in *our* children? What solid evidence have scientists come up with to date regarding causes, and what does the latest research reveal?

In this chapter, we'll look briefly at the history of LD research and then go on to examine three main areas of etiological concentration: the structure of the brain and central nervous system, their function and relationship to learning, and environmental influences. But, in the interests of perspective, it's nice to start with an explanation offered by the researcher Leon Eisenberg in his paper "Definitions of Dyslexia": "A group of disorders exists which does somehow correspond to the Loch Ness monster — i.e., a category of patients who fail to learn to read in the absence of any of the ordinary causes for poor reading."

How It All Began

If you have [an LD kid], you may be surprised to hear that the rationale behind his or her remedial curriculum is probably 40 or 50 years old, going on 100. This does not mean that the program is a bad one, but it does mean that the program is not based on current scientific theory in the areas of human learning and thinking.

> *Sylvia Farnham-Diggory in*
> Learning Disabilities: A Psychological
> Perspective

Remember William Pringle Morton, the ophthalmologist who constructed the first known definition of LD in 1896? His definition of the term *word blindness,* the congenital inability to recognize familiar words despite apparently normal intelligence, set the stage for a century of research. Actually, his research was predated by more than thirty years: in 1860 Paul Broca postulated the dominance of the left side of the brain over the right, and theorized that the left side was the seat of language functions. Dysfunctions such as aphasia (the inability to express spoken or written language), he felt, were caused by brain lesions. (Lesions are harmful changes in the tissue of an organ, and can be caused by injury, disease, or malformation.) Many current researchers cite Broca as their direct theoretical ancestor.

Another Scottish ophthalmologist, James Hinshelwood, actually predated Morton's definition of LD by a year, in 1895, but he focused on acquired word blindness, probably the result of brain damage. Drawing from case histories of adults who had suddenly lost the ability to read or perceive other visual stimuli, Hinshelwood postulated that there were separate places in the brain for everyday visual memory, visual word memory, and visual letter memory, and that trauma to any one of these areas would lead to the loss of the corresponding function. Although Hinshelwood may not have been exact about where in the brain these control centers existed, his theory — that certain functions resided in certain discrete areas of the brain — has been the basis of neurological research ever since.

Hinshelwood, however, was talking about acquired brain injury, while Morton was postulating word blindness present from birth for no apparent reason. In order to examine the connection between the two, Hinshelwood looked at children *without* histories of traumatic brain injury who still could not read, and decided that dyslexia could, in fact, be due to a *preexisting* injurious condition in the brain — in other words, the damage did not occur as the result of a fall, a blow, or an illness. Like Broca, he attributed the cause to tiny lesions — congenital lesions that had occurred during prenatal development.

No one has yet come up with solid evidence to disprove his supposition and, in fact, most subsequent research has taken this theory as its root. Hinshelwood's most famous theoretical successor was the American physician Samuel T. Orton, who in 1925 published a paper that took Hinshelwood's theory one step farther and presented for the first time the notion of hemispheric imbalance — or cerebral dominance — as a possible cause of dyslexia. Neurologists were already aware that the left hemisphere was responsible for language functions, but little was known about the nature of the brain's right hemisphere. Instead of being a structural aberrance in the way the dyslexic brain was formed, Orton believed that, since both sides worked equally instead of the left side dominating as it should, dyslexia was a *functional* distortion — an imbalance in the way the brain operated rather than in the way it was built. As a matter of fact, he never worked on an autopsied dyslexic brain, so he had no direct experience of the brain's structure.

But Orton's work is still invaluable to modern researchers. Not only did he characterize the functions of the hemispheres, but he also described the different cortical tissues that were, he felt, responsible for different parts of the activity we have come to know as reading. Orton hypothesized the separate uses for which each hemisphere and each type of tissue was responsible. He went farther than Morton and Hinshelwood, describing the problem as one that involved not only word-recognition blindness, but also memory and associative blindness: the inability to connect the printed symbols with their learned meaning.

While perception of a word, and recognition of it, can be handled by either the right or left hemisphere (and thus can occur even when one half of the brain is damaged), the associative functions need both hemispheres to operate. Orton's tongue-twisting name for the problem was *strephosymbolia* — a Greek term that, in English, means "twisted symbolism." (Keep in mind that Orton and the others were concerned chiefly with reading and language disabilities, but that the main tenets of their work can be applied to other perceptual disabilities as well, although we still don't have direct evidence of those connections.) Today, the worldwide Orton Society is a preeminent institution in promoting understanding, treatment, and prevention of dyslexia, which they also call specific language disabilities. Some critics feel the methods espoused by the Orton Society don't go far enough toward remedying the myriad problems encountered by LD children and adults, but their success rate in terms of academic remediation is undisputed (see chapter 8 and Appendix A for more information about the Orton Society).

After World War II, investigations into the problems of brain-injured veterans accelerated the knowledge of congenital disabilities. Using research on brain-injured soldiers, which indicated that behavioral disturbances persisted even after wounds had healed, the physician Alfred Strauss hypothesized that the same types of behavioral disturbance — notably hyperactivity and volatility — could be attributed to brain injuries in children. Strauss used the terms *endogenous* and *exogenous* to indicate congenital and ac-

71

quired injuries, and specifically concentrated on those children whose injuries occurred exogenously — outside their genetic development.

It's important to note that Strauss concerned himself only with mentally retarded children, although his theories can be extended to children of normal intelligence with either congenital or acquired dysfunctions. The typical behavior associated with such injuries — emotional instability, perceptual disorders, and distractibility — came to be known as the Strauss syndrome, and can still be used to describe learning disabled children. But today's "definition" of LD, such as it is, rules out the presence of verifiable physical abnormalities as the primary cause of learning problems. In addition, neither mental retardation or low IQ is a factor associated with LD.

There were, however, several serious lapses of logic in Strauss's theory. He felt that the location of the injury didn't matter as much as its size, so he didn't think it was necessary to pinpoint the location in order to infer damage. In addition, he felt that, if nonspecific brain injury caused Strauss syndrome behaviors, then Strauss syndrome behaviors implied nonspecific brain injuries.

We now know that the location of the injury is extremely important, and that Strauss's theory was only partially correct. Impulsive behaviors and perceptual difficulties can have a host of causes unrelated to brain injury of any kind — psychological disorders and sensory impairments are just two possibilities. But Strauss's influence, like Orton's and those of the other LD research pioneers, is still reverberating through the field, and the historical basis of today's research into the structural, functional, and environmental causes of LD reflects the work of these early pioneers.

The Structure of the Brain

Many factors have been suggested to explain the origin of learning disabilities. There are functional causes (defects in the way the brain works), head injuries, birth traumas, and sensory deficits. There are environmental causes such as malnutrition and language deprivation, allergies and toxic substances. There are theories that point to inner-ear disorders, vitamin deficiencies, and even laziness. But the main thrust of contemporary research focuses on the structure of the brain itself, and on the cellular abnormalities that seem to be at the root of all types of learning problems. It is this research that provides us with the most substantial and promising attempts to explain the etiology of LD.

Before we look at the latest discoveries, however, let's take a quick look at the structure of a "normal" brain. The brain is divided into two hemispheres, each of which handles a different group of functions. The brain can also be classified another way, though. The "triune" (or three-part) brain reflects not the shape of the brain, but its evolution from the earliest simple formation to the current large and complex system. Amazingly, the brain still retains the basic features that reflect our ancestral relationship to reptiles and early mammals, and it is this evolutionary consistency — the primitive structure lying within the more complicated system — that provides the key to much of our understanding of the way the brain operates.

While they are radically different in structure and chemistry, these three formations — the R-complex, the limbic system, and the neocortex — constitute a hierarchy of three brains in one. The R-complex, located in the midbrain, influences the primal patterns of behavior in all mammals — our impulses and compulsions, or routine habits, our urge to mate, to breed, and to conform to the rules of our species.

The limbic system, located in the layer surrounding the midbrain, is the seat of our emotions and aspects of our personal identity, as well as our sleeping and dreaming functions and our short-term memory. Drugs often act on the limbic system in the brain, and dysfunctions here cause uncontrollable emotions.

The largest outer layer of our brain, the neocortex, is responsible for all of our higher functions (although it does share some functions with the limbic system). Here reside our reason, linguistic expression, muscle activity, verbal memory, and speech. Our perceptual functions are controlled by the neocortex, although all three systems interact in a complicated interchange of electrical impulses and chemical discharges.

It is the neocortex that is divided into those two hemispheres we spoke about earlier. The relationship between the hemispheric division and the triune division is complex, to say the least, and any brief explanation is an oversimplification. In lower animals,

73

the connections among the three levels are quite direct. As we move up the evolutionary scale, however, they become more complicated, appearing in newly developed regions of the cortex by way of complex associative connections.

Much has been said about the division of labor in the brain, but it's important to realize that none of the areas of the brain functions alone. The theory that the left brain is the more advanced — the "smarter" side — is nonsense. After all, the right hemisphere has to be providing some important advanced functions, or the law of evolution would have rendered it obsolete and atrophied long ago.

The two sides of the brain operate on the principle of complementary specialization, with both sides of an equally advanced level of complexity. Functions are generally divided, but complex activities result in the interplay between left and right hemispheres, and many basic functions have seats in both hemispheres.

The concept of hemispheric dominance has been at the center of LD brain research for years. Remember Orton's and Strauss's theories from fifty years ago? Studies have since shown that they were right — certain simple tasks are "grabbed" by one hemisphere before the other because that hemisphere is more specialized for the task, although the other could do it if necessary. In other words, the part of the brain that's right for the job does the job, although another part could do it if necessary. It's an impressive system of checks and balances, insuring that our body's functions are taken care of in one way or another.

Having said that, let's look at the basic division of labor between the two, aware that the list is both tentative and oversimplified.

Left	*Right*
Speech and writing	Spatial identification
Main language control	Music awareness
Right eye, hand, ear	Left hand, eye, ear
Calculation	Simple language
Analytic and abstract reasoning	Recognition of patterns
Sequential functions	Intuition
Specific concepts	General concepts
Familiar thinking	Creative thinking
Logic	Emotions

In spite of "complementary specialization," it's interesting to note that no other mammal is predominantly controlled by one

74

half of the brain the way humans are, which is why cerebral dominance is such a crucial concept for understanding the etiology of LD. Although the right and left halves of the brain are roughly equal in size, in about 65 percent of the population the surface area of the left side (the side that controls reason, higher language, and abstract reasoning) is larger. In many dyslexics, however, the sides are equal, and in about 10 percent of the population, the asymmetry is even reversed. Not only are the language centers in the right side as large as those in the left, but there are actually more brain cells in the right than in the left, which may result in a real rivalry between the right and left sides of the brain. It is a well-accepted theory that this tension is what causes the confusion and distractibility apparent in so many LD kids.

So the concept of two hemispheres and hemispheric dominance must be looked at in the light of another important theory: the asymmetry of the brain. Most brains are asymmetric — it's the nature of the imbalance that accounts for learning problems. The right and left sides are generally asymmetrical, but asymmetries can also be structural — the size, shape, density, and distribution of the cells in each side are different. Research has shown, for example, that the curves and curls of the sylvian fissure (a large fold near the base of the cortex) differ consistently between dyslexics and nondyslexics. And they are chemical, too. Research has shown imbalances in biochemicals such as choline, norepinephrine, dopamine, serotonin, and the hormone testosterone.

This, then, is the first bit of physical evidence that the brains of dyslexics are actually different from those of the general population. Albert M. Galaburda, a neurologist at the Harvard Medical School, feels that these differences in asymmetries are the real key to understanding the pathology of LD, and, in its graphic simplicity, this etiology offers a very clear explanation of the connection between the nature of the brain and the behavior of the individual.

Galaburda calls it the study of cerebral architectonics — an elegant and evocative phrase that describes the complex physical structure of the organ. He has proven that "the surface of the brain shows striking variation in organization. There is strong evidence to support the notion that distinct architectonic areas have distinct connectional patterns and functions." In other words, the differences in size, density, and distribution of brain cells are what create the differences in the way our brain (and our CNS) functions.

So the architecture of the brain is a likely cause of LD. But what are the mechanisms that *cause* this difference in hemispheric development? The two sides of the brain are connected by a large bundle of nerve fibers called the corpus callosum, which carries incoming sensations to appropriate areas in the neocortex, connects different parts of the brain together, and carries impulses out again to the muscles. If this area is not functioning properly, the message may never get to its appropriate site. In other words, a failure of the messenger, not the receptor site itself, may be responsible for the improper reception of incoming stimuli. A good way to visualize this concept is to think of a game of catch. A ball is thrown in a straight line, and a catcher is ready to receive it, but an unseen and unexpected force suddenly interrupts the pitch, which ricochets out into left field. The actions and intentions of the pitcher and catcher were right, but, through no fault of theirs, the ball ended up far from where it was supposed to be.

How does this breakdown in communication evolve? Galaburda and his predecessor, Norman Geschwind, who pioneered this area of research, looked for the answer in the fetal development of the brain, particularly in the development of neurotransmitters, the chemical messengers of the brain and the CNS. Scientists know of more than fifty of these messengers and postulate the existence of as many as two hundred.

During pregnancy, genetic messages pass daily through the fetal brain to various receptor sites and stimulate growth there. The end result, when it works right, is a fully wired brain — a process that is begun when the structure is developing in the womb and continues throughout childhood. As the child matures, the brain and the CNS mature, anatomically and biochemically. Cell function improves, and the number and complexity of connections increase.

When this architectural progression — building receptor sites, one upon the other, to create a fully operative structure — goes awry, problems occur. Millions of cells are migrating to their predestined sites and interconnecting with millions of others in a process that would defy even the most sophisticated computer. If one cell fails to arrive at the proper site at the right time, all subsequent development will be affected. The astounding thing is that it doesn't happen more often.

Abnormal development and alignment of brain cells in the second trimester of pregnancy are thought to be the cause of most learning dysfunctions, because that is when the structure for higher functions such as thought and language is being erected. Researchers have found evidence of structural abnormalities in fetuses as young as twelve weeks, and they suspect that some of these abnormalities may be the organic root of language development problems, among other things.

There are several working theories about what might be interfering with the building process:

• maternal use of drugs, cigarettes, or alcohol
• unknown virus that seeps through the placental walls
• poor maternal nutrition
• small stroke
• maternal or fetal stress

Factors unrelated to the second trimester include:

• slow fetal growth rates
• twin births
• labor and delivery
• fetal position
• fetal birth weight

But those are all external, or epigenetic, factors, affecting the outcome of the fetus's development. Galaburda and his associates believe that the culprit is something more integral to the process of fetal development — the male hormone testosterone. Altered levels of this essential chemical appear to interfere with the normal pattern of nerve cell migration, resulting, among other things, in an imbalance in the development of the two hemispheres. Specifically, Galaburda theorizes that the right hemisphere is formed more rapidly if there is testosterone interference during 18 to 24 weeks' gestation.

The testosterone theory makes sense, especially since it offers an explanation as to why there are four times as many male LDs as females. Until recently, it was commonly thought that there were more male than female LDs because the male brain was slower to develop, and because the female brain had stronger left-brain activity. Galaburda and Geschwind decided that the opposite was, in fact, the case. Female fetuses affected by an abnormal testosterone variation are much more severely affected by it than males and thus are much *less* likely to survive to gestation than male fetuses. In fact, statistics reveal that, while there are fewer female LDs, they usually are more severely affected by the problem.

Galaburda's work indicates that dyslexics (by the way, he confines his studies to dyslexic brains, but argues that the same theories hold true for people with other learning problems) have larger right-hemisphere language centers than the nondyslexic population. And he is by no means the only researcher to come to this conclusion. Another study, conducted by Judith Rumsey of the National Institute of Mental Health, indicates that dyslexics show greater than normal activity on the *left* side of the brain. These two results are not as contradictory as they seem. The left side of the dyslexic's brain will, indeed, have to work harder in order to compete with the more highly developed right side, and studies indicating extra blood flow and more electrical activity show that that's exactly what's happening. The efforts of dyslexics to read can be excessive and inefficient, like spinning one's wheels in place.

A third study, by Arnold Scheibel, looked at the individual dendrite structures (the treelike nerves that relay information through the brain and CNS) of both hemispheres of each subject's brain. He found that the structures differed dramatically in several ways from the left to the right side of each individual — a clear indication that the structure determines the function of the separate areas of the brain. Scheibel considers this "organic proof that specific talents (for art or music, for instance), as well as specific disabilities, are reflected in actual brain tissue," and his evidence is persuasive. Other work connecting various anatomical asymmetries directly to learning disabilities are equally convincing.

The evidence is dramatic. But we still haven't gone back far enough. What caused the altered testosterone level, or the small stroke, or the bioelectrical imbalance? *Why* did the brains of those dyslexics, or those musically talented individuals develop differently in the first place? The answer to this fundamental question brings us to a common underlying factor in LD etiology: the role of *genetics*. Time after time, studies with natural and adoptive families and with identical (monozygotic) twins have definitely proven that there is a genetic factor linking traits such as abnormal testosterone levels, irregular brain patterns, left-handedness, and learning disabilities through generations of inherited genetic codes.

William Critchley's research indicated that up to 88 percent of all dyslexics had inherited their disability from a parent (more often along the male lines than the female). Monozygotic twins (the dual product of a single egg) showed a 100 percent concordance — that is, if one twin was dyslexic, the other was sure to be, as well.

Norman Geschwind was a pioneer in the field of genetic linkages. He took the study of bioneurology to new heights of complexity and made several important breakthroughs in the field of LD. "Although [the function of the brain in dyslexia and other disabilities] has been studied for more than 120 years," he said, "its biological foundations and relationships have received only scant attention . . . until the past fifteen years."

Geschwind set out to remedy that situation. He theorized that the genetic coding that produced LD was connected to other conditions, and proved that there was a common mechanism operating in utero that was responsible, indicating a predisposition toward occurrences of specific disorder types and an inherited vulnerability that influences the ordering of behavior.

Geschwind found that a common defect in the genetic cell pool affects cells migrating not just to areas that affect learning, but to those that affect other body functions as well. In particular, he studied left-handedness as an indicator of a whole field of conditions. He found that 30 percent of the population has anomalous — or mixed — dominance, which means that neither hemisphere is stronger than the other. The other 70 percent of the population has a stronger left hemispheric dominance. Of the anomalous dominant (AD) population, however, only one third are strongly left-handed. The AD population as a whole, however, has a greater tendency than the other 70 percent of humans toward several seemingly unrelated conditions. Geschwind was able statistically to link left-handedness to the following:

migraines	skeletal malformations
allergies	thyroid disorders
dyslexia	depression
stuttering	premature graying of hair
hyperactivity	immune system disorders
childhood autism	

But Geschwind was the first to warn that the presence of left-handedness, or any of these conditions, was not *causally* linked to the others. In other words, just because a child is left-handed, or dyslexic, does not put her at greater risk of immune disease. "Left-handedness," he said, "is a factor, not a cause of developmental disabilities. Both are the result of a common genetic factor which favors the occurrence of any of those possible conditions, but does not predict them."

Similarly, Galaburda has found higher incidence of several immune system diseases in the families of dyslexics, particularly on the female side (testosterone again). But, as he says, "although a gene can predispose to a particular condition, that condition is not necessarily the cause of the LD."

In addition, Geschwind pointed out that, while people with such genetic predispositions may have higher rates of the above syndromes, they also have lower rates of other conditions, and higher rates of some higher cognitive functions, particularly those of the right side of the brain.

All this is to comfort the parent who may fear that the LD child is in danger of contracting a severe physical ailment. There is, I repeat, *no causal connection* between learning disabilities and the physical diseases mentioned above. Geschwind's point was that the genetics of dyslexia should not be studied in isolation, and that family patterns of other related conditions should also be examined. The study of family patterns of LD and related conditions may prove to be the most valuable predictive tool we have for early intervention in the treatment of LD.

If you know, for instance, that there is a history of thyroid disorders in your family, or a history of reading problems that were not diagnosed as LD (since the term did not exist more than a generation ago), then you might be quicker to act on suspicious symptoms. Your pediatrician should be able to help you investigate this matter further, and if she is not aware of the current research, you might want to direct her attention to it.

The theory of nerve cell migration, of a common influence — perhaps even a single chromosome — affecting the development and function of very disparate cells is a fascinating resolution of the heretofore unexplained connection between our brain and our behavior. Drs. Herbert and Marie-Louise Lubs are heading a group at the University of Miami Medical School that is doing exciting work isolating a specific gene on chromosome 15 that they believe is responsible for dyslexia. Given the clear genetic coding involved, it's not surprising that whole families have strains of LD running through their histories, whether the disorder was diagnosed or not. Look back through your own family tree and see if you can come up with an uncle who never did learn to read well, or a brother who never did well in school.

To prove their fascinating theories, researchers now have the kinds of tools at their disposal that Strauss and Orton could only have dreamed of. After all, dyslexic patients have to be alive and reading for us to understand how their brains are working. Computerized axial tomography (CAT scans), positron emission tomography (PET scans), nuclear resonators, and regional cerebral blood flow tests make it possible for scientists to watch the brain while it is actually in the process of reading. In 1987 Dr. Frank Duffy, of Children's Hospital in Boston, pioneered the use of brain electrical activity mapping (BEAM) and found distinct differences in the electrical activity of several regions of the brains of pure dyslexics — adults with a lesion–induced loss of the ability to read. George Ojeman has mapped living brains of patients using a BEAM-type scan and found that there are, indeed, tiny brain sites for different functions, distinguishable for different tasks.

High-technology procedures such as BEAM can be used not only to study the structural abnormalities of other disabilities, but also, perhaps, to *predict* predispositions toward them in early childhood. Dr. E. Roy John at New York Medical College has created the Quantitative Electrophysiological Battery — QB for short — which measures brain waves and extracts an exhaustive profile of brain function. According to Dr. John, it can differentiate among learning problems caused by unfocused attention, poor short-term memory, auditory inefficiency, or information-processing problems. It also maps delta waves, and he has found fascinating evidence that LD children have much more delta activity than non–LD children.

With this information, John hopes to be able to give detailed information on the best prescriptive process for LD kids, and also to identify at-risk children virtually from birth. So far, his research has not provided us with practical applications such as broad-based testing, but the implications for research are enormous.

IT'S easy to see how new research into the structural abnormalities of the brain can offer us exciting revelations about the nature of LD. Galaburda says, "As yet we have no way to see the wiring diagram of a brain in action — our tools are not precise enough. But this is the first step toward finding better predictive markers at a very young age."

But there's a danger in putting too much store in the predetermined nature of the brain. For parents, these new technologies do not yet have much practical value. The tests are still expensive, experimental, and not widely available. Besides, they may not tell us much more than we already know about what we can do for our children — knowing that our child's electrical brain waves are different from those of his peers does not help us know what might be done to remedy the problem.

The configuration of our brain should no more determine our lives than the color of our skin. Geschwind himself said it best: the differences in our brain, like the differences in our skin color, are "the biological basis of human diversity. To treat all of these special learning deficits as abnormalities is probably wrong in most cases. Most of these children are normal variations of the human species."

How the Brain Functions

It is impossible to separate the structure of the brain from its functions. The structure determines the function. But there are differences. We cannot infer the nature of a structural dysfunction by looking at the nature of the behavior it produces. Just because a

child can't see words doesn't mean she's blind. We can, however, study the structure of the brain to increase our understanding of its function, and we can work the other way as well, studying function to understand structure.

So far, our examinations into the causes of LD have presupposed certain structural problems in the brain itself. When we look into functional problems, we must realize that, in many cases, they are inseparable from structural abnormalities. The only way we can divide our exploration is in terms of the approach of the researcher. The functionalists tackle the job in terms of what the brain does: how it processes information, how it acquires language, how it produces and controls behavior. Whereas Strauss, Geschwind, and Galaburda were mainly concerned with genetic and developmental factors occurring *before* birth, functional theories look more at postnatal factors, particularly at the processes we develop in order to interact with our environment — the way we process information, the way we acquire language, and the way we adapt our behavior in order to function most effectively in the world.

The bases for these functions, of course, are structural. But they also have a lot to do with what's going on inside the body after birth. Even without the external environment to act on them, the central nervous system and the brain do not stop developing when a baby is born. As the child matures, they change dramatically in size, complexity, and function. Simple cause-effect relationships evolve into highly structured transmission systems.

This is because the brain is a living organism, which never stops developing. New neurons and synapses are constantly growing to replace old tired ones. Perhaps that's why experiences that were so fresh in our minds last year fade to distant memories, even though we're sure we'll never forget that face, or the name of that great restaurant where we ate.

The brain operates by processing information that comes in through the five senses. Assuming that the senses are operating normally, and that the receptor sites are not congenitally awry, we then have to look at the system by which the information is transmitted. Structurally, this means those neurotransmitters we were talking about earlier, but what does it mean from a functional point of view?

Information-processing tasks are handled in various parts of the brain, and no one area handles any one task. It's not a simple procedure — here are some of the tasks involved in processing information about something as simple as an apple:

Perception: recognizing the apple by perceiving its
- color
- size
- texture
- smell
- taste
- (sound)

Organization: putting the perceptual information into the right order by
- distinguishing it from its background
- telling it apart from similar objects
- connecting it with familiar objects in memory

Integration: adapting the sensory information by
- translating information between senses
- integrating all the salient features
- remembering what they mean
- associating them with memories of other apples
- connecting them to the proper word

All of these tasks must take place before we can say, "Apple!" much less decide if we want to eat it or not. And reading the simple sentence "I want that apple" is an even more complicated process.

In addition to the above tasks, more advanced skills are required, including:

visual motor skills — to manage the physical act of reading;

sequencing — to put letters, sounds, or words in order;

comprehension — to understand a system of symbols;

motivation — to apply all these skills to the decoding process;

maturity — to integrate these skills.

It is when one or more of these processes break down that functional deficits are to blame. And, since we are dealing particularly with learning disabilities in this book, our eyes and ears are the primary senses to consider.

Deficits in the processing of information are most commonly structural in nature — that is, there is some neurological deficit that prevents information from flowing through the proper channels to the proper destination ("Apple!"). As we saw earlier, the simplest lesion in one of those billions of neural pathways may have resulted in many changes in the way the brain functions.

But researchers who focus on the function of the brain — on processing deficits — say that those deficits can be remedied by repatterning those pathways. In other words, the structural deficits that caused the dysfunction are not permanent; they can be changed, or other equally effective alternative routes can be created, through processing therapies.

We'll go into more detail about the research, in our chapter on remedial therapies. Aside from a few dissenters, the majority of the functionalists believe that LD is a perceptual processing deficit. That means there is some dysfunction in the way the brain makes use of the information that comes in. This idea, of course, presupposes that all the senses are in good working order — the eyes and ears are physically able to take in sights and sounds. That doesn't mean that the information is taken in properly — visual and auditory processing deficits indicate that the eye or ear is not seeing or hearing the same thing that a "normal" eye or ear does.

Once beyond the organ itself, problems can occur when the brain is trying to relay the information to the proper site, or when the information is trying to interact with related information stored in long- or short-term memory. There can be tie-ups in the sorting process that would put the information in the proper place, in the sequencing process that would put it in the proper order, and in the conceptual process that would allow the child to make generalizations about the information. Then, of course, there can be a host of difficulties in getting the information back out again — in expressing the thoughts, in using the right words, in setting them on paper.

It's almost a wonder it happens right as often as it does. Galaburda likens the brain's architectural system to an immensely complicated field of dominoes — if one piece falls, all the others are affected. But, unlike the game of dominoes, one piece down doesn't mean the game is lost. The brain has a remarkable recu-

85

perative ability, finding alternative paths and compensatory skills so that we can play on and win. A twelve-year-old I spoke with about his long-standing LD came up with a wonderfully resilient approach to dealing with his problem. "When one part of my brain isn't working," he crowed, "I just use the other part!"

The Root of Processing Deficits

Now let's look at some of the causes that might result in perceptual-processing deficits. Developmental immaturity is one commonly cited cause. Quite often, a child is simply not ready to handle the complex series of information-processing tasks required to speak, read, or write. (Let's not forget the motor skills involved in these tasks as well. Physical immaturity in the development of fine motor skills, from the inability to hold a pencil to the inability to track visually from one line of print to the next are also essential.) Children develop at greatly varying speeds, and the five-year-old who cannot differentiate between a *b* and a *d* is no more disabled than the one-year-old who cannot walk. It is only when those inabilities persist beyond the wide range of normality, as discussed in chapter 2, that there is cause for intervention.

Learning style also plays a role in the processing skills of all children, whether LD or non-LD. There are visual learners, who learn by seeing, and auditory learners, who learn by hearing. The visual learner may have trouble with spoken directions, while the auditory learner may learn to read later than the visual one. Similarly, the child who responds well to physical stimulation may take longer to acquire such skills than the child who is visually oriented. Often, developing a multitude of skills to work in concert takes extra effort. In addition, the active child who has a short attention span may have a focusing or attention problem — or he may not be ready to master the complex skills involved in reading and writing simply because he is busy learning other things.

We'll talk more about learning styles and temperament in chapter 6, when we talk about remediation. But let's go back for a moment to those attentional disorders. Aside from information-processing deficits, attentional and behavioral deficits can also be a cause of LD.

But what causes hyperactivity or ADD? Researchers speculate that it is probably a transmitter dysfunction similar to that which inhibits the processing of information once it is acquired. Often, biochemical interference is the suspected culprit. Or it could be the additional electrical activity caused by a greater number of right brain cells, or the interference of the right brain in the left's efforts.

Interference can also be external. Children who are overly sensitive to outside stimulation often find it difficult to attend to one particular task when their senses are being bombarded by a variety of other stimuli. When we concentrate, our brains can filter out unimportant stimuli, enabling us to focus on the matter at hand. The ADD child doesn't have that ability and must constantly sort through a confusing barrage of information before settling on the appropriate input. Think about trying to read while a television news program is blaring loudly in your ear, and you'll get a good idea of what it must be like for an ADD child to concentrate on a task.

Language deficits are another functional root of LD. The acquisition of language is one of the most complicated tasks the human brain performs. No one knows quite how language began. Did words evolve from gestural symbols? How was the connection first made between the object and the symbol? How complicated is the communication system of nonhumans?

A baby learning to speak has an enormous job to do. Imagine what it would be like to try to learn Greek without a dictionary or a translator, without even having English as a base of reference. Yet babies do learn, not only how to match nouns to objects, but also how to express complicated abstract concepts in the convoluted system of symbols we call language.

Since language is necessary for learning, we have to learn language before we can learn almost anything else. Language acquisition is a process, like everything else. And it is an architectural process — those first simple words are the building blocks of complex sentences. If the process goes awry at any stage, it's easy to see how a language deficit would lead the way to complex difficulties in reading, writing, speech, and abstract thinking.

Research has shown that children learn differently. Some learn descriptive words first, while others develop expressive language. And it appears that those children who develop descriptive skills earlier are the ones who have a higher chance of success in school, although there is no inverse correlation between learning an expressive vocabulary and school failure.

Furthermore, children who are emotional or physically active are liable to learn language later than and differently from their more concentrated peers. Of course, it's hard to say which comes first. The fascinating connection between children with active, emotional temperaments who learn language later and who have learning difficulties in school is just being examined in depth.

A FEW possible organic causes of LD are not related to processing or behavioral deficits. Some researchers have found connections between LD and disorders of the vestibular system, which governs our sense of balance and muscle control and influences our sensorimotor development. Children with vestibular disabilities are unable to walk a straight line or coordinate their body and eye movements, disabilities that result in a whole range of learning difficulties.

Dr. Harold Levinson of the Medical Dyslexic Treatment Center feels that inner-ear disturbances, either congenital or acquired through persistent ear infection, are at the root of the majority of LD diagnoses. Coordination, balance, speech clarity, emotional stability, and concentration are all much more difficult when the inner ear is disturbed. Levinson's controversial theory and medication therapy have given him dramatic results, although they have not yet been independently proven.

Other researchers have provided similarly controversial evidence that cites improper visual development as the cause. Developmental optometrists have found that children who are given the usual optometric testing and found to have "perfect vision" in fact can't move their eyes properly at all. Standard eye tests evaluate the stationary eye, but it is the moving eye — moving from line to line on a printed page, moving from blackboard to paper or looking up to find a fly ball on the baseball field — that is involved in reading skills. Therapies to strengthen the weak musculature of the eye can result in dramatic improvements.

The Irlen Institute has received a great deal of attention because of Dr. Helen Irlen's contention that a large number of children and adults with reading problems can be greatly assisted by the use of tinted reading lenses. The lenses, predominantly in pink and red tones, reduce glare and help the reader separate the printed word from the background page. This theory, too, has yet to be independently confirmed.

Metabolic imbalances have also been implicated, particularly the inability to metabolize certain amino acids in the diet and the absence of certain essential trace biochemical elements. Despite many reports of benefits by proponents, research in all these areas is still in its infancy, and few of these theories have been proven to standard satisfaction.

The Effects of the Environment

When we talk about functional causes of LD, we can postulate developmental reasons for various dysfunctions, whether we're talking about congenital disorders, processing disorders, or plain old immaturity. But what about external causes? What effect does a child's environment have on her learning skills?

Human beings are the result of an exquisite integration of congenital and environmental factors — what we are determines what we make of where we are. A great home environment might not make up for a genetic disability any more than a poor one might squelch a great talent. On the other hand, those born into families where their skills are nurtured and their weaknesses forgiven stand a far greater chance than those who must fight so hard for survival that their skills never have a chance to emerge.

There is a great deal of evidence to support a causal link between a child's performance in school and her environment. The following factors have been implicated in the presence of learning disabilities — some well proven, others the subject of ongoing debate:

Poor maternal health: a mother who smokes, drinks, eats improperly, or has an untreated illness during pregnancy (proven)
Complications of birth: cord around neck, breech delivery, prolonged labor, use of drugs, low birth weight (proven)
Poor childhood nutrition: diet poor in proteins and complex carbohydrates, and high in sugar and processed foods, especially

those containing preservatives and artificial colors; vitamin deficiencies; hypoglycemia (supported but not independently proven)

Allergens: mold spores, pollen, food compounds, additives (not yet independently proven)

Environmental toxins: lead paint in the home where an infant can ingest it, or mercury poisoning (proven)

Radiation stress: from color TV cathode rays (not yet independently proven)

Sensory deprivation: lack of stimulation during infancy (widely supported but not yet independently proven)

Language deprivation: lack of adequate verbal and auditory input (proven)

Educational deprivation: poor or improper schooling (proven)

Emotional factors: family stress and/or emotional deprivation (proven)

Economic deprivation: lack of financial resources to avoid all of the above (proven)

Since so many of these factors are unalterable, it seems pointless to distinguish them from organically caused problems, especially when external factors such as those contributing to poor maternal nutrition could be responsible for a neurological dysfunction resulting in LD. And some children may suffer from environmental deprivation without having "diagnosable" learning disabilities, but their performance in general is affected by many of the above factors.

But there are those, the U.S. Department of Education among them, who feel that the definition of learning disabilities should be narrow enough to rule out these environmental factors so that the definition covers only children who fail to perform "in the absence of emotional disturbances, environmental, cultural or educational handicaps."

This argument seems to beg the point. What about the child with ADD who is a victim of lead poisoning, or the adolescent whose years of poor nutrition have led to poor physical and cognitive development? In the final analysis, how much does it matter what it was that caused LD in the first place? This is a conclusion that most parents come to in their own private search for answers, and it is a conclusion that must make sense on a larger scale. We don't much care, when it comes right down to it, whether our child's LD was caused by a rogue hormone or an overdeveloped left hemisphere. We can go over and over our child's prenatal and birth history, looking desperately for some fact that would make the light bulb flash on: "Eureka! That's the answer!"

We might find it, but we probably won't ever know with any great degree of certainty, what made it happen. And we come to realize that we don't really care. What we care about is making the best of it now, and in the future.

Priscilla Vail lists four very pragmatic and comprehensible main causes for learning disabilities:

> genetic — inherited
> pediagenic — inappropriate schooling
> chronogenic — inappropriate development (immaturity)
> sociogenic — inappropriate environment

Her point seems to be that the emphasis on the inherited and developmental factors should not obscure the fact that children have other perfectly legitimate reasons for the compound system of failures that indicates an LD diagnosis. Should we not help because the child's poor diet is to blame instead of the father's passed-on genetic predisposition?

There is a growing body of thought that says it is all the same. The psychologist Howard Gardner says that the cause of LD is the system itself:

> Unmusical or inartistic children are not labeled [MBD]. Talents are distributed asymmetrically throughout the population. We live in a society in which a child who has trouble learning to read is in difficulty. In an illiterate society, such a child might have superior skills. In most cases, we are not talking about disease, but about children who have run up against the demands of this society for a particular set of talents.

This may be comforting news for parents, but the truth is that our children have to learn to live and function in our society, and we have to help them do that. At the same time, we can work to broaden society's acceptance of alternative types of intelligence by fostering our children's creative strengths and welcoming these strengths in others.

There is an optimism afoot for children with proven organically caused learning problems. Studies have shown that patterns of cerebral dominance may not be set until after the first few years of life, offering hope for remediation through early intervention. Says the neurobiologist researcher Fernando Nottebohm, "In the not-so-distant future, it may be possible to treat local regions of the brain to activate genes to induce . . . patterns of growth. It may be possible to rejuvenate underused portions of the brain to restore lost functions. We are . . . at the threshold of an optimistic era, a new neurology."

For children whose LD is a result of environmental deprivation, however, the future may not be so rosy. But that is an issue to be dealt with at the larger, political level. For us parents, the facts remain the same, regardless of our child's LD etiology: our children *must* be able to function in this society, regardless of its weaknesses, or theirs.

So, onward, to confront the problem of diagnosing our child's particular difficulties, learning what to do about them, and how to get this task done.

CHAPTER 4

How Do We Find Out?

Question: "When did you first know your child had a learning disability?"

Answers: "I knew something was wrong with him when he was a toddler. I could just tell he wasn't dealing with the world the way the other kids were. But nobody seemed to have any answers when I asked if anything was wrong. They all said he'd grow out of it, or that it was normal. I thought there was something wrong with me. It wasn't until David was in the third grade that a teacher suggested I have him tested."

"Rebecca was tested in a routine nursery-school screening program, and the teacher told me she might have trouble learning to read because of her problems with shape perceptions and things. I thought she was crazy — Becky was only three! But the more we thought about it, the more it became obvious that she was confusing things she saw. Thank God I finally listened."

"I didn't really know until she was tested in the first grade. But, looking back, I can see the signs I might have missed. The delayed speech development, the low frustration threshold, the fine motor skill difficulties. But that's all hindsight, and what good is hindsight now?"

WHAT good indeed? Plenty, if you know how to use it once you've decided that your child *does* have a learning problem. In spite of your doubts, which are completely understandable, it might comfort you to know that parents have shown themselves to have a very realistic view of what their children are like — their strengths and weaknesses, skills levels and areas of difficulty. You know what kind of sleeper your daughter was and how she handled new information, even before she could walk or talk. You know if she was able to stack blocks at eighteen months, or hold a pencil at three, even if you don't know what these skills mean.

That information is extremely valuable now that the evaluation process is about to begin. And it's not only the past that can be helpful. Your knowledge of your child's current behavior patterns at home will provide information that is essential to her diagnosis and remediation.

Besides, what good is it to feel guilty about what you should have known but didn't? There *was* no way to be sure, or even a reason to be unusually suspicious. Those well-meaning friends and teachers were most likely right when they said that your child would grow out of this behavior, or that it was normal. In spite of the developmental charts, and how much farther along "the other kids" seem to be, the range of normal behaviors for any one age is extremely broad. The child who cannot stack blocks at eighteen months will probably stack them very well at two years, and the child who cannot hold a pencil properly at three will probably grow out of it — or, rather, into it — by the time he's four.

But every parent has doubts about the development of *every* child. After all, we spend so much time watching them and being with them, and we are so emotionally attached to them, that it would be impossible *not* to ask questions of ourselves and others about them. Once we decide to do something about our doubts, we remember those questions and wonder why we didn't act on them sooner. We feel angry, ill equipped, and, most of all, guilty.

This, too, is a normal response, but will become a productive one only when we decide to stop beating ourselves over the head and begin using that thorough knowledge of our children to help them get the proper diagnosis and the proper help. We'll be more effective, the experts remind us, if we stop feeling like failures, so that our children can see us respond in a positive, constructive fashion.

This doesn't mean that we should not get upset if nothing is done about the problem. Suzanne Stevens says in her book *The Learning Disabled Child: Ways That Parents Can Help* that hysterical mothers and angry fathers can be the strongest source of support an LD child has.

> Hysteria in the mother of an LD child is typical. It's logical. And it can be productive. The power of the hysterical mother, if used creatively and to its fullest extent, can be very effective in getting help. Parents *do* know when something is wrong with their child. No one should be able to convince them otherwise without overwhelming proof.

A Plan of Action

How can we use our hysteria creatively? We need a plan of action to help us channel it effectively. We need to

1. decide what it is we want to examine about the child;
2. insure that the proper tests are being done so that the nature of the problem can be determined;
3. decide whom we want to do the examining;
4. look closely at the results of the tests to see if they make sense to us, and do something about it if they don't;
5. agree with the evaluation team on a positive, achievable goal and method of remediation;
6. keep an eye on the remediation process to insure that the goal is being achieved.

That sounds like a lot of work — it *is* a lot of work. But research has shown that effective advocates are those who are clear about what they want, and who stay with their task until they are satisfied that they've gotten it. Not only do successful advocates get results, but their LD children seem to do better, too, although there is only anecdotal evidence to support this notion. Maybe it's because they get better services, but it's possible that the kids do well when they know they have someone in their corner.

Still, the process is time-consuming and often frustrating. And it's not as if looking after this child's needs were the only thing we have to do. Our families, our work, and our homes need attention, not to mention our LD child's often excessive demands. It may seem that the last thing we need is another battle. But the fight is worth it, and the results will be long-term for us and for our LD child.

If we break down our plan of action into more digestible increments and examine them one at a time, maybe we can get a better idea of how to proceed without feeling overwhelmed.

What Is It I Want to Examine?

As we have seen, the LD child often has a dizzying array of symptoms, all of which are worrisome to us and of some concern in school. But just because we have decided that there is a problem doesn't mean we know how to begin to get it evaluated. Do we test the child for hearing problems or for speech problems if he doesn't seem to be able to respond verbally to directions? Or do we give him a psychological evaluation, or an IQ test, or a neurological workup?

The answer is yes — we want to do all those things, and more. Remember, we don't know for sure yet that LD is the problem. We just know that there *is* a problem, and that testing is the way to find it. That means looking at every aspect of the child's abilities, performance, and behavior, even if they don't seem to be related or affected.

Of course, we're not the only ones doing the looking — thank goodness. Teachers still instigate the majority of LD screenings in U.S. public schools, although the percentage of parent-or-guardian–initiated evaluations is on the rise. (School officials other than teachers can also initiate a request for evaluation; staff psychologists or LD specialists might spot an at-risk child whom a teacher or parent misses.) An alert teacher or specialist can often help us see what we have been unable — or unwilling — to see before. However, be forewarned that it's unusual for a school to mandate a full evaluation, even if the teacher has been the one to suggest it. And, in many cases, they're right. It's not always necessary to get a full complement of tests done on every at-risk child right off the bat. But, as parents we should always be prepared to err on the side of overtesting rather than undertesting, regardless of a reluctant administration.

The first thing we want to do is rule out any primary physical, neurological, or emotional disabilities that may be responsible. We call them primary because, as we know, learning disabilities themselves may cause symptoms of a wide variety of disorders, both physical and emotional. If LD is the primary cause, then the secondary symptoms will be resolved as the LD is treated. But if a reading problem can be taken care of by a new pair of glasses, or if ear surgery can solve a speech problem, then we certainly want to solve those issues first.

That means a complete physical. All public schools and most private schools require a physical exam before the child can enter, but that doesn't mean the pediatrician will automatically look for problems beyond the very obvious. Faced with a seemingly well child, the doctor can only assume that there is nothing wrong. Without your input, doctors have no way of knowing how the child is behaving outside the office. It's up to you to ask your pediatrician to look more closely at any aspect of your child's behavior about which you feel uneasy. Does your son consistently ignore you when you call him? Make sure his ears are being checked. (Most reading problems are not the result of hearing disabilities, but it helps to rule them out first.) Does your daughter have trouble focusing on you when you speak to her, or finding her place on a page of print? Ask for a more thorough vision check than the simple eye chart offered by most pediatricians.

These things are almost always included in well-child checkups right along with the required immunization schedule. But if they're not, or if you are not satisfied with the results of the evaluation, you must see to it that more is done.

We have seen that LD problems are probably caused by neurological inefficiencies, abnormalities, or dysfunctions. In addition to the physical exam, it may be helpful to get a complete neurological evaluation for your child, although this is not always indicated. In any case, the kinds of problems that cause LD may not show up, even in the most sophisticated testing procedures. In dealing with brain functions, it's hard to pinpoint sources, more difficult still to determine levels or extent of damage.

Emotional issues are even trickier, since it's nearly impossible to tell which came first, the symptom or the cause. Virtually every child with a learning problem (or with a physical problem, for that matter) will suffer some kind of emotional disability as a result. Is an LD child unhappy because of her LD or is her learning problem the result of some deeper emotional disorder? It's not an easy question to answer, even for experts. Anger, frustration, low self-image, and depression are some very real and difficult by-products of LD, and they need the same kind of attention that the educational problems receive.

For the purposes of getting the best type of treatment, though, it would help to establish that there is not a primary emotional or psychological condition that is preventing the child from learning. A child with a severe emotional problem may also have LD, but it may be necessary to address the emotional issues first, or at least carefully tailor the remedial program to meet the child's complex needs. Basic psychological testing to determine attitudes, learning styles, behavioral profiles, and self-concept is often useful. If necessary, more intensive projective testing will be prescribed by the psychologist.

This doesn't mean that children with secondary emotional difficulties arising from an LD are not in desperate need of proper treatment. It just means that the primary (but by no means the only) focus of the treatment will be on relieving the learning difficulties that create the emotional problems, in much the same way that treatment of a child suffering from family stresses would focus on relieving those stresses. However, psychological malfunctions that are clearly the result of a learning problem must be treated as part of the federally mandated IEP, which must consider the whole child and not just his academic status.

Once the medical component of the tests has established that the child is physically, mentally, and emotionally able to learn, there is a whole battery of education-related tests to determine why he can't, and exactly what the learning problems are. These include intelligence tests, perceptual and motor skill tests, speech and language tests, achievement and behavioral tests. They will determine the extent of a child's learning disability and pinpoint in exactly which areas the problems lie: visual, auditory, oral, manual, perceptual, and behavioral.

These tests may overlap with the medical tests, since the source of these skills is either physical, mental, or emotional. In addition, there may be testing by an occupational or physical therapist (to gauge a child's motor skills and coordination), by a speech and language specialist (to gauge his language abilities), or by a social worker doing a home assessment (to determine the family situation). The end result is to get a comprehensive picture of the child, and *you* are responsible for seeing that it is done, and done right.

How Do I Insure That the Proper Tests Are Being Done?

Fortunately, you don't have to arrange all this yourself. Most often, a teacher or specialist will conduct the initial screening and provide a referral for further evaluation if he or she thinks it's necessary. Many states now have laws requiring compulsory screening of all kindergarten children, and most have also extended their voluntary screening procedures to children as young as twelve months (more on early intervention in chapter 9).

But if this hasn't happened, and you're getting nervous, it's up to you to start the ball rolling. In spite of administrative reluctance, remember that federal law allows a parent to demand a complete evaluation of a child if he or she thinks it is necessary. (In chapter 5, we'll discuss at length your rights under the law.) This is sometimes called a core evaluation, and it provides for a battery of tests in all the areas we mentioned above. There are many different kinds of tests: standardized tests, which compare the performances of same-age children; achievement tests, which measure what the child knows; aptitude tests, which measure what he is able to learn; intelligence tests to measure how "smart" he is, and diagnostic tests, which indicate his learning or behavioral style. LD assessments usually draw from all of these, although standardized tests are the least effective, since the child is clearly not performing like the rest of the population.

In each evaluation there is no set group of specific tests, since there is such a variety to choose from, and many test the same skills. But a good investigation should include at least one test from each of the areas mentioned above, and several in a particular area where trouble is suspected.

The partial list below of tests used in the educational and psychological components of an evaluation may be confusing, but don't be intimidated. You can't ask for specific tests, anyway. But it will give you some familiarity with some names you may see, and let you know what sort of information is being examined in each case. The use of one test over another in a specific area is the decision of the individual tester; although different tests concentrate on different aspects of each area, one is not necessarily better than another. A few of the more commonly administered tests are described briefly, and many of them have self-explanatory assessment targets, though they are certainly not as simple as they sound.

Intelligence and Readiness Tests: Intelligence tests are a much-disputed source of information. Ideally, they are meant to measure a child's ability and knowledge. In the 1940s and 1950s, they were much relied upon to determine a child's potential and to explain a lack of it. But for many years the use of IQ tests has come under fire for a number of reasons. While they are geared to specific ages, they measure only a particular kind of information, which every child of that age may not yet have acquired. In addition, children's scores can vary from day to day, just as a child's performance in school may vary. And, if a poor reader scores low on an IQ test because he cannot read it, do we blame his poor readership on the resultant "evidence" that he has a low IQ?

At best, the tests can show what a child remembers of what he has learned relative to other children his age. Most of the tests listed below have been adapted to account for racial, social, and cultural variations, although the charge that white middle-class children do better on them is still valid. Regardless of how often they have been tested, most children continue to score within a fairly narrow range (the range between 100 and 115 is considered average on the Stanford-Binet and WISC tests). However, LD kids often display a greater variation in scores. As they get older, LD kids have greater difficulty performing the higher-level skills required on the tests, so their scores may appear to drop precipitously. And children with a developing history of failure may experience decreasing scores.

Readiness tests measure similar attributes, concentrating on the child's preparedness to perform higher-level tasks. While some readiness tests are geared toward prereading children and take the form of picture drawing, motor skill evaluation, and oral responses to determine basic cognitive level (for example, a knowledge of colors, the ability to say the alphabet or count to ten), the intelligence tests are usually written. A sample question: "The sun rises in the east and _____ in the west. (Fill in the blank.)"

Stanford–Binet Intelligence Scale
Wechsler Intelligence Scale for Children-Revised (WISC-R)

A few words about these two very common tests: intelligence test scores are expressed either as an intelligence quotient (IQ) or as a mental age (MA). The Stanford–Binet gives only these two scores, while the WISC-R gives a more in-depth reading, with as many as twelve subtest scores divided into two categories (all measured as IQ). The verbal one requires the use of language and measures ability, asking questions such as "What is the difference between a car and a truck? What does 'jump' mean? What would you do if . . . ?" The performance component does not rely so much on what the child says as on what she does, and measures her developmental skill level, as the child completes or reproduces pictures, looks for missing elements in pictures, and puts objects in a particular order. Often it is the wide discrepancy between these two sets of scores (in either direction, although the verbal is more often higher than the performance score) that is a tip-off of a learning problem and an indication of the specific areas of difficulty.

Verbal	Performance
information	picture arrangement
vocabulary	picture completion
comprehension	block design
mathematics	object assembly
similarities	coding
digit span	mazes

Devereux Child Behavior Rating Scale (administered to parents)

Devereux Elementary Behavior Rating Scale (administered to teachers)

Leiter International Performance Scale (for deaf or speech-impaired children)

Hiskey-Nebraska Test of Learning Aptitude (for language- and/or hearing-impaired children)

Hayes Adaptation of Stanford-Binet (for visually impaired children)

Peabody Picture Vocabulary Test

Vineland Social Maturity Scale

First Grade Screening Test

Wide Range Achievement Test

Detroit Tests of Learning Aptitude

Denver Developmental Screening Test (infants to six years)

Gesell Developmental Schedules (infants to six years)

Bayley Scales of Infant Development (children under two years)

Perceptual Development Tests: These tests measure the developmental levels of a child's sensory skills, alone or in various combinations. They may indicate problems with fine or gross motor skills, or they may look for problems with the ability to integrate motor skills with visual perception, such as the ability to copy a figure correctly or make a simple block construction.

The majority of these tests focus on variations in visual skills, although auditory and kinesthetic abilities are also evaluated. A child may have difficulty with analyzing what he sees, with synthesizing that information with what he already knows, or with grasping abstract concepts about it.

Perceptual development also takes into account various disabilities associated with memory. Some children have poor verbal memory and are unable to remember what they hear, while others have poor visual memory and cannot recall what they see. In addition, memory problems may involve either short- or long-term inabilities. Complex memory skills, involving the integration of a combination of these processes, is another problem that can be identified by these tests.

A sample: The child must copy a stick-figure of a man, using the correct structural components and putting them together in the proper arrangement.

Slosson Drawing Coordination Test

Illinois Test of Psycholinguistic Abilities (ITPA)

102

The ITPA was originally developed by the researcher Sam Kirk to help teachers identify brain-injured, cerebral-palsied, or emotionally disturbed children. Since it measures the psychological aspects of language acquisition, it has come into general use in the testing of LD children, and it can provide a fascinating insight into what goes on in people's heads when they use language — both how the message comes in and how it goes out.

Beery Visual-Motor Integration Test
Bender Visual Motor Gestalt Test
Bender Test of Visual-Motor Integration
Wepman Auditory Discrimination Test
Frostig Developmental Test of Visual Perception

Marianne Frostig, a prominent California researcher, who developed the test that bears her name, believes that there is a direct correlation between learning problems and visual perception. The test pays particular attention to a child's ability to separate figure-and-background illustrations.

Benton Visual Retention Test
Sentence Memory Test and Digit Memory Test
McCarthy Scales of Children's Abilities
Southern California Sensory Integration Tests
Rey-Osterreith Figure Copy Test
Goldman-Fristoe-Woodcock Test of Auditory Discrimination
Test for Auditory Comprehension of Language
Lincoln-Oseretsky Motor Development Scale
Graham-Kendall Memory for Designs
Purdue Perceptual-Motor Survey

Speech and Language Tests: These tests measure a child's ability to communicate. Some are used to measure more than one element of a child's performance or ability — that's why the ITPA, which correlates language with perceptual abilities, appears here as well as in the previous category. These tests are often quite specific in terms of what they measure; minute variations in a child's ability to distinguish between and reproduce sounds can signal a speech problem even though it is not discernible to the average listener.

Typical questions involve naming ability (name colors, name

103

the objects in a picture, identify common objects), semantic ability (What does "dog" mean?), syntactic ability (sentence construction), and linguistic concepts (Does lunch come before or after dinner?).

Goldman-Fristoe Test of Articulation
McDonald Deep-Screening Articulation Test
Expressive One-Word Vocabulary Tests
Peabody Picture Vocabulary Test
ITPA (see above)
Wepman Auditory Discrimination Test (see above)
Northwest Syntax Screening Test
Porch Index of Communicative Ability in Children
Roswell-Chall Auditory Blending Test
Assessment of Children's Language Comprehension

Achievement Tests: While intelligence and readiness tests measure a child's aptitudes, achievement tests measure what the child has learned so far. These are the tests you will often find in periodic minimum-competency testing programs that are mandatory in most states. Some achievement tests — those used in mandatory testing programs — measure a child's achievement against others of his chronological age and grade level. Others measure the child's own performance level in greater detail. Most test specific skills in reading decoding, reading comprehension, spelling, math applications, and math computation.

Wide Range Achievement Test
Metropolitan Achievement Test
California Achievement Test
Kaufman Test of Educational Achievement
Gray Oral Reading Test
Peabody Individual Achievement Test
Diagnostic Reading Scales
Dolch Basic Sight Word Test
Durrell Analysis of Reading Difficulty
Gates-MacGinitie Reading Tests
Woodcock Reading Mastery Tests

Emotional Development and Personality Tests: These are the tests used to measure a child's underlying emotional makeup, which is so often a factor in learning problems, although it is more likely to be the result than the cause of LD. The tests are also known as projective tests because they provide a neutral ground (a stick-figure drawing, an inkblot) onto which the child can project her feelings. Drawing a family, or a house, or finishing sentences will, it is hoped, provide insights into the emotional makeup of the child, enabling the interpreter to measure the child's social skills, feelings about his family and feelings about himself. Psychologists rely on projectives to give them an in-depth look at the connection between a child's performance and the underlying causes for it.

Because such tests often open a frightening Pandora's box of problems, school psychologists are hesitant to administer them unless there is a very clear reason to do so — for example, if a child is clearly suffering from a debilitating hostility or depression that affects his schoolwork and may or may not be related to his learning problems.

Another problem with personality tests is that they are so subjective and open to the interpretation of the evaluator. Children with ADD often respond with primitive imagery on the Rorschach and Thematic Apperception tests, but an inexperienced evaluator might draw other conclusions, such as that the child is frightened and/or severely depressed.

If you decide to have such testing done, check carefully into the testing situation; speak directly with the person who will be doing the testing and make sure she knows something about your child and your family history. If your child's evaluation team suggests a battery of such tests, make sure that the evaluator knows a little bit about you and the child before the results are written up. The school may balk at the extra time (and money) a personal interview involves, but parents can insist.

Children's Apperception Test
Thematic Apperception Test (TAT)
Draw-a-Person Test
Tasks of Emotional Development
Kinetic Family Drawing
Play Therapy Observation
Sentence Completion Test
California Test of Personality

Children's Personality Questionnaire
Rorschach Inkblot Test
House-Tree-Person Projective Technique

Neuropsychological Tests: Again, these tests are not always indicated, and should be performed by a qualified neuropsychology evaluator. Neuropsychology tests can determine the presence of brain dysfunction and various perceptual and cognitive abilities. They are being used increasingly to determine attention and concentration disorders such as those characteristic of ADD.

Reitan-Indiana Neuropsychological Test Battery
Vigilance Tests
Wisconsin Card Sort Test
Connor Scale of Hyperactivity and Conduct Problems
ANSER System (see chapter 2, Appendix B)

Histories: Getting Other Information: In addition to the educational and psychological tests, a good evaluation should include the following material, gleaned from extensive interviews or questionnaires:

- An educational history of the child's performance to date and current classroom performance (as reported by teachers and school records)
- A family history, including genetic and medical information on family members and an assessment of the current family situation (as reported by family members)
- A personal history of the child, including prenatal, birth, and early childhood information and information on his current behavior at home (as reported by parents and medical records)

The following comprehensive history form, drawn from the University of Tennessee Center for Health and Sciences, is an excellent example of the kind of exhaustive and probing questions that should be asked in order for an evaluation to be complete. It also demonstrates the extensive input parents should expect to provide for their child's evaluation. You'll notice that a complete medical work-up is included in this form, and it might be a good idea to use it as a checklist for your child's physical, since it focuses carefully on possible trouble areas for LD kids.

106

Obstetrical History (parents' and medical records)
number of pregnancies
number of living children
number of miscarriages (cause,
    if known)
child's birth order
high-risk factors:
    infections
    toxemia
    diabetes
    bleeding
    trauma
    excessive nausea and
        vomiting
    other factors
weight gain (or loss) during
    pregnancy

medications during pregnancy
excessive use of tobacco, alco-
    hol, or drugs
exposure to toxins and/or
    radiation
length of gestation
mother's age at conception
father's age at conception
mother's past medical history
father's past medical history
prenatal care-giver
hospital for delivery

Perinatal History (parents' and medical records)
labor — induced or sponta-
    neous/duration/
    complications
delivery — presentation/for-
    ceps/complications
condition at birth
Apgar score
onset of cry and respiration
birth weight
discharge weight
head and chest circumferences/
    length

sleepy, irritable, lazy
jaundice/cyanosis/convulsions/
    tremors/vomiting
feeding problems
other problems
attending physician
breast or bottle fed
number of days in nursery
discharged with mother or not

Developmental History (documented from "baby book" if
    possible)
smiled
followed objects with eyes
laughed
held head up
rolled over

first tooth
sat alone
pulled self up
crawled
walked

ran
talked in words
talked in sentences
regression of speech abilities
toilet trained

enuresis (bed–wetting)
rode tricycle
rode bicycle
comparison with siblings

Past Medical History (medical records)

estimate of general rate of
  growth (compared with
  siblings)
serious illnesses
serious accidents
hospitalizations and operations
high fevers
convulsions or neurological
  problems
staring spells or blackout spells
head trauma with loss of
  consciousness

anorexia, vomiting, diarrhea
  causing dehydration
medications taken and dosage
childhood diseases and/or vac-
  cines (give dates):
measles
German measles
mumps
scarlet fever
roseola
other
immunizations and severe
  reactions
estimate of general health
attending physician
any current disorders being
  followed?

Review of Systems (pediatric examination)

general health
allergies
head
eyes
ears
nose
throat
lungs
heart
gastrointestinal system
skin

central nervous system review:
  parents' appraisal of intellec-
    tual status
  eye blinking or strabismus
    (wandering eye focus)
  dysphagia (difficulty swal-
    lowing) or drooling
  spasticity or hypotonia
  coordination problems —
    fine/gross
  ataxia

lymph nodes
bones and joints

speech problems:
  delays
  articulation
  stuttering

Educational History (school records)
nursery performance
kindergarten performance
grades completed
grades repeated
current grade performance
previous testing and results

parents' observations of:
  word or letter reversals
  handwriting difficulties
  difficulty following multiple
    directions
cnild's school attitude

Social History (parents)
household members
father's occupation
mother's occupation
marital history
problems or crises in family
  continuity
discipline methods:
  by whom
  type
  frequency
  response

relationship and/or problems
  with siblings
passive or aggressive with
  other children
sleeps away from home
close friends (ages)
living quarters (indoor plumb-
  ing, own room)

Family History (parents)
construct a family tree with
  ages, sex of all family
  members
mental retardation
neurological problems
learning disabilities
emotional disorders
diabetes

cancer
sickle cell anemia
cardiovascular problems
renal problems
metabolic problems
hearing or speech problems

Behavioral History (parents)
evaluation of motor activity
attention span
distractibility
impulsiveness
destructiveness
emotional lability (mood
  swings)
reaction when frustrated
cruelty to animals or other
  children
hobbies
favorite TV programs
favorite (and worst) school
  subjects
additional organized activities
plays with older/younger/
  same-age children

sleep habits:
  hours out of 24 hours
  night-light and/or other
    security objects
  bedroom shared
  nightmares and night terrors
  bizarre night habits (sleep-
    walking, sleep-talking,
    bruxism [tooth-grinding])
  enuresis (bed-wetting)
  resists going to bed
  comes to parents' bed
particular fears
nervous habits
tic
ritualistic activities
parents' description of child's
  worst habit
discipline problems at home
evidences of poor self-concept

Nutritional History (parents)
24-hour dietary history
food likes and dislikes
pica (eating wall plaster, dirt,
  etc.)

food allergies
diet modifications tried

As you can see, a history like this is an ambitious undertaking, and both parents should plan to spend some time together filling it out. Corroborating records should be consulted whenever possible and, if parents have two separate answers, this discrepancy should be noted.

Looking at the questions, you will probably recognize much of the material from the lists of causes and symptoms we discussed in chapter 2. Because there are so many possibilities, it's best that no stone is left unturned in examining the child's history and behavior. The result of an investigation such as this (and the questionnaire you receive may be different) are obvious: a complex picture of your child as *you,* the one true expert on the subject, know her.

Who Will Do the Examining?

A family history, used in conjunction with carefully selected and executed testing, can produce the most precise picture possible of the child. But how can we be sure that the testers will select the right tests, execute them well, and evaluate the results properly? This is a difficult question. Much depends on who is doing the testing. An educational specialist may place more weight on achievement and aptitude tests, while a psychologist looks more closely at the behavioral indicators and a neurologist spends time on developmental analysis.

These specialists will choose the tests they feel will provide the best answers. It's only natural, then, that a certain amount of professional bias should seep into the conclusions that are drawn. Good testers should be able to administer the same test to the same child and come up with the same results, but many tests are open to some interpretation, and similar tests measure the same thing in different ways. That's why it's so important to get a well-rounded evaluation, and why it's up to you to give your child's evaluators the clearest possible picture of the nature of your child's problems so that they know where to look for those answers.

In addition, the relationship between the child and the tester, regardless of his professional bias, is crucial to the success of the test. If a child is uneasy about her tester, she's not going to feel comfortable with the tasks he assigns her — particularly if the child has a hard time with testing in the first place, as so many LD children do. Testing can be a frightening prospect to the child, partly because the bright LD child knows she's got a problem, but doesn't know what it is.

The best way to prepare a school-age child for testing is to explain very calmly that you (and the child's teacher) would like to find out some more about how she learns so that you can help her to learn more easily. Tell her that, on most of these tests, there are no right and wrong answers, and that she will not receive a grade. Explain that no one else in her class will see her scores. Your mood will set hers, so don't make too big a deal out of it. Make sure she gets a good night's rest the night before and eats a good breakfast on the day of the tests, and don't spend too much time trying to find out from her how she did, since she will have no way of knowing.

Younger children (preschool age) don't even need to be told that much, unless they ask. You can simply tell a three-year-old that he is going to play some games, and that nothing is going to hurt him.

A well-trained tester will spend time making the child feel as relaxed as possible under the circumstances. The site of the testing, the number of tests administered at one time, and the time of day are also important factors to be considered. It's a good idea to be sure that more than one person is conducting the tests and that they are spread out over several hours and even days.

If the school is doing the evaluation, each component of the test will be done by a particular specialist. Independent clinics will often do the same thing. If you are paying for a private evaluation by an individual, you may want to be sure that the tester knows your child's limits and plans to take time to get to know her as well as to build relaxation, exercise, and snacks into the schedule.

School evaluations are your child's legal right, and are free of charge. They're a good place to start, especially if you stay involved in the entire process and can monitor the course of the evaluation. That, too, is your right — to be an equal member of the evaluation team and to attend all meetings (your child's testing sessions are off limits, though, since your presence would probably skew the results). Many evaluation teams would just as soon meet at their convenience, especially if they work in the same place. Make sure that nothing is done without your *informed* consent. (See chapter 5 for a more thorough discussion of your legal rights.)

Sometimes, though, a school evaluation is not enough. Some parents feel that school evaluations are inadequate, that the red tape involved is too much, that the specialists are overworked and undertrained. More important, some feel that it may be in the school's best interest to find as little as possible wrong with a child, since it is the school system that must pay the cost of remediation.

It's a delicate subject, and one that many school systems are working hard to overcome. Naturally, the more of a presence *you* are in the whole process, the more likely it is that your child will get her due attention. Nevertheless, there are school systems that are so overburdened and understaffed that the evaluation process suffers. And there are parents who are not satisfied with the results. In that case, the next option is a private evaluation service.

Private evaluations, whether done by local clinics or by individual educational evaluators, can be an expensive proposition. A basic testing format can start at $300 and go up into the thousands, if sophisticated technological tools are used or many hours are put into the interpretation process. Most clinics and professional evaluators use a sliding scale, and some public funds are available if the school system isn't paying for it (again, see chapter 5). In many cases, the schools must pay — although it might be for an independent evaluator of their choice.

Evaluations are also time-consuming, although they shouldn't take *too* long. If an evaluator says he can test your child in three hours, don't trust him. If he says it will take several weeks and thirty hours, don't trust him either. Six to ten hours of testing time should be adequate for a sound initial diagnosis. The law also provides for a child who isn't completely comfortable and proficient in English to be tested in her native language.

How Can I Examine the Results of the Testing to See If It Makes Sense to Me?

If you are satisfied with your choice of evaluators, you should trust that they will be doing a good job evaluating the results of your child's testing. And if you have been interviewed closely and your child's history has been carefully examined, then you should be satisfied that you made the right choice. You have the right to examine your child's actual test work, as well as the "raw" scores (see the Glossary), but they will probably make little sense to you.

It's better to plan on a lengthy session in which the evaluator explains the results to you in detail. He should also plan on explaining them (perhaps in somewhat less detail) to your child, if the child is old enough (this would be at your discretion). *The first (and possibly the most important) step in remediating the problems caused by LD should always be to tell the child exactly what is going on.* Tell him that he is not stupid or crazy. Explain that testing will help everyone understand the nature of the problem and help decide on the best course of action. Let him know what kinds of changes he can expect once the results are in, and let him know that you are on his side.

After much agonizing, we finally sat down with my daughter and told her that the reason first grade had been so hard on her was that she had something called a learning disability. It wasn't painful, it wasn't catching, and we were going to do the best we could to help her with it. She asked us if it would ever go away, and we said that we didn't know, but that life was certainly going to get easier for her now that we knew about it, because there were things we could do. We drew her the squiggly diagram mentioned earlier to help her understand what it meant to have a learning disability. Her relief was visible and made us feel a lot better. Your child will feel the same way.

The Evaluation Process: Developing a Plan

Once the tests have been done, the process of evaluating them and coming up with a plan of action begins. According to Public Law 94-142, Section 303.343 (c), "a meeting must be held within 30 calendar days of a determination that the child needs special education and related services." This should *not* be a meeting at which you are handed a completed educational plan for your child. You are legally entitled to be in on the development of that plan (see chapter 5 to find out how to insure this legal right), and it may not be completed without your input.

The evaluation meeting should consist of you, your child's teacher, educational specialists, a school administrator or evaluation team chairperson, and anyone else who has been involved in the process. There may be more than one meeting, especially in public schools, where it's often impossible to get everyone together at once for a lengthy session. Premeetings might have been held between, say, the LD specialist and the school psychologist. Your child may or may not be present. Someone (not you) will probably act as chairperson of the team. Make sure that the chairperson knows how to reach you to let you know about *all* meetings, and make it a point to attend *all* meetings other than testing sessions.

114

You are entitled to have someone attend the session with you — a relative, friend, or child advocate, if you feel it might be necessary. It's a good idea to bring along someone you trust, if only because the amount of information you receive may be overwhelming and you may not think of all the questions to ask yourself. You may ask to have copies of the evaluations provided to you before the meeting, so that you are prepared.

Professionals often find it difficult to discuss their work with nonprofessionals. If the evaluators don't explain their results in terms you understand, stop them and remind them that you *must* understand clearly and completely before you will allow them to proceed. For those whose native language is not English and who don't feel comfortable with their comprehension level, the law provides them with the right to request that the evaluation meeting, like the tests themselves, be done in their native tongue.

You need to know the good news along with the bad, and an evaluation meeting should be able to provide you with a description of your child's strengths as well as her weaknesses. You should also be told what learning styles will work best for her, and why.

Make sure that you get the complete results in writing, as well. Remember that nothing can happen without your informed consent — your written signature on a document that you must read and understand before you can sign it. Don't let anything happen without you!

Here are some testing terms you may come across during an evaluation session:

Converted Scores: raw scores put into a table to compare performance with others of the same age, grade level, and/or sex

Grade Equivalent: a test score measured by the child's grade-level performance (for example, a student may test at a grade equivalent of 4.6, which means the sixth month of fourth grade)

Intelligence Quotient: the number derived from adjusted scores on standardized tests

Mean: average, the sum of three scores together, divided by three

Median: the point where half the scores are above and half below

Mental Age: a test score measured by a child's age level (for example, a child may test at a mental age of 9.4, meaning 9 years, 4 months)

Norms: results of the performance of groups of individuals to whom the test is being administered when it is being standardized

Numerical Score: how many correct answers on a test

Percentile: where one student scores in relation to 99 others — measures relative performance

Raw Score: the numerical total of the test taker's right answers

Stanine: a standardized scoring system using numbers from 1 to 9 in sets of 10 (comes from "standard nine")

How Do I Get Everyone to Agree on a Goal for My Child, and on the Remediation Necessary to Achieve That Goal?

Once the evaluation team has reported to you on the findings of their tests, they must also provide you with a clearly defined set of goals for your child, and a program of remediation to help her achieve it. This is known as the *Individualized Education Plan,* or IEP, and it is mandated by law. The IEP is the most important tool you will have in helping your LD child. It is the goal of the testing and evaluation procedures and the unit by which you may measure your child's progress. The IEP must take into account all aspects of your child's disability and come up with acceptable ways to address those separate aspects.

By law, the IEP *must* include:

- a statement of the child's handicapping condition(s) as it relates to his education;
- a statement of the present educational levels of the child;
- a description of the annual long-term goals and short-term treatment steps necessary to achieve annual goals;
- a statement of the least restrictive treatment conditions necessary to achieve goals;
- a statement of the specific educational services to be provided in the course of such treatment;
- an explanation of the rationale behind a particular treatment plan;

- projected dates for initiation, frequency, and the anticipated duration of such services;
- what, when, and where and whose services will be received;
- appropriate objective criteria for measuring progress and for determining the continuation and/or level of need.

The IEP is the most powerful weapon you can have in helping you to help your child battle an LD problem. It is a communication tool for letting you know precisely what the problem is, a management tool for letting you know what should be done, a monitoring document to see that it is done, and an evaluation device to measure its effectiveness. Because it serves so many critical functions, the IEP must be very specific, and very clear. A copy of a sample IEP appears on pages 118–121 so that you can get an idea of just how specific it should be. It is taken in part from *The IEP Primer* by Beverly School and Arlene Cooper, an extremely useful handbook for parents and teachers.

Ideally, your child's written IEP should not be presented to you until after the evaluation meeting has been completed and a remediation plan has been agreed upon. After all, you are a part of the evaluation team, and if the paper is presented to you at the meeting, that means it was created without your input, as a fait accompli. In a perfect world, the evaluation meeting would end with a discussion of the IEP, which would then be presented at a second meeting.

In reality, this may be too time-consuming, and you are interested in getting results as quickly as possible. In addition, you could not be expected to know what particular remediations are indicated by the results of the tests; that's why you've called in the experts in the first place. So, if the evaluation has been conducted by professionals you trust, using extensive information from you, you can expect the resulting IEP to reflect your input.

However, you do know your child better than anyone else, and even if the plan seems highly technical, you should look at it very carefully. Don't be afraid to ask questions. A list of some of the things you may want to verify follows.

Are the recommendations based on a well-rounded evaluation, or just on test results, or on classroom behavior?

Individualized Education Plan

DATE: 10/14/88 SCHOOL DISTRICT: Webster
NAME: David Morris SCHOOL: Curry School
BIRTHDATE: 11/18/76 CURRENT GRADE: 6th grade
PHONE: 205/555-6022 TEACHER: Mrs. Holmes, Rm. 204
HOME LANGUAGE: English

EVALUATION TEAM PARTICIPANTS AND ROLES:
PARENT: Deborah and Kevin Morris
TEACHER: Evelyn Holmes
LD SPECIALIST: Mary Briggs
CHAIRPERSON/SCHOOL PSYCHOLOGIST: Mark Harper

STUDENT PROFILE: David is keeping up well with his classmates, but recent testing in math and reading indicates some gaps in learning. David is weak in phonic analysis and comprehension skills. In math, David is doing very well with computation skills, but is weak in applications of math concepts: money, measurement, time, and word problems. In English, he has difficulty with sentence structure and grammar.

REGULAR CLASSROOM PARTICIPATION:
all_____ most_____ part_____ none_____ of school day at 6th grade level

SPECIAL EDUCATION ASSIGNMENT(S) AND PROJECTED DATES (CHECK ONE):
☐ Regular classroom (9/88–6/89)
☐ SLD tutoring in LD room 4 × week for 30 minutes (9/88–6/89)

CRITERIA FOR MOVEMENT TO LESS RESTRICTIVE ENVIRONMENT: when David is able to read at least one year above grade level as indicated on the Spache Diagnostic Reading Scales and perform successfully in the classroom in math skills and English

ADDITIONAL PLANS:
TRANSPORTATION: none
PHYSICAL CONSTRAINTS: none
STANDARDIZED TESTING EXEMPTIONS: none
SPECIAL TESTING REQUIREMENTS: additional time allotment
GRADING: unofficial grades to eliminate pressure
NOTE-TAKING: notes to be Xerox copied to eliminate copying difficulty
SPECIAL DISCIPLINE REQUIREMENTS: behavioral contracts

STUDENT'S NAME: David Morris
SCHOOL YEAR: 1988–89

Instruction Area A: Reading Comprehension
ANNUAL GOAL: David will improve his ability to comprehend text.

Short-Term Tasks	Methodology	Success Criteria	Time Frame	Progress
1. David will use context signs in figuring out meanings of unfamiliar words.	Specific skill serves: "Using the Context," "Drawing Conclusions," "Getting the Main Idea"	80% accuracy	8–10 weeks	
2. David will tell the main idea of a passage he has read.	Same as above	80% accuracy	8–10 weeks	
3. David will draw conclusions from material he has read.		80% accuracy	8–10 weeks	

Instruction Area B: Reading
ANNUAL GOAL: David will improve his ability to sound out words.

Short-Term Tasks	Methodology	Success Criteria	Time Frame	Progress
1. David will use phonic elements or small syllables to sound out new or unknown words.	Teacher observation of David's oral reading	Consistent improvement in sounding out words	12–16 weeks	

Instruction Area C: English
ANNUAL GOAL: David will improve his written expression.

Short-Term Tasks	Methodology	Success Criteria	Time Frame	Progress
1. David will write complete sentences with proper capitalization and punctuation.	Unit texts and specially prepared worksheets	80% by the end of the year	End of year	
2. David will write grammatically correct sentences.	Teacher analysis of written work	Consistent improvement in performance	End of year	

Instruction Area D: Math
ANNUAL GOAL: David will improve his ability to use mathematical concepts.

Short-Term Tasks	Methodology	Success Criteria	Time Frame	Progress
1. David will be able to translate word problems into computational form.	Special worksheets Oral work	Teacher evaluation	8–10 weeks	
2. David will use common forms of measurement and manipulate them in math problems.	Teacher workbook Repetition	Teacher evaluation	8–10 weeks	
3. David will be able to compute problems involving hours, minutes, and seconds.	Training clock and worksheet Repetition	Teacher evaluation	8–10 weeks	

Instruction Areas A–D:

PARENT/GUARDIAN RESPONSE:

☐ I accept the educational plan as written.

☐ I accept the educational plan with revisions (see below).

☐ I postpone a decision until the completion of an independent evaluation.

☐ I accept the finding of no special needs.

☐ I reject the educational plan as written.

☐ I reject the finding of no special needs.

☐ I request an independent evaluation.

CERTIFICATIONS AND SIGNATURES:

(all members of team)

What is the reasoning behind these particular remedial approaches?

Why are these approaches the best?

What training has the specialist received who will be working with your child?

How many times per week will the child be receiving services?

What is the size of the class? What sorts of facilities are there? Are there aides? What transportation will be provided, if needed?

Are there any special discipline policies that we need to know about?

When can we reevaluate?

What happens if I move?

What can I expect in the way of other problems (emotional, social) as a result of this plan? How do you plan to handle them?

What can we do at home to implement the IEP?

Usually, the first thing an IEP indicates is your child's *placement level* — that is, the classification of the remedial program that is considered most appropriate. Each state develops its own separate codes to describe the type of placement. Massachusetts, for instance, has twelve "prototype levels" ranging from 502.1, a regular classroom program with only a slightly modified curriculum provided by a teacher or consultant, to 502.10, a program for children in need of special education who reside in state facilities (the twelfth allows for an individually designed placement for older children).

Since each state has a different system, classification can be confusing. But Suzanne Stevens has generalized seven "variations" on the usual categories, which cover most placement classifications (the eighth and ninth are my own):

1. Nothing is done.
2. The classroom teacher does the best she can on her own.
3. The classroom teacher does the best she can under the supervision of a specialist.
4. The child is removed from the classroom on a regular basis (for varying periods of time, depending on need) to work with a specialist.
5. The specialist works separately with the child outside the classroom *and* helps the classroom teacher in the classroom.
6. The child is removed from the classroom (for varying periods of time, depending on need) for LD tutoring and also for instruction in areas directly affected by his disability (for example, a special math class).
7. The child is given all his instruction in a self-contained LD classroom.
8. The child goes outside the regular school, either part- or full-time, to a special school or education program.
9. The child goes outside the regular school, either part-time or full-time, to a residential, hospital, or at-home program.

It seems to be most effective and easiest for the child if he moves gradually from a lower to a higher classification, so that his progress can be gauged in the least restrictive setting before moving him to a more restrictive one. However, some educators feel that this wastes valuable time and confuses and upsets the child. An IEP, if properly designed, should clearly indicate the setting that will provide the child with the greatest degree of help in the least restrictive environment. If your child is being moved from one setting to another because the plan doesn't seem to be working, you might consider questioning the IEP or asking that it be reevaluated.

A Few Words about Mainstreaming and Least Restrictive Environment

If we keep in mind that the IEP will provide our child with the least restrictive environment possible, given the restrictions determined by the evaluation, the placement system is pretty easy to understand. But the term *least restrictive environment,* which is a legal one, is often confused with another term: *mainstreaming.*

Least restrictive environment (LRE) means that the IEP must conform to the minimal amount of intervention necessary to achieve maximum results — in other words, the child must be able to learn effectively in the environment most close to normal that he can manage, given his disabilities. By law, a child's IEP must place him in the LRE that still guarantees his constitutional right to an appropriate education. Although there is no dispute about least restrictive environments, there is some difficulty with what constitutes an appropriate education. Some states set standards; in Massachusetts, for example, the child must receive "maximum feasible benefit" from his placement — he must get the best education he possibly can, given his handicap, and he must receive it in the environment that is closest to normal, given his handicap.

Mainstreaming means that the child is placed as soon as possible in a nonrestricted environment, or that he moves through the placement levels with that goal in mind. Even children who spend most of their time in a regular classroom should be moved toward a greater degree of nonintervention. If the child now spends half of his time in a resource room, the goal of the IEP might be to have him spend only 25 percent of his time there within a year. In other words, all LD children should theoretically be working toward a less restrictive environment than the one they are already in.

The concept of mainstreaming first developed in the early 1970s as a reaction to the labeled segregation of "special education" students that was routinely going on in American public schools. Children who were labeled slow learners were plopped into special classes regardless of the reason for their "slowness." (Remember, the definition that separated LD kids from retarded or

123

physically handicapped kids was not developed until the mid-sixties, and not implemented until a decade later.)

There they were expected to stay until they were old enough to leave school and find some other safely limited environment. The concept of moving out of a special classroom into a regular one was unheard-of, since no one considered slowness to be any more "curable" than retardation or paraplegia. Besides, went the reasoning, it would be traumatic for both the normal and slow learners to be thrust together.

But the prevailing winds of education and psychology changed, and professionals began to see that not only did children have different types of disabilities, but almost all of them had some prospect of improvement, given the proper instructional environment. Studies indicated that there was no sound reason to consign special-education children to the figurative back of the bus; they were both able and entitled to move as freely through the educational system as their disability allowed. The idea was to achieve a learning situation as near to normal as was constructively possible.

The concept that children of varying abilities and degrees of "normalcy" could learn together, and could even mutually benefit one another, was considered radical in the late 1970s, and it achieved much attention. Parents were particularly anxious to have their children functioning in the mainstream of life, not considered second-class citizens destined for a life of exclusion and limitation.

Although some critics argued that putting such children into regular classrooms put undue and unfair stress on them, parents felt that they were sacrificing a short-term struggle for a long-term victory. Their child might feel better if removed from the stress of a regular classroom situation and placed among other LD types, but what would happen when he or she got out into the real world? Better to have a child adjust to reality as soon and as much as possible — with support, of course.

And the idea seemed to work. By interacting with their non-handicapped peers, children felt more normal, and parents felt that their prospects for the future seemed to improve. It was thought by psychologists that children would pick up on sorely needed social skills from their peers much as they would pick up academic

124

skills from their teachers. They were no longer ostracized, and no longer thought of themselves as different. Not only that, but the non-LD children were learning a good lesson in tolerance and compassion by working with their LD peers.

In addition, public school systems stood to save a lot of money by avoiding costly restrictive placements unless these were absolutely necessary. The need for separate classrooms containing only a handful of children was diminished, saving space in crowded school buildings. And, with good support, the regular classroom teacher would be able to handle the more diverse class load, to the enrichment of all involved.

In fact, the idea of mainstreaming as many children as possible into the least restrictive environment looked good to everybody involved. In 1975, the passage of Public Law 94–142 (see chapter 5) made the concept of "least restrictive environment" a requirement of federal law. Every state had to "assure, to the maximum extent appropriate, that handicapped children [including LD] were educated with children who are not handicapped, and that special placement occurred only when the nature or the severity of the handicap was such that regular education in the classroom, with the use of supplementary aides and services, could not be achieved satisfactorily."

Although this definition did not mention mainstreaming (the word was originally coined to refer only to completely noninterventionary placements), the two terms, *least restrictive environment* and *mainstreaming,* came to be interchangeable. Today, "mainstreaming" generally refers to a placement in the least restrictive environment — that is, in a regular classroom — for as much of the day as possible, as well as to movement toward nonintervention within the remedial system. IEPs routinely make provisions for mainstreaming, whether it's from a residential placement to a special class in a public school or from a daily tutorial session to a full-time regular classroom situation.

But, as with most theories (look at the never-ending juggle between phonics and sight-reading), the prevailing winds changed again in the mid–eighties and the concept of mainstreaming once again came under a lot of fire. Many experts and parents wondered if the benefits of inclusionary education were as real as they had seemed a decade before. The self-image of an emotionally fragile

LD child might suffer irreversible damage from constant comparison with peers who were easily able to do what came so hard for the child.

In fact, a study reported in the *Learning Disability Quarterly* in 1988 showed that children who are in classrooms with non-LD peers do have lower self-images than children in special self-contained classrooms. The social isolation that comes from being considered dumb or different does not seem to disappear just because the children are in a regular class — in fact, it can be worse. By the time they are ready for "the world," instead of being shocked by reentry problems, these children may be already crushed.

This isn't always the case. For some students, particularly those with strong self-images and sound social and physical skills, being with non-LD children is a positive experience, and really does fit the "least restrictive environment" requirement of the law. But many LD children do not have strong self-images, social skills, or athletic prowess. For them, the regular classroom may be a crippling environment — the *most* restrictive placement rather than the least.

In addition, mainstreaming can work only when there are expert regular classroom teachers to implement it. They must be willing and able to work closely with the child and with a specialist. They must have special training to learn how to handle the special academic and emotional needs of LD children. Even for those few teachers who have such training, the burden is great in terms of time and energy spent. The variety of special requirements may make it impossible to work effectively with anyone. School systems are finding themselves under fire when LD children don't thrive in mainstream placements, and several landmark legal cases have been awarded in favor of the "most appropriate" rather than the "least restrictive" environment.

Today the pendulum seems to be swinging again in the direction of support for mainstreaming, although there is an alarming amount of attention being paid to the money it saves as opposed to the good it does a child. Valid arguments are still being heard on both sides of the issue. Teachers are maintaining that they are not equipped to handle the wide variation of learning styles in one crowded room, especially when public funds for special-education support services are often the first to be cut out of school system budgets. Schools are beginning to recognize that "extra" money spent on increased intervention in the early years is not wasted, since the cost of special services increases as the child gets older and needs more extensive help. And parents, who have long fought to have their special-needs children placed in the environment most near to normal, are once again caught in the dilemma of weighing the benefits of a special education against the possible damages to self-esteem.

There is still much to be said for mainstreaming, and the concept of "least restrictive environment" is still legal and valid. Problems arise only when the quality of the instruction or the well-being of the child comes into question. "Mainstreaming," said one special-needs administrator, "is only effective if the system is willing to support the child in that environment." If you suspect that your child is in a "least restrictive environment" that is turning out to be a more restrictive one in terms of her self-image, or in terms of the quality and level of help she's getting, you have every right to see that it is changed.

How Can I Keep an Eye on Things?

By law, the IEP must be reviewed and revised annually, and a new plan set in place for each new school year. Sometimes this will amount to nothing more than a reiteration of the previous year's plan, and you will need to remind the evaluation team that a new plan may be called for. The child's IEP *must* be written so that there are measurable increments of progress. If those goals have not been met within the one-year period (or within the individual quarters in that period), then the school has not upheld its part of the contract.

During the course of the year, there is much you can do to keep track of progress. Without putting yourself in an adversarial position, let everyone in your child's school know who you are, and that you are keeping a close eye on things. Arrange for regular meetings (via phone or in person) with your child's teacher and/or specialist. Review the IEP yourself on a regular basis so that you can ask intelligent questions to make sure that the particulars of the IEP are being carried out. Inform them of any dramatic changes at home or in your child's behavior there. Look over any work your child brings home from school. Does it seem to be in keeping with the plan? Ask your child questions. Is she being given extra time if she needs it, or extra assistance with a project?

Consider your role as an educator as well. Some parents are willing and able to put a lot of time to help their child with homework and schoolwork on which she needs extra help. Certainly home assignments should be monitored closely to see if they are in keeping with the IEP. But ask your child's teacher how you can help your child in accordance with the terms of the IEP. He may need a certain type of instruction that you need to learn how to provide.

Some parents, however, find assisting the LD child with schoolwork is an impossible task that erodes the quality of the parent-child relationship. They find themselves unable to provide the necessary patient instruction. They are unable to understand the material themselves, or how to provide it in a particular way. Tutoring is an option to be considered in such cases, and the school can help provide resources in this regard as well.

Your child should be completely reevaluated every three years. Her academic and emotional needs will change dramatically in that time, so don't let the second evaluation slip by without using it as a chance to look closely at any new issues, and make sure they are addressed in the new IEP, even if they were not in the previous plan.

Testing: Is It the Answer?

If we do not have a sound evaluative foundation, we have no basis on which to judge progress. And what if we can't trust the testing system to give that sound foundation to us? Many professionals question the validity of the current evaluation system, either in part or in whole. William Cruickshank says that "there is no curricular potential in the WISCs, the WPSIs, the Binets, Leiters, IQs or MAs [Metropolitan Achievement tests]. There is every potential in observing how children function, [in the] continuous evaluation and constant penetrating inquiry into the learning needs of children."

According to some researchers, like Cruickshank and Sylvia Farnham-Diggory, many tests are simply not sufficiently pure measuring tools to be of value. They may serve as useful negative indicators, to tell us what is *not* wrong with the child (for example, severe brain damage or physical dysfunction), but not as indicators of a specific LD problem with an eye to correcting that problem. They may tell you what's not wrong, but they won't tell you what *is*.

IQ tests come in for particular criticism because it is so difficult to measure overall performance on one set of tests given at one point in time. Many professionals argue that all an IQ represents is the score a child received on that particular test. They feel that the only validity of WISC-R and other tests like it is a reflection of the information the child has acquired thus far.

Some tests seem particularly skewed against a nontraditional population. The researcher Alan Ross found that even the ubiquitous WISC-R (revised) sample of "normal" included no more than a 15 percent nonwhite population, no bilingual children, nor any children whose family profile fell outside the 1970 U.S. Census's "representative range" for occupation, location, size of family, income, et cetera.

It's difficult to imagine the precision of a test that judged all children against a sample that did not include such a large segment of the population. Other tests have also come under fire because minority children constantly score lower on them than nonminorities do, or because they require a degree of cultural literacy that nonnatives or economically deprived children may not have. Imagine showing a picture of a VCR to a Haitian child whose family has never owned a television set and you will understand why so many Haitian children score low in many testing formats. The law excludes economically and culturally deprived children from the LD umbrella, but, until tests can be developed that do not discriminate against them, they will continue to fall into that category and be treated accordingly, rightly or wrongly.

There are other, more fundamental, reservations about the validity of current testing methods. What methods have the testers (and society as a whole) used to devise these tests? What sorts of skills do they measure, and are those the only skills we consider important? Says Ross, "We have arbitrarily decided that circle-drawing is a better indication of intelligence than dart-throwing. [Based on that criterion], the average child is a statistical myth, nothing more."

Howard Gardner, in his important book *Frames of Mind,* challenges the entire structure of our educational system by arguing that there is more than one type of intelligence. "The problem," he says, "is not the technology of testing, but in the way we think about intelligence." His careful scientific research has uncovered seven types:

musical: skill at mastering rhythm, pitch, timbre
kinesthetic: bodily mastery such as dancers, actors, mimes, and athletes have, and the ability to handle objects skillfully, as artisans, craftsmen, and inventors do
spatial-reasoning: visual sense of orientation of objects in the external world such as architects, sculptors, and navigators have
intrapersonal: ability to understand oneself ("access to the feeling life")
interpersonal: ability to understand others
logical-mathematical: love of abstraction, problem-solving
linguistic: the ability to master language and memory for reflection as well as communication

Instead of identifying LD kids as being at risk, Gardner says that they may be "at promise" for other kinds of tasks than those for which we are testing them. "It should be possible to identify an individual's intellectual proclivities at an early age and then draw upon this knowledge to enhance that person's educational opportunities and options."

The Parents' Perspective

But a learning disability is still a learning disability, and our children still have to be raised in a society in which different forms of intelligence, or different learning styles, are not well tolerated. We are still the parents of children who fail in school, who present problems at home, who undermine their own strengths because of their feeling of inadequacy.

We are still left with a tremendous responsibility and a flood of our own emotions to deal with at the same time. The entire process of finding out that our child has an LD problem takes a long time and a great deal of energy, but, at some point, every parent who goes through it is going to be hit with a wave of sadness. Even if we've suspected some dread condition, and the diagnosis of LD comes as a relief, we are still going to feel that grief. It has become apparent that our perfect child isn't perfect, and all of our dreams for her must be reevaluated.

In addition, there is the recognition that life is not going to be simple for us, or for the child. Even if the adjustments are minor, and even if we believe that they may be short-lived, they are difficult to adopt without a struggle. LD kids *are* more difficult to raise than non-LD children, and they have a harder time growing up than their LD peers. The brightest LD kids are painfully aware of this, and that only increases our sorrow.

There are things we can do to adjust. We can talk with our child's teachers and members of her evaluation team, if they are supportive. We can talk with our pediatrician, and possibly get help from a counselor or therapist. We can share our feelings with relatives or friends who would be most likely to provide positive support. We can seek out the parents of other children who are in placements similar to our child's.

Parent support groups are the most effective way of handling our own overwhelming emotions, and Appendix A lists a variety of groups that have regional or state branches. Many school systems have developed local groups of parents, and some even have school funding and administrative support. In Massachusetts, for example, there is a statewide network of parent advisory councils, which are divided into regional and local councils, all under the auspices of the state Department of Education. The regional councils conduct informational seminars to help parents in the local districts set up their own councils, and the state provides training to the local councils, helping them find effective ways to address academic support, child advocacy, and community outreach.

But the best thing about the local PACs (parent advisory councils) is that they offer parents a network of other parents with the same concerns. A meeting set up to investigate computer learning materials may end up being a round-table discussion of the social problems encountered by high-school LD kids. There is an opportunity for parents to share sympathies with other parents whose children are going through similar experiences, or to learn from parents who have found alternative ways to cope. The sense of shared problems and triumphs is the best possible means of support to a parent, who can then pass on renewed strength and new ideas to her child.

(More information on the parents' perspective and on the emotional price paid by LD families can be found in chapters 6 and 7.)

CHAPTER 5

How Do We Make It Happen?

Question: "How was your child's evaluation handled?"

Answers: "Basically, they told me that Megan's problem was an emotional one. The burden of proving that she had an attentional problem that was organic in nature fell to me. Ultimately, I had to use the courts to prove that what I knew about my own daughter was true."

"We took Allison right to Children's Hospital. We knew it was the best program in the city, and we wanted to know everything we could about her before we made any decisions. It turned out to be the best thing we could have done."

"The testing procedure was so ghastly! I blame a lot of David's problems on the trauma of that time. It took us over a year to get everything done the way it was supposed to be done, even with our pediatrician working with us. The school just didn't want to face the fact that they had to deal with David's LD in a different way than they handled all the other LD kids."

IT seems fairly cut-and-dried. We recognize a problem in our child, or a teacher recognizes it. We agree that an evaluation is necessary, and then go about arranging for one, either through the school or by private means. The evaluation team collects information from us, does the required testing, then meets with us to discuss the results. A course of remediation is decided upon, to which we agree, and which we follow up with careful scrutiny and occasional reevaluations. Our child makes slow but steady progress, and everyone is satisfied that the right thing has been done.

Of course, things don't always go as smoothly as that. In fact, given the number of variables, not the least of which is the erratic performance of the LD child himself, it's probably safe to say that they *never* do. From the moment you recognize the need for action to the time when action is finally taken, at least a dozen people, and as many months, may intervene. It's highly unlikely that the course you travel in getting the proper help for your child will be without bumps and pitfalls.

That's only natural. Such ups and downs are to be expected, perhaps even welcomed, since they may give you a chance to reassess your child's progress. But what happens when the system itself breaks down and your child's rights are not attended to? What if the school system refuses to acknowledge that there is a problem worth its considerable time and effort to evaluate? What if the evaluation you do get is clearly unacceptable?

That's when you need to know more about your child's rights and the laws that protect them. That's when you need to know about Public Law 94-142 and Section 504.

PL 94-142: Landmark in Education

Public Law 94-142 is like an IEP written for the states by the federal government. Its full name is the Education for All Handicapped Children Act, and it was born in the early 1970s. Before that time, handicapped children were given short shrift by local and state school administrations. Quite simply, they were not considered a good investment. Why waste time and money teaching the unteachable, when no return could be expected by society?

134

Children with minimal or moderate mental, physical, and emotional handicaps were tossed together into classrooms that were more like day-care centers than learning institutions. Children with learning disabilities were not even recognized as such; they were either classified as handicapped in some other way or left to fail in regular classrooms. And LD kids got off relatively lightly. Those with more severe difficulties were barred from school altogether. As recently as 1970, nearly every state had laws excluding handicapped children from compulsory school attendance.

But this was the coming of age of civil rights, and the constitutionality of such statutes was brought under sharp scrutiny. Attitudes about the rights and educability of the handicapped changed, and a series of legal battles determined that public school systems could not discriminate against children because of their limitations. In cases such as *Mills* vs. *The District of Columbia Board of Education* and *The Pennsylvania Association of Retarded Citizens* vs. *The Pennsylvania Board of Education,* schools were ordered by the courts to find appropriate placements for such children, and were legally barred from restricting their access to education because of budgetary constraints.

Public Law 94–142 was passed by the Senate on June 18, by the House on July 29, and signed into law by President Gerald Ford on November 29, 1975. It was drafted by a committee of educators and lawyers, with considerable input from parent and child-advocate lobbying groups. Its purpose, quite simply, was to insure that "all handicapped children have available to them a free appropriate education which includes special education and related services to meet their needs."

But the law is not as simple as that. Public Law 94–142 is extremely comprehensive, specific in detail, and precise in parameter. In addition to defining and insisting on free appropriate education for all children, it serves as a financial, administrative, and enforcement policy. It provides for federal aid to reimburse state and local education agencies for a portion of the additional costs of providing special education, and sets down conditions and obligations with which those agencies must comply in order to receive such funds.

This law provides services for children if they have difficulties in these areas:

- hearing
- speech
- vision
- learning disabilities
- chronic or long-term health problems
- emotional disturbance
- mental retardation
- physical impairments

The regulations contain basic principles of nonexclusion, assuring that no child is barred from his constitutional right to a public education. They also contain sections pertaining to the specific appropriate educational processes for such children, precise requirements for their identification, evaluation, and placement, and extensive procedural safeguards. Even noneducational "related services" are considered, including:

- social work services
- psychological services
- physical or occupational therapy
- transportation
- speech and language therapy
- vocational education
- parent counseling and training
- before- and after-school care
- medical services
- residential services

PL 94-142 is a mammoth piece of legislation, since it serves such a broad range of functions. Most of the law is couched in dense legalese, with very specific regulations regarding disbursement of funds, requirements for qualification, and program-monitoring guidelines. It lays down a foundation for the states to follow, and addresses the terms by which they must follow it. However, despite the numbing attention to legal, fiscal, and procedural detail, the law's major thrust remains obvious — to identify and address these major educational issues:

- free appropriate education for all
- public involvement in providing such education
- least restrictive environment for that education
- identification and evaluation procedures
- IEP placement and implementation
- parent participation in all aspects of education
- due process for protecting the above

We won't bother to reproduce 94–142 in its entirety. Teams of legal specialists would be needed to decipher it, and most of it only applies to us indirectly. But the following outline, adapted from the one offered by Joseph Roberts and Bonnie Hawks in *The Legal Rights Primer for the Handicapped,* breaks 94–142 down into its major components.

1. Section 601: Statement of Findings and Purpose — The first section states that, because of inadequate services within the public school system, over 8 million U.S. children are not receiving the proper educational services to which they are entitled. State and local agencies have the responsibility to provide it, and the federal government will assist them.

2. Section 602: Definitions — This section defines the terms used to describe various handicaps and the kinds of services to be provided. Phrases such as "orthopedically impaired," "instructional materials," "special education," "free appropriate education," "individualized education program," "excess costs," and "related services" are precisely described and their parameters established. The term "specific learning disabilities" is included, but not clearly defined until Section 620 (see below). Using a "zero reject" philosophy, the statute does not allow for the possibility that some children are too severely handicapped to be served.

3. Section 606: Employment of Handicapped Individuals — A later amendment to the basic bill, this section insures that the state makes positive efforts to employ handicapped individuals.

4. Section 607: Grants for the Removal of Architectural Barriers — This is another amendment that allows for payment of funds to increase handicap access to schools.

5. Section 611: Entitlements and Allocations — This deals with the financial disbursement of funds based on per-pupil expenditures, number of pupils served, and percentage of growth of funding over the course of five years. It also describes the age limitation of the bill (originally ages five to seventeen, extended to ages three to twenty-one).

6. Section 612: Eligibility — This sets down conditions that the states must meet in order to qualify for funding (states must establish their own "free appropriate education" laws and create education plans equal to or greater than those of 94–142); it sets

137

down extensive administrative procedures states must follow to receive such funds.

7. Section 613: State Plans — This section entails educational guidelines the states must follow in establishing and implementing their plans. It places responsibility for implementation of guidelines with local school districts in accordance with state standards. It demands that the IEP be all-inclusive, extending to related services if necessary.

8. Section 614: Application — This elucidates extensive record-keeping procedures and public availability requirements, defines required state provisions for a system of evaluation and individualized education plan review, and provides state safeguards for compliance of local programs.

9. Section 615: Procedural Safeguards — This sets forth procedures for hearings and civil action suits and defines district courts' jurisdiction.

10. Section 616: Withholding and Judicial Review — This establishes the right of the state to petition for review.

11. Section 617: Administration — This enumerates regulations regarding implementation and rules about confidentiality.

12. Section 618: Evaluation — This contains regulations for reporting numbers of children to be served and methods for authorizing and evaluating programs available to them. The right of students to participate in regular classroom activities to the greatest extent practicable (the basis for the concept of mainstreaming) is established here.

13. Section 619: Incentive Grants — This establishes guidelines for additional services to three- to five-year-olds.

14. Section 620: Payments — This section provides regulations for disbursement and contains the federal working definition of specific learning disabilities:

> Specific learning disability means a disorder in one or more of the basic psychological processes involved in understanding or using language, spoken or written, which may manifest itself in an imperfect ability to listen, think, speak, read, write, spell, or do mathematical calculations. The term includes such conditions as perceptual handicaps, brain injury, minimal brain dysfunction, dyslexia and developmental aphasia. The term does not include chil-

dren who have learning problems which are primarily the result of visual, hearing or motor handicaps, of mental retardation, or of environmental, cultural or economic disadvantages.

Other Numbers: 99–457 and 504

In 1986, when the statute of limitations on the original bill ran out, President Reagan signed a bill (PL 99-457) that reauthorized and extended the provisions of 94-142. By 1991, special education is mandated for all children aged three to five and seventeen to twenty-one who need it (children from six to sixteen are already covered), and policies for intervention for handicapped children from birth to two years are set forth. Secondary and postsecondary educational programs are addressed, and workplace discrimination is covered more comprehensively. In addition, funds for research, training, and dissemination programs are established to spread the effectiveness of the law.

But the other most important number to remember is Section 504 of the Federal Rehabilitation Act of 1973. Section 504 puts the teeth in 94-142 and its subsequent amendments. Legally, state compliance with both 94-142 and 99-457 is voluntary (forty-nine states signed on right away, and New Mexico agreed to join the plan shortly afterward). Section 504, however, is mandatory, and makes it illegal for a state to deny handicapped individuals access to education, employment, or housing. Effectively, it makes it illegal for them to ignore 94-142.

Section 504 is the quintessential civil rights law. It says that "no otherwise qualified handicapped individual in the United States . . . shall, solely by reason of his handicap, be excluded from participation in, be denied the benefits of, or be subjected to discrimination under any program or activity receiving federal assistance." It means that no public school can qualify for any federal money unless it complies with the particulars of 94-142.

The original 1973 Federal Rehabilitation Act was amended in 1977 specifically with PL 94-142 in mind. Section 504 is divided into seven subsections, which cover employment practices, program accessibility, and education on all levels right up through college. More than a demand for an end to discrimination, Section 504 insists on positive programming to remediate limitations. It's not enough, says 504, to allow a blind child into the school system; Braille books and specialized instruction must be provided so that the child can learn to read.

The Law and the LD Kids

Together, 94-142, 504, and the slew of state laws that they mandate have changed the face of education for handicapped children. But what, specifically, have they done for our LD kids? First of all, it was largely because of the efforts that resulted in 94-142 that the term *LD* came into popular national usage, although we know that even today, everyone means something a little bit different by the term. Nevertheless, the number of children identified as LD after the passage of 94-142 and 504 jumped dramatically from 800,000 in 1976 to 1.8 million a decade later.

Part of the reason for the great increase can be attributed to the growth of the field. Ten years ago, we were barely aware that the problem existed; today it is a major focus in educational and medical research. New testing procedures allow for more precise identification and placement. The passage of 94-142 allowed parents to insist that their children who had formerly been identified as mentally retarded or otherwise handicapped be moved to more appropriate LD placements.

By including LD kids under the aegis of the two federal laws, legislators and educators were making several important assumptions: first, that learning disabilities were a recognizable and remediable condition, and second, that they were worthy of special treatment. Children with learning disabilities now had the legal right to be identified, evaluated, and educated in the most appropriate and least restrictive manner. Public schools were required to provide these services in order to meet state requirements, receive federal funding, and avoid prosecution.

Although much of 94-142 and 504 seem to be directed at the needs of children with severe physical and mental handicaps, the law makes no such distinction, and parents of LD children must learn not to be put off by the extent of the statutes. The rights of LD children are overlooked as often as those of more severely handicapped children — perhaps even more often than theirs, since the LD child appears "normal" and has so many other strengths on which to draw. But we can use the letter of the law to assure our children of an appropriate education when it appears that their problem is being ignored or diminished in any way.

There is, of course, a flip side to the positive aspects of the inclusion of LD (actually, there it's called Specific Learning Disability, or SLD) in 94–142. For a law that states as its primary intent the dissolution of negative classifications, 94–142 seems to have stepped into its own pothole with such extensive categorizations of handicapping conditions. True, it tries to provide the most nonjudgmental definitions, but the very act of special classification sometimes creates a barrier to children so identified. There are still some skeptics who feel that the passage of 94–142 simply creates another caste system to replace the old one.

Others have protested that the passage of the law creates a battle for funds that will eventually deplete the monies that are channeled into regular educational programs. Already several states have encountered battles with parents and local school systems that argue that dollars are being taken from enrichment programs like sports and the arts in order to fund the rapidly rising costs of special education programs for LD kids — who represent, by the way, the largest percentage of the special needs population in most school systems. Increases in the levels of federal support have not been forthcoming to remediate the financial shortfall in regular programs, which pits parent against parent in a battle for limited funds. Unfortunately, this promises to be a growing concern at both local and state levels.

The guidelines set for LD children by federal law — that they be performing at least two years behind their age-appropriate grade level — also comes in for criticism, particularly since it seems to indicate that school systems must wait until a child has demonstrated at least two years of school failure in order for him or her to be eligible for evaluation and remediation. For a child who has the capability of performing well above grade level, working one year behind can indicate a need for help. On the other hand, is every kid working below grade level a potentially LD child? Not necessarily, and it's a question that testing should — but too often doesn't — answer effectively. Fortunately, most states now have in place mandatory screening programs that determine if children are at risk for developing learning disabilities, and state special education laws provide for intervention well before a child is in her third year of public school.

School systems reluctant to provide services have tried to use the two-years-behind definition to avoid providing services, although several court cases have struck them down in favor of the early-intervention clauses provided in Section 504 and the 99-457 amendments. By and large, however, the passage of 94-142 has liberated the LD child by providing him with a free education appropriate to his needs, in the least restrictive environment, and by offering parents the chance to take an active role in the process.

The Appeal Process

Nearly 2 million children were identified as LD in 1987. That number reflects a 144 percent increase in the number of identified LD kids from a decade before, and 24 percent of the total number of handicapped children served under 94-142. Regardless of the reason for their growth, those numbers do not lie. LD children need special attention as much as any other handicapped children do, and 94-142 is the strongest weapon in our arsenal to acquire that help for them. Remember, our children's rights are clearly mandated by the laws. And, if we don't think those rights are being served, our rights as parents are also laid out in no uncertain terms.

What are our rights? Under the law, there are six avenues of action open to us:

1. An independent evaluation
2. A hearing before a neutral hearing officer
3. An administrative appeal
4. A complaint to the state education department
5. A complaint to the federal Office for Civil Rights
6. A lawsuit

Before we examine these steps in detail, however, let's backtrack a bit. The law, as we have seen, has all sorts of protections built into it to insure fair, careful, and thoughtful evaluations and placements. Due process of law protects every citizen, and *this* law provides the following protections:

- regular consultation between educators and parents
- disagreement resolved by hearings within a reasonable period of time and at a convenient place
- prior notification of all actions
- all information provided in parents' native language and in understandable terms
- advisement of legal rights and right of appeal
- parental consent
- confidentiality of information
- parental access to records
- independent appraisal
- surrogate parents' or guardians' rights

With such extensive guarantees, how can the law possibly fall short? Obviously, even the most comprehensive legal guidelines will fail if they are not implemented by well-trained and committed personnel. Teachers who are not trained to spot LD symptoms will not find LD kids in their classrooms. That leaves the burden of proof on the parent, who must then convince a sometimes reluctant school administration to spend the time and money on an evaluation.

You are the primary source of a referral for evaluation. If your child is in preschool or kindergarten, required screening procedures may detect a problem. A school-age child is more likely to be referred by a classroom teacher, although school officials, judicial officers, family doctors, and other custodians of child welfare may do so.

But, as I say, by far the primary source of a referral for evaluation is the parent. And then, even if the teacher is willing to start the evaluation process, and even if the administration agrees that the child merits the expenditure, a poorly trained evaluator may not administer the right tests in the right way, so the results of the evaluation could be seriously affected. Then, once a diagnosis has been reached, poorly trained (or untrained) specialists will do no good at all.

Thanks to due process of law, you do not have to settle for less than the best. According to PL 94–142, you have the right to challenge your child's school if you think

- that the evaluation was unsatisfactory, inadequate, or discriminatory;
- has not taken place within a reasonable time from your request
  (you do not have to provide a reason for your refusal to accept
  the results of the evaluation, but most advocates admit that it
  does help if you provide the school with that information);
- that an initial evaluation does or does not need to be done, contrary to the school's opinion;
- that your views were ignored or unfairly represented by others
  involved in the evaluation process;
- that the IEP developed for your child is not responsive to his
  individual abilities or needs;
- that the services being offered are not what your child needs in
  order to learn;
- that promised services have been excessively delayed or denied;
- that your child is showing no progress or insufficient progress
  in her placement;
- that your child should spend more (or less) time in a more (or
  less) restrictive placement.

Clearly, you have a tremendous degree of authority in making
these decisions, and a tremendous responsibility to see that things
are done right. The law is *very* clear about the ultimate rights of
the parent to decide what is best for the child. "The parent is entitled to complain with respect to any matter relating to the identification, evaluation or educational placement of the child, or the
provision of a free and appropriate public education to such child."

But you must be prepared to back up your claims with facts.
To this end, it is important for you to keep a file of all your child's
records, both educational and medical; of all previous assessments,
regardless of when or where they were done, and a record of all
your communications with the school. Keep a family history and
your child's comprehensive history (see chapter 4) on hand and
updated. Do your homework in other ways, by finding out about
other sources for evaluation so that you don't have to use a school-
supplied independent evaluator (see pages 149–152 for discussion
of the independent evaluation process), and by talking to other
parents to get support if you feel your school system is not being
cooperative. The prospect of class action can intimidate even the

most reluctant school system, and the legal history of such suits weighs heavily in favor of parent and child.

Find out what your legal options and alternative actions are. Consult your local advocacy office (see Appendix A) and see if you might need legal advice as well. Your state's department of education should also be able to provide you with a handbook on state appeals processes (see Appendix A). Be prepared to argue against bottom-line tactics and laissez-faire educational placements. The more ammunition you have, the greater your ability to challenge the decision of the school, and the more likely your success.

Step-by-Step: How to Do It If You Have To

Robert Schoonover, in his *Handbook for Parents of Children with Learning Disabilities,* has created a very clear flow chart to help parents understand the process by which a learning disabled child is recognized, tested, and, one hopes, treated:

Step 1: Referral (*by parents or teacher*)

Step 2: Notification (*of parents and appropriate personnel*)
Parents must be notified within 5 working days if teacher has initiated referral.

Step 3: Screening (*review previous history, if applicable*)

Step 4: Consent (*terminate or appeal*)
Parent has 30 days to decide whether or not to go ahead with evaluation process.

Step 5: Evaluation
Must take place within 30 days of agreement to proceed.

Step 6: Evaluation Meeting (*written summary*) (*appeal*)
6a: Discussion
6b: Mediation
6c: Hearing
6d: Administrative Appeal
6e: Civil Suit
Parent has 30 days to decide whether or not to accept IEP.

Step 7: IEP
Must go into effect immediately after parent's acceptance.

Step 8: Implementation (*monitor and review*)

Let's say that everything has not gone according to plan, and you are not happy with the way your child's problems are being handled at school. What do you do? The best way to describe the lengthy and complicated process is probably to follow an appeals case from beginning to end, so we'll pick a hypothetical situation and develop it step-by-step.

Let's call our child Kate Perkins. Kate is in the third grade, and is having a lot of trouble with her reading, spelling, and math computation skills. In addition, she is beginning to present quite a behavior problem, being loud and disruptive during class. There have been several meetings between Kate's teacher and her parents to discuss Kate's situation, and all agree that the matter must be looked into more closely.

Step 1. The Referral: Kate's parents requested an evaluation, in a letter directed to the school system's bureau of pupil services, with copies sent to the teacher and the principal of Kate's school. In return, they received a consent form asking them to allow the school to conduct a fairly complete battery of tests (Kate's parents checked off the tests they thought should be done, after conferring with the teacher). Tests were to be conducted in the areas of educational status and achievement, hearing and vision, and psychology. A family history would be completed by a social worker in a home visit. Other tests, such as psychiatric, occupational therapy, and speech and language, were waived by the Perkinses.

Step 2. Notification: In addition to the letter to Kate's parents, other appropriate school personnel were notified of the testing, and a schedule was drawn up by the team leader, who was the LD specialist for Kate's school.

Step 3. Screening: This step was not taken in Kate's case, since she had already been screened by her teacher, and a need was found. If Kate's parents had requested the evaluation without pre-

viously consulting with the teacher, Kate would have been screened by the school to determine if, in fact, there was a need for an assessment. If someone other than Mrs. Perkins had been the source of the referral, and she had not been involved in the initial decision, she would have been notified no later than five days after the referral had been made. But the final decision rested with the Perkinses, although the school has rights of appeal if they feel parents are unjustly keeping a child from his legally mandated education. In turn, if the school had not agreed to the testing, the Perkinses could have appealed that decision as well.

Step 4. Consent: Kate's parents signed the form authorizing the school to go ahead with the evaluation.

Step 5. Evaluation: All the tests were to be conducted by school department specialists on school property over a thirty-day period. Kate's parents told her that she was being tested to help find out why she was having trouble in school, and that they were confident that they could help her overcome her difficulties once they knew more about them.

Step 6. The Evaluation Meeting: At the evaluation meeting, Mrs. Perkins was disappointed. Despite the extensive history of behavioral and emotional difficulties documented in the classroom and at home, the evaluation team felt that Kate's difficulties were largely developmental, and that she would grow out of them. Kate's academic problems were, the team felt, also a result of this maturational lag, although they conceded that some remedial efforts were in order to help her catch up.

According to the IEP they developed (this was the first time Mrs. Perkins had seen it, despite the fact that she should have been invited to participate in its creation), Kate was to remain in the regular classroom and receive remedial reading tutoring three times a week. Clearly, the school did not intend to do anything to help Kate learn nonacademic coping strategies, like controlling her temper and managing her impulsive volubility.

Mrs. Perkins wasn't satisfied with the way the tests had been interpreted. She didn't feel the classroom teacher was equipped to handle Kate's behavior in class, much less her special curriculum needs in math and spelling. She felt that the amount of intervention provided for was not nearly enough to address Kate's academic needs or her behavioral problems — a self-contained classroom, she felt, would be more appropriate. Despite their efforts to explain the rationale behind their IEP, the evaluation team could not convince her that their placement decision was in Kate's best interest.

The Perkinses' rights had been followed to the letter of the law (except for the fact that the IEP had not been provided to Mrs. Perkins before the meeting). Kate had been tested within the legal time limits, and the results had been processed within the given time frame as well. Kate's parents had been advised of all meetings other than the IEP development meeting, which was done in bits and pieces by the various evaluators and pieced together by the team chairperson, and Mrs. Perkins had been present at the evaluation meeting.

Still, they knew that they had to go further to insure that Kate got a more effective diagnosis and placement. They were not yet prepared for the possibility of appeal. What were their options, once they decided not to accept the school's recommendations?

Step 6a. Discussion — Try to settle differences at the local level: At the evaluation meeting, Mrs. Perkins told the team that she did not believe the IEP adequately reflected Kate's needs. Was the team willing to revise them? The team leader said she would stand by the team's results. Mrs. Perkins refused to sign the consent form at the end of the IEP until she had talked again with the classroom teacher, who was not at the meeting, although she should have been. (The teacher had already signed the IEP forms.) She also wanted to discuss the results with her husband, who was not present. By law, she had thirty days either to accept or reject all or part of the evaluation. If she had accepted it, services would have begun immediately. If she rejected it, Kate would remain in her current situation (that is, without any special services at all) until a new plan was agreed upon by all. Mrs. Perkins could have accepted a portion of the plan, such as the reading tutoring component, but she felt it wasn't adequate.

— **Keep records:** Mrs. Perkins requested a copy, not only of the written evaluation, but of the actual tests that Kate had been given. Even though she could not interpret them, she wanted to include them in her files. In fact, she did not receive the tests themselves, but did get copies of the individual evaluators' reports on the tests. She then spoke with the classroom teacher, who agreed that Kate would probably not do well at the intended level of remediation and indicated that she did not feel capable of providing Kate with additional individualized instruction and behavior management. Young, and inexperienced with special-needs children, the teacher had signed the IEP plans, she told Mrs. Perkins, because she felt she had no alternative.

Mrs. Perkins also talked with the vice principal, who was sympathetic but pointed out that the school did not have room in the budget to place every "immature" child in a special classroom situation. He pointed out that the concept of "least restrictive environment" meant that, by law, Kate had to be placed in the most nearly normal situation. Besides, he said, he was certain, with his long experience, that if Mrs. Perkins accepted the school's finding, Kate would probably grow out of the problem.

In each case, Mrs. Perkins jotted down a record of the meeting, describing what had been discussed and what the response had been to her concerns. She also kept records of phone calls she made to a local community legal service agency to find out how she should proceed. Mary Lutens, a child advocacy specialist, was assigned to help her decide what to do and how to do it.

— **The independent evaluation:** In looking over the tests, Mrs. Perkins told Ms. Lutens, she and her husband had felt that not enough emphasis had been placed on psychological testing, and that the educational testing was cursory, given the degree of difficulty described by parents and teacher. The two women agreed that more action was necessary. Ms. Lutens told Mrs. Perkins to proceed with a request for an independent evaluation and to base further actions on those results.

Advocates often encourage clients to get an independent evaluation, for a number of very valid reasons. Since the school evaluators are often also the service providers, they may be under personal pressure to keep services to a minimum so that they are not unduly burdened.

Other evaluators hired by the schools expressly for the purpose of evaluation may be under financial pressure to do the same thing and keep special education costs down. Some school districts rely on evaluations made by personnel who are not trained testers, a situation that would make their interpretations questionable, to say the least. In general, unless you feel completely satisfied that your child's problems have been clearly described and effectively addressed by the IEP, you can request an independent evaluation without giving an explanation of the reasons behind your request.

In reality, it makes more sense to be as helpful as possible and explain your reasons to the school. If there are components of the evaluation that you do not reject, there is no reason to spend money on repeating them. There is also the danger that the child begins to feel "overtested," making his performance in subsequent tests less reliable. Taking these things into account and being positive but firm in your requests will make the school more likely to cooperate without a fuss. But the bottom line *must* be your child's welfare, and being pushy is sometimes the only alternative.

On the basis of her own feelings and Ms. Lutens's advice, Mrs. Perkins rejected the IEP, explaining that she thought it did not address her daughter's needs adequately, and requested that an independent evaluation be conducted. She was very specific about what she did not agree with, pointing out that the teacher did not feel capable of dealing with Kate within the classroom, and that the amount of tutoring Kate was to get was not sufficient to address her academic disabilities. She closed by saying that the concept of "least restrictive environment" did not apply when her child's chances for educational success were being limited by the placement. In fact, she considered the IEP a more restrictive environment, since it denied her daughter access to an appropriate education.

As legally required, the school provided the Perkinses with the names of several independent evaluators within the allotted time frame. But Mrs. Perkins, in talking to friends who had been through similar experiences, decided not to use them. She felt that Kate's evaluation should be done by someone who had no connection at all with the school system. Ms. Lutens provided her with names of two clinics in the next town, and the Perkinses chose one because it was also recommended by a friend.

They also had to come up with an additional $400 to pay for it, although the clinic operated on a sliding scale of charges and they were eligible for a slight reduction because of their income level. The school system provided funds for outside evaluations on a prorated basis (set by the state's rate-setting commission), and would not pay more than $300 out of the total $700 fee.

Some estimates the Perkinses had received had gone as high as $1,500, which was totally out of the question for them financially. The Perkinses could have decided to go with the school's choice of an independent evaluator, but felt that they would encounter many of the same limitations they had in the first evaluation, so they chose to pay the additional money. Ms. Lutens told them there was a slight chance they could recover some of the money retroactively, but warned them not to expect it. The advocate explained to them that, in any case, the results of the second evaluation would be considered valid in determining the outcome of Kate's appeal, and urged them to incur the cost regardless of whether it was eventually repaid.

The results of the second evaluation came much closer to what the Perkinses believed was appropriate for Kate. The wide battery of tests indicated that Kate had moderate to severe visual processing problems, poor motor coordination skill, and a poor attention span. There were other deficits indicated in language synthesis, spatial orientation, and social maturity. The results confirmed the Perkinses' suspicions that Kate needed the broader interventions of a special classroom. Now they had to convince the school of that.

In Kate Perkins's case, the results of the first evaluation were the impetus for the Perkinses' appeal. Aside from an unacceptable assessment, there are other reasons for beginning an appeal process. There might have been resistance on the part of the teacher or the administration to administering the tests, in which case appeals would have been made in order to enforce the child's right to an evaluation. A child in first or second grade — or even in preschool — might not be considered eligible for an evaluation by the school, since she has not demonstrated that she is at least two years behind in her academic skills. As the law reads, however, children are eligible for intervention well before they have reached school age, and this eligibility may have to be the basis for the appeal. State mandatory preschool testing laws make it nearly impossible for a child to be turned away from an evaluation because she has not yet demonstrated the two-years-behind component.

Even more frequently, appeals are conducted on the basis of an infringement of constitutional rights of the child as laid down by 94-142 and 504. If a child is denied access to a mainstreamed classroom, for example, or if the evaluation process was not conducted according to strict guidelines, appeals are warranted. If, in addition, the Perkinses' legal rights had not been observed — if Mrs. Perkins's native language had been Haitian Creole and the information given her had been in English, or if the school had placed Kate in a self-contained classroom before evaluation and without consulting her parents — the appeals process would be necessary.

Step 6b. The Request for Mediation: As Mrs. Perkins had feared, the IEP team at school looked over the results of the independent evaluation but did not recommend any additional services for Kate (the independent evaluation had come up with a recommendation for Kate — a separate classroom placement —but the school was responsible for creating the IEP). The time had finally come to proceed with the appeals system available to all families by federal law, which is based on a judicial system whereby both sides present their cases and accept or reject the verdict handed down by a third party.

The Perkinses wrote another letter, again rejecting the school's IEP for Kate and asking that it be rewritten to include the recommendations of the independent evaluation. A copy of that letter was forwarded to the school's bureau of special education appeals, and, within the five-day limit required by law, the Perkinses got a response. Before going to hearing, the BSEA asked if Mrs. Perkins was willing to have her case heard by an impartial mediator from the bureau.

She agreed, and a meeting was arranged with Mrs. Perkins, the evaluation team leader, and the BSEA mediator. Although she could have had Ms. Lutens or legal counsel with her, Mrs. Perkins went alone. She had been told that most disagreements are worked out in the informal hearing process, and she was hoping that would happen in her case.

However, after going over Kate's records, looking at the second evaluation, and listening to both sides of the story, the mediator was unable to suggest any compromises that were agreeable to both parties. He agreed that the two evaluations differed, but felt that the results of the first were valid, and that neither Kate's nor her parents' rights had been violated in the process.

As soon as she could, Mrs. Perkins called Ms. Lutens, who told her that a more formal hearing was the next step. A second decision could have been made without a hearing, based on all available information, but, since the "impartial" mediator seemed to have in mind the school's best interests rather than her child's, Mrs. Perkins felt it was best to have the formal hearing.

— **Keeping things calm at school:** In spite of the growing disagreement between the Perkinses and the school, every effort was made to insure that Kate was not affected by the process. She remained in her classroom, and the classroom teacher did her best to work with the child during the course of the appeals. Had the conflict been over a proposed change in placement, such as a child moving from a self-contained classroom to a regular classroom, the child would have been legally required to stay in the current placement until the appeal was resolved. Although this concept is usually to the child's benefit, reducing the stress of changes until absolutely necessary, in Kate's case it was exacerbating her problem, since she was doing so poorly in the class. This only made the Perkinses more convinced that the IEP was inappropriate.

Step 6c. The Hearing: The BSEA scheduled the Perkinses' hearing within twenty days of the receipt of their request for it. Before the hearing, Kate's parents had presented their extensive file and the results of the second evaluation to the hearing officer. In return, they had been given access for their own examination to all school records regarding Kate, and the independent evaluators had used these records in making their recommendation.

The hearing was held at school administration headquarters, and the Perkinses brought in Ms. Lutens as well as a specially trained lawyer provided by Ms. Lutens's advocacy office. The school had its own lawyers present, and several administrators, as well as the members of the original evaluation team and Kate's classroom teacher. Mrs. Perkins had requested that both the vice principal and Kate's teacher attend, and both were required to corroborate their statements to Mrs. Perkins. The Perkinses decided to keep the proceeding closed to the public, and they elected not to have Kate attend.

The hearing was a lot like a courtroom trial, with the hearing mediator asking both sides to present their evidence and state their cases. The hearing officer had been chosen from a list of available professionals who had no connection with either the school system or the Perkinses, and who had no reason to benefit in any way from the outcome of the proceedings.

The written record Mrs. Perkins had kept was extremely valuable here, since she was able to document that the vice principal had told her that budgetary concerns were involved in the decision to limit Kate's remediation to twice a week in her IEP. Mrs. Perkins was allowed to question the school official herself, and the classroom teacher testified that she felt Kate needed more help than she was getting. At Mrs. Perkins's lawyer's request, the hearing officer admitted into evidence a tape recording of Kate telling the independent evaluator that she hated school because it made her feel dumb, and that kids picked on her because she couldn't read. She said she wished she could go somewhere else to school or, preferably, stay at home with her mother.

— **The results:** Forty-five days after the hearing, the hearing officer presented her decision. She ruled in favor of the Perkinses, and directed the school to provide an alternative IEP based on the information in the independent evaluation. The school had ten working days to come up with a plan that took into account Kate's need for a broader range of academic supports as well as a series of behavior contracts designed to help her function in the special classroom.

Step 6d. Administrative Appeal: Everything went well for the Perkinses at the hearing level, as it does in the vast majority of appeals. However, if any step in the process had violated the rights of the Perkins family — if, say, the information provided by the second evaluation was not considered in reaching a decision, or if the legal time limits had not been observed — the Perkinses could have gone several steps farther, beginning with an administrative appeal to the state department of education.

An administrative appeal is not available if the hearing was conducted by the state department of education in the first place, as it is in most cases. Administrative appeals are usually conducted only in cases where procedural rights have been denied, although parents can institute one if they do not agree with the results of the hearing.

At an administrative appeal, the results of the hearing would be reviewed, but no new evidence would be introduced unless requested by the appeals board. If a parent has been using advocacy advisement up to this point, a lawyer would probably be called in, to deal with the complicated procedural issues involved in an appeal and because civil suits are often instituted concurrently with administrative appeals. The judgment of the appeals court, handed down within thirty days, would be binding, unless the parents felt they had to go even further to insure their child's rights to a free and appropriate education.

Step 6e. Civil Suit: The final step is a state or federal lawsuit, and, again, this is usually done only if civil rights have been violated on the basis of race, sex, religion, or handicap. This is most often the case in the situation of physically or otherwise handicapped children, and rarely used for LD. But it's certainly an available avenue for appeal, laid down and protected by law. If, for instance, the Perkinses' request for Kate's initial evaluation had been denied at every level, or if a school board member had served as hearing officer, and these issues had not been remediated at the state administrative appeals level, then there would be grounds for a civil suit. If, in addition, the IEP called for placement in a situation that was physically inaccessible to a handicapped child, or that blatantly violated the provisions of PL 94-142, civil law would be engaged.

Federal law requires states to have complaint management offices, which investigate civil suit claims and resolve them if possible. Civil suits are different from administrative appeals, since they call into play the state and/or federal civil rights laws, which protect the rights of children and parents under both 94–142 and 504. Some state agencies will render faster results than federal courts, but you may feel it is necessary to go all the way to the federal level, especially if there is gross violation of the law or you are part of a class action suit, a suit that is filed by an individual or an advocacy agency on behalf of a group of citizens with similar complaints.

The federal Office for Civil Rights (OCR) is charged with seeing to it that Section 504 and 94–142 are administered by the Office of Special Education and Rehabilitative Services (OSER). A complaint registered with either of these offices would result in a federal investigation of your charges, and could affect federal monies received by a school district if the district is found to be in noncompliance with either law.

Lawsuits result in direct court orders being issued requiring public officials to obey the law and provide your child with services or else risk fines, reduced funding, or imprisonment. It's important to list all the local, city, and state officials involved in your child's case, since they are legally charged with carrying out the letter of the law. The law also provides for repayment of legal fees, which are extensive in a legal battle of this magnitude.

Step 7. The IEP: Based on the finding of the appeal judge, the new IEP was written to the Perkinses' satisfaction. Kate Perkins was finally placed in a self-contained classroom in a nearby school that had six other learning disabled children ranging in age from seven to ten years. In addition, she was judged eligible to attend weekly sessions with the school psychologist to help her work on coping strategies outside the class. The new placement was to go into effect immediately.

Step 8. Implementation: Mr. and Mrs. Perkins kept a close eye on Kate's progress, and were satisfied that she was getting the best help possible. At the end of each year, her IEP was reviewed and revised, and, after three years, everyone agreed that she was ready to return to a regular classroom for half her school day. She continued to get support in and out of the classroom.

Practical Issues

There are some practical questions that need to be answered regarding you and your child's legal rights. There is a distinction between advocacy and legal advice. The list of resources in Appendix A will help you locate advocacy offices and law information centers in your area that can provide you with both information and assistance about your legal rights. Should the need for a lawyer arise, these professionals will be able to direct you to lawyers who concentrate on special education law. In general, it's wise to get in touch with an advocacy office as soon as you have decided to reject an IEP (or sooner, if the evaluation process is not going according to the rules). A lawyer should be called in if it appears there are going to be continued negotiations beyond the mediation level.

If you can't find a qualified specialist in child advocacy law through your local resources, you may have to do some hunting on your own. In order to be sure you're getting the best qualified legal assistance, you'll want to ask some questions first. Then, once you've made your choice, you'll have to ask some more. The following list of pertinent questions, from Sally Smith's book *No Easy Answers,* is by no means complete, but it gives you a good idea about where to start. (By the way, these questions would do just as well when talking to advocates.)

1. Are you familiar with PL 94–142 and Section 504?
2. Are you familiar with the related state laws?
3. Have you defended other parents in similar cases?
4. What's the first step to take in our particular case?
5. Have you successfully handled cases in my school district?
6. What kind of preparations must I make in order for you to present my case?
7. What can be done short of a hearing, and how are you prepared to help me do it?
8. What is my role in a hearing and/or appeal?
9. If we settle before the hearing, will the town pay my legal costs?
10. Will there be any repercussions for my child, and how can you help me insure against them?

11. Whom shall we ask to speak as witnesses for us, and how do we go about insuring their cooperation?
12. What will the guidelines be for the hearing officer's decision?
13. What will the cost of your services be?

Cost is big consideration when you're considering hiring a lawyer to help you in your appeal process. Regardless of their commitment to the cause of children's rights under the law, lawyers are expensive. Many advocacy offices provide services similar to those provided by an attorney, and legal aid societies offer legal services on a sliding-scale basis. But the most important thing to remember is that you can get the school to pay your legal fees. In the 1986 amendments to 94–142, appeals courts at the local, state, and federal levels were given the power to order school systems to pay court costs — *if the ruling is in favor of the parents.*

If it is not in your favor, you will be saddled with the legal bills. In addition, if the school brings you to an appeal, you may be sued for the school's court costs. There are a number of circumstances under which this might happen: if a parent ignores or refuses a school request for evaluation; if a parent refuses a special placement and the school believes it is acting in the child's best interests; or if the parent keeps the child out of school as a result of a placement dispute.

Even if action is brought against you by the schools, you have the same legal rights laid out above. Above all, your informed consent is required before the school can take any action, and the burden of proof lies with the school to demonstrate need.

The other major consideration is time. By law, the school must adhere to a pretty strict schedule in terms of getting your child evaluated, diagnosed, and placed in the proper remedial situation. The time line that follows is an example of the Massachusetts legal restrictions on how long the evaluation and appeals process can take. Massachusetts has among the most stringent laws; other states' regulations may vary (write to your state's department of education — see Appendix A).

Massachusetts 766 Guidelines

1. If someone besides the parent refers the child, notice must be sent to the parent within 5 DAYS.

2. Following the date the school receives the parents' written consent, the evaluation must be completed in no more than 30 WORKING DAYS.

3. Following the completion of the evaluation and the evaluation team meeting, the IEP must be provided in written form to parents within 8 WORKING DAYS.

4. An informal discussion period of up to 30 WORKING DAYS can occur in order for the parents to review their IEP and make a decision.

5. If the parent requests an independent evaluation, it must be completed within 30 WORKING DAYS. Within 10 WORKING DAYS after receiving the results on an independent evaluation, the IEP team must meet to discuss those results.

6. Following the completion of the independent evaluation and team meeting recommendations, a parent must make a decision within 30 DAYS.

7. After receipt of rejection of IEP, the school committee must send notice to the Bureau of Special Education within 5 DAYS.

8. After receipt of rejection of IEP from school committee, BSEA must send notice to both parents and school within 5 DAYS. There may be another 30 DAYS discussion period, known as mediation, at this time.

9. No later than 5 DAYS after the request for a hearing is received, the BSEA will send notification to parents. The hearing must be scheduled within 20 DAYS, and a decision rendered by the hearing officer within 45 DAYS.

If the parent disagrees with the result of the hearing, he or she may appeal to the State or Federal Court within 30 DAYS.

If you add it all up, that's nearly 100 school working days from start to finish just for the evaluation process to be completed. That's nearly half of a 210-day school year. And, if a parent has rejected an IEP and plans an appeal, the time frame can run into additional months. It's important, then, to make sure that the legal limits are being observed, and to be aware that it may take a while.

The ins and outs of conducting an appeal are indeed daunting, and the amount of time and money that can be spent is considerable. But the prospect of a favorable result should outweigh the short-term aggravation, and it might help to remember that you are the resource of last resort for your child. If you don't help him, he might not get the proper help at all. And the law is very much on your side, all the way down the line. The Massachusetts Office for Children offers a motto to parents who are looking for advice: "If you don't like the IEP, mediate. If you don't like the mediation, appeal."

What's Wrong with This Picture?

We've already discussed some of the problems inherent in special education for learning disabled children as provided by the law. The twin concepts of maximum feasible benefit and least restrictive environment are sometimes not as compatible as they seem. Comprehensive evaluations can leave as much room for error as for precise diagnosis when not conducted properly. Although the law guarantees that appropriate services will be provided, there is no guarantee that they will be provided in a quality environment, by a well-trained specialist or teacher.

There's a lot we can do to prevent these problems. But there are some things we can't do. We can't simply assume that the mere existence of PL 94-142 is going to insure that our child's needs are going to be served in the best possible fashion. We have to monitor constantly, and advocate strongly, on their behalf.

And we can't prevent the weakness inherent in the law itself. PL 94-142 addresses many essential issues, but it seems to shy away from the problem of those children who suffer from handicaps imposed on them by a harsh environment. The majority of children classified as LD under 94-142 come from working or middle-class families in which at least one parent is willing and able to participate in the child's school career. For the very poor, the uneducated, and foreign-born families, such attention is not always possible. It may be true that the LD children of these families do not suffer primarily from LD, but it's certainly true that they need help as much as other children do.

"The most unfortunate exclusion in the PL 94-142 rules," says the critic Leon Eisenberg, "is that regarding kids who suffer from 'environmental, cultural or economic disadvantage.' The legislation, unhappily, abandons those most in need of help in favor of those whose families already command the largest share of resources."

Fortunately, civil rights legislation such as that represented by Section 504 of the Rehabilitation Act of 1973 provides for much more active intervention. Any child who is being denied special education services because of racial, economic, or cultural disadvantage can insist on his right under that law, and parents of all children can insist that the rules apply to every child. Parents who have learned to speak out on behalf of their LD children can also speak out on behalf of other children in need, and see to it that their school meets those needs as well. It's part of the empowerment of parents, and speaking out does us almost as much good as helping our own children.

CHAPTER 6

Meanwhile . . . What Happens When School Gets Out?

Question: "How does your LD make you feel?"

Answers: "I know I'm not dumb — everybody tells me how smart I am and that it's just my learning disability and all. But sometimes I feel so bad that I just want to stop trying." (Age 14)

"I'm so frustrated. Everybody makes me feel like a jerk." (Age 9)

Question: "How does your child's LD affect your life?"

Answers: "My marriage was, and is, very much affected by Bruce's problem. My husband does not want to accept the responsibility associated with our son's learning disability. His solution is to be very firm with Bruce. I'm too easy. This has led to terrific disagreements about our son. At times, the situation is so desperate I've thought of taking Bruce and leaving my husband."

"I spend so much time thinking about Ellen, and so much energy arranging her life for her. The other kids are always complaining to me about it, and they take it out on Ellen, too. And then I think, my God, I'm probably ruining her by doing so much in the first place. . . ."

LET'S assume that your child's evaluation and placement process has been satisfactory, or that you've successfully appealed an unacceptable placement and gotten one that's appropriate. Your child should now have a program that, in addition to reflecting her specific educational needs, addresses her specific emotional needs in school as well. The result might mean a different classroom placement, visits to a school psychologist or an adjustment counselor, occupational or speech therapy, or a special disciplinary contract for behavior management.

Those six hours between eight and two are no longer a nightmare for everyone concerned. Your child is functioning, the school is in control of the program details, and you're relieved. You no longer have to worry about panicked phone calls from the guidance office at all hours of the day, and your child seems to be making slow but steady academic progress — a state of affairs that you secretly admit you *never* expected to come about.

Then the school day ends, and your daughter comes home. All the progress you worked so hard to insure at school seems to evaporate as soon as she walks in the door, and emotionally, you're right back to square one. She refuses to do her homework, doesn't seem able to connect with any of her classmates, and won't join the local soccer league because she's afraid of fouling up the game. Her room is a mess, her clothes are buttoned awry, and she needs to be asked six times to brush her teeth after dinner.

In addition, your other children are complaining that she gets too much of your attention and embarrasses them in front of their friends. Your husband is wondering why you're always rushing to her defense and when you're going to have a moment to spend with him that's not taken up with arguments about how to handle the kids. It seems as if you're spending 110 percent of your time and attention on your LD child — and that it's like pouring all that energy into a black hole. Nothing seems to stick.

In short, whatever academic progress is being made at school is useless to you and your family and not particularly helpful to your LD child in her social relationships. Although those six hours a day spent on schoolwork may be going well, the other eighteen hours are a nightmare. And what good are improved reading and math skills if your child suffers from inadequate social skills, tense familial relationships, and a low self-image?

Not much. Experts agree that educational remediation without emotional support is ineffective. It may work for a while, especially if the child's educational progress boosts her self-esteem. But sooner or later the unhappiness at home and with friends will erode any new confidence, and the vicious cycle of failure will begin again.

Larry Silver, in *The Misunderstood Child,* says, "I find it helpful in understanding LD kids to realize that they have had only one brain all their lives, and they don't know it is different from anybody else's. They don't realize they are harder to understand, more distractible, or more active than any other child. They are trying just as hard to learn. Their experiences constantly confuse them. Why don't they succeed? Why do they constantly fail?"

What can we do to interrupt that painful pattern? We can reduce stress at home, educate our family members in ways to cope with each other, and assist our LD children in developing social skills. And, although these are time-consuming tasks, they're not impossible ones. If we use the IEP as our model, we can teach our children these skills in small, carefully structured increments that virtually assure success. What's more, life at home may actually improve while the learning process is going on.

But how do we know where to begin, and how can we decide what specific skills our children need? First, let's examine the various areas of friction — from both the LD child's point of view and our own. Once we've acknowledged the source of some of this painful maladjustment, we can look more effectively for strategies that can realign our lives and prepare our LD children to live theirs more confidently. The following are admittedly bleak pictures of life as an LD child (and as the parent of one), but they are not altogether exaggerated, and they serve to point up some of the very real emotions that LD kids experience.

From the Kids' Point of View

You know the story about the real estate agent who told his clients that the three most important considerations in buying a house are location, location, and location? In the emotional life of an LD child, the three most important considerations are probably self-image, self-image, and self-image.

That doesn't mean that other factors — the child's developmental history, the way his family treats him, his success in school, even the nature of the specific learning problem itself — aren't crucial to an understanding of his emotional makeup. And it doesn't mean that there aren't plenty of positive factors to offset some of the negatives. But the common denominator in all LD kids, regardless of the reason for their LD, the nature of their problems, or the level of their school remediation, seems to be the negative effect of years of frustration and failure on the child's confidence and self-concept.

And when we, as parents, are trying to make his life — and ours — more bearable, experts tell us that that's where we should start: by building a renewed sense of worth and helping the child learn that his actions can have a positive effect on the world around him. Sure, a learning disability can affect every area of a child's life. But he is still a child with many other strengths and weaknesses. The sooner he recognizes that LD is not all he is — and the sooner everyone around him learns to treat him as a whole person — the happier everyone will be.

Of course, that's more easily said than done. The accumulated emotional debris of years of failure, doubt, and guilt cannot be swept away with a few words of praise. Most LD kids are far too smart to believe their parents when they heartily declare, "Hey, son, you're terrific, and don't let anyone tell you otherwise!" They know that they must struggle over tasks that come with great ease to their peers, they know that they stumble and move clumsily, they know that their peer relationships are not satisfactory.

What they don't understand is *why* life is so much harder for them. And they're angry about that — and the anger fuels more self-doubt and further undermines the child's tenuous self-image. What are they so angry about, and why? Priscilla Vail has identified six emotional difficulties that can attend a learning disability:

1. Fear of failure
2. Disorganization — the inability to make sense of the world because of lack of affect
3. Fear of depletion — unwillingness to offer what little skills or energy is available
4. Learned helplessness — lack of a sense of control over life because effort brings no results
5. Guilt
6. Depression

Not all LD kids have all of those feelings, and they are usually present in varying degrees. But, with feelings like that, it's no wonder the LD child has so little self-confidence and such low self-esteem. And really, that's what all those difficulties boil down to: a sense of being a failure as a person. The behaviors that result — anger, withdrawal, aggressiveness, noncompliance — are natural outgrowths of cumulative frustration.

Let's take a look at the LD kid's life from his point of view and see how it must feel to him. (Note that we'll be focusing on the reactions of children seven or eight and over, as reported by several noted researchers. Younger children certainly have similar kinds of feelings, but they take different forms.)

1. Life with Parents: Of course, parents are the most logical target for anger. The LD child may blame himself deep down inside, but acknowledging that is too painful. It's much easier to blame parents, since they're responsible for his being here in the first place. If they really loved him, the LD kid feels, they wouldn't have let this happen to him. If they were really good parents, they would do something about it. (Parental guilt plays right into this scenario, but we'll deal with that later.)

So he's angry at them — partly because he blames them for his condition, and partly because, in spite of that condition, they insist on having expectations. He has to do his schoolwork and his chores, maintain some degree of hygiene, and be a contributing member of the family. They ask a lot of him, and he resents that, too. It's bad enough that they caused his learning disability, but why do they have to try and make him be "normal"?

And, in trying to get him to be "normal," they may be pushing him into areas in which he doesn't feel comfortable or confident. As a matter of fact, since he doesn't feel comfortable or confident anywhere, he's reluctant to do anything on his own. He relies on them to negotiate with the world on his behalf — to make excuses, to advocate, to explain things to him. They are his buffer against the world, and, if he resents that feeling, he's also terribly needy.

In addition, he's acutely aware of their frustration and disappointment in him (more on this later, too), and that sense only fuels the fire of his self-hatred. He knows he's not easy to live with, but he can't control himself in order to meet up to their expectations.

He literally does not feel he can survive without his parents, and so he clings to them even more. Separation issues loom large in his life, and he resents his dependency on them as much as he resents their liability, and their expectations. His low self-esteem drops even lower every time he needs them to do something for him.

2. Life with Siblings: Anger and dependency — that's a tough hand to be dealt for any child, but especially for an LD child, who has a hard time sorting out information and emotions. No wonder he's volatile, distractible, and easily provoked. And no wonder he's such a prime candidate for a stiff case of sibling rivalry. All the family issues that arise in his interactions with his parents also arise in his relationships with his siblings, but, since he's dealing with other children, who have their own needs, the situation can get even further out of control.

There's his older brother, who pleases his parents by getting good grades, making the baseball team, and bringing home lots of friends. And there's his younger sister, who delights everyone just because she's so cute, and who seems to reach new heights of achievement every single day.

The angrier he feels about his siblings, the less in control of his emotions he's going to be. He fights with them, ruins their projects, embarrasses them in front of their friends. And, if they retaliate in any way, he feels put upon and defeated. He demands even more time and energy from his parents, creating even more jealousy in his siblings, who, though they feel guilty and sorry about his learning disability, are nevertheless angry at his unfair demands. The cycle continues, and the LD kid's self-image deteriorates even further.

3. Life with Other Kids: The tensions of life at home are real, but, especially for the school-age LD kid, they often pale beside the painful realities of his attempts to make social contact with his peers. At home, at least, there are familiarity and a degree of security that comes of knowing his family so well. Within the bosom of the family, the LD kid also knows he is loved, even though he may not be sure why or how much.

Out in the world there is no such safety net. Relationships with peers are usually predicated on shared outside interests: sports, arts, listening to music, dressing in a certain style. In many of these, the LD kid cannot — or will not — participate. Either he perceives the activity as being beyond his ability, or he cannot cope with the rapid adjustments to unfamiliar situations and social cues that may result from, say, a trip to the local record store or mall.

The LD kid wants desperately to belong, but can't make himself fit the mold. He can't adapt his behavior to the necessary parameters, can't recognize social cues just as he can't recognize letters of the alphabet. As a result, he may be subjected to teasing or, even worse, to ostracism. Children are notoriously cruel to one another, and, regardless of the school's (or the parents') attempts to mainstream the LD child socially, he is often perceived as different — a terrible stigma in childhood.

Studies conducted on the social life of the LD youngster by James and Tanis Bryans have yielded some fascinating insights into the ways in which children judge one another. LD children are perceived by their peers not only as different, but also as less desirable playmates. However, children often cannot put their finger on the reason for their judgment. There is definitely a correlation between perceived intelligence and popularity, and, although the LD kid may be more intelligent than his classmates, he is certainly judged by his peers on the basis of his performance, not his aptitude.

But that's not the reason most children give for their low social rating of an LD child, and the reasons they do give are often unclear. Some of the factors most commonly cited relate to the same kinds of perceptions adults have of LD kids: poor attentional abilities, negative behavior toward others, lack of cooperation, and insensitivity to social cues. To a certain degree, they are skills that all children must work to acquire. Perhaps the real reason why some children are so harsh in judging their LD peers is that they sense not only the differences but also the similarities between them, and are frightened by the degree of identification.

Socially, girls seem to have a rougher time than boys, who can often find relief in physical outlets. White LD kids seem to suffer more than black LD kids from ostracism, but that may be because black children are more routinely excluded from white social circles. Naturally, the more severe the degree of learning difficulty, the more severe the social handicap, although, interestingly enough, children with physical disabilities are not judged as negatively (perhaps because of that identification factor).

LD kids, of course, are painfully aware of how they're seen by their classmates. Some respond to it by becoming class clowns, others by becoming class bullies. Others may not respond at all and retreat into a policy of quiet nonintervention. Some stick it out by following along the best they can, absorbing whatever flak they get when they misread a cue or behave inappropriately, and continuing to follow along despite these failures. Some are inordinately shy, others provocatively vocal. Some have no trouble making friends, but can't seem to keep them. Some cope by playing with much younger children, some by choosing as friends children with other problems that may make them unsuitable companions.

Yet the LD child is unable to control this important aspect of his environment. He can watch others at play and wonder what it is that he is doing differently, yet be unable to manage his behavior when the time comes. He can gauge the effect of his behavior, but not until it is too late to undo the damage. It is hard for him to anticipate what is expected of him, especially in the volatile world of children's relationships. Whatever the method of coping, or not coping, the LD child's sense of worth is not helped by his social situation. Nowhere else are his differences so apparent and so much of a burden to him as there.

4. Life with Other Adults: Teachers, too, have attitudes about LD kids that can color their relationships with them. Although teachers tend to be more positive toward younger children with learning problems (younger LD kids are easier to manage and may elicit a more sympathetic response), they seem to become less tolerant as the child grows older, a tendency that coincides with the LD kid's own slowly escalating lack of self-esteem.

A study of teachers' perceptions of students showed that their rating of a child's competence and behavior was a good predictor of how the child would fare in that classroom — and LD children consistently rated lower than their peers in those categories. Even when an LD child is treated more tolerantly by his teacher, his self-image is affected negatively, because he experiences the jealousy of his peers because he is a "baby," or "teacher's pet." However it is manifested, the teacher's lower expectations of the child's capabilities are passed on to the sensitive LD child, with predictable results.

When dealing with adult strangers, LD kids can have a difficult time because they are not familiar with the basic social skills required for polite introductory conversation. They may stare, or mumble incoherently, or ask inappropriate questions. And, because they do not look "abnormal" in any way, they may be perceived as being intentionally rude or obnoxious. Dealing with relatives who are unfamiliar with his condition can be a particularly painful experience for the LD child, who knows that his family is attached to these strangers and who wants to perform well for them but cannot. More damage to that fragile ego results.

5. **Life in the World:** Home life may be hard enough during the school year, but what about after school and during vacations, when there isn't even the structure of the school day around which to build a consistent schedule?

LD kids may be relieved to be out of the classroom situation, but finding an enjoyable structured activity may not be easy. After-school programs often focus on nonacademic cognitive skills that are as difficult for the LD kid as reading and writing, and the staff may not be aware of the problem or may not know how to deal with it. As in the classroom, more ostracism results when the child is singled out, whether for lack of participation or for special help.

Even if the child's skill levels are good, transitions to unfamiliar environments — new drama club, computer group, even a new baby-sitter — are very difficult for a child who has trouble reading social cues even in the comfort of his own home. The LD kid feels that every unfamiliar situation may require a whole new set of rules — and he may be right. But he lacks the ability to decipher these rules without help, and the idea of being left in a strange environment without any guidelines is as frightening to him as it would be for us to be left alone in a strange darkened room. For this reason, new situations require a lot of preparation on the part of parents — more intervention that the LD child may need, but resent.

For the same reason, summer vacations may not be as much fun as parents hope they will be; too many new variables can throw the LD kid into a panic of anxiety. Summer camp programs are often needlessly competitive, and, like the after-school programs, their concentration on physical agility usually insures that the LD child will be perceived as clumsy and incompetent yet again.

6. Life as an Adolescent: The extra pressures experienced by LD teens have been well documented in a number of books (see the Bibliography), so the myriad special problems of LD teens will be only briefly discussed here. All teenagers feel the need to belong to the group, to conform to its style and live up to its expectations. This may not be possible for the LD adolescent, who feels increasingly different as he grows older and his own expectations are forever being foiled. Added to his sense of being on the outside is the isolation of being LD, especially if there are no other similarly affected teens in the neighborhood. And, since LD kids tend to be less mature than their non-LD peers, he is in fact less ready to face the complicated world of adolescence.

Even more alarming for him, hormonal changes can create physical discomfort and confusion. Bodily changes necessitate the need for new self-awareness and attention to hygiene, which the LD teen may not be prepared to meet. Issues of sexuality are complicated by feelings of social inadequacy — how can the LD boy deal with having a girlfriend if he can't maintain any successful relationships with his peers? His feelings of incompetence are magnified by the increased pressures in high school and increased isolation from his age group.

If he doubted during his childhood, the LD teen is now certain that no one understands him, that he is doomed to failure, and that it is all his own fault. No wonder several studies indicate that LD children whose problems go undetected and unremediated in childhood have a much higher rate of delinquency and drug use than their non-LD peers. The learning disability does *not* cause the juvenile delinquency, but is an effect of years of erosion to the youngster's ego. This is particularly true for children whose families do not seek early intervention and remediation.

Drake Duane, a noted LD researcher, says that the most common complication of LD is chronic success deprivation. Clearly, the effect of all of this frustration is a shattered self-image. The LD kid's needs are complex, and his reactions to the world around him are colored by his perceptual problems. It's a tribute to the resiliency of our LD kids that they don't knuckle under sooner and more often.

From the Parents' Point of View

And what about us? How do we feel about having this unhappy creature in our midst? Listen to this quotation from the sociologist C. M. Anderson in his book *Society Pays,* and see if it rings a bell:

> Taking care of a child who does not respond as other children do, and who makes parents feel that they never get through to him, verbally or emotionally, is a very hard load to carry, for love is ordinarily a reciprocal experience. Trying to maintain some semblance of stability in the home with a child who overreacts to practically everything, who has temper tantrums on almost no provocation, who seems to gravitate to most undesirable companions, or who cannot be made to understand why the reins must be tighter on him than on "normal" children would try anyone's patience.

Sound familiar? Let's look from our perspective at some of the issues mentioned above and examine our feelings about them.

1. Parenting: We feel lousy. We feel guilty, angry, helpless. We feel a loss of control over our ability to be parents, to protect and affect our child's life. We feel incompetent and inadequate, and we think the LD child is right — that we are, after all, to blame. Our failure lives with us every day, reflecting back our own pain and magnifying it. And, as the child grows older and his LD does not disappear but rather changes in form, presenting new problems as quickly as the old ones are solved, we feel an acute loss of the future and the possibilities it holds. So we feel grief — grief for the child we hoped this would be, the one who would meet and exceed all of our hopes and expectations for him.

Often, the way we react to our LD child is directly related to the way we feel about ourselves. If we have unresolved issues about our own childhood, they will affect the way we behave as parents to our children. If those issues have to do with control, with performing well in the world, with the way we express our emotions, then those are going to be the weak spots in the way we relate to our LD child. Our expectations for our children come from our expectations of ourselves, and if we do not feel that we've lived up to our own self-images, the reality of our LD child's problem is going to be magnified, and much more difficult for us to deal with.

A parent who is feeling inadequate or overburdened with work pressures is going to have a double bind when it comes to helping his LD child with homework. The sheer amount of time and patience required will tax an already overstressed schedule, and the fact that the child is performing poorly will only reinforce the parent's sense of inadequacy, resulting in an overreaction, which will probably escalate the child's poor performance level.

That sort of personal pressure cooker is going to affect our marriage as much as the presence of the LD child himself. Depending upon the individual issues each parent brings to the raising of the children, there may be a great discrepancy between the ways in which the two handle the LD child. One parent is often more lenient, or more involved, or more protective than the other, and all of those behaviors are going to reflect back on the marriage itself. There will be a strain between parenting styles, and anything that goes wrong may be blamed on the parent who did too much, or on the one who didn't do enough. We often feel guilty in either case, and then we overcompensate by focusing again on the child, which is detrimental to our relationship with our spouse.

Parents sometimes blame each other for the problem to begin with, either by pointing to genetic traits in the spouse's family or by citing the spouse's effect or lack of effect as a parent. Parenting is a difficult balancing act between compromise and cooperation, and any tensions between partners is sure to be exacerbated. The need for attention to all aspects of the marriage is essential in a situation like this — even more than it may be in a marriage that is not stressed by the difficult child. Parents often report that the LD child is the largest source of conflict in their marriage, when in fact the child may only be the catalyst for conflicts in the marital relationship.

But the LD child *does* cause a great deal of additional tension in the marriage. The sheer bulk of time and energy spent on him often assures that there will be less of both brought to the husband–wife relationship. When the needs of other children are involved, and two careers come into the equation, the marriage is usually put on the back burner, and can deteriorate dangerously. And of course the LD child is aware of this fact, but can do little to stop it. In fact, he may respond in his shame by exacerbating the problem, inserting himself even more obtrusively into the marriage. Parents blame themselves, they blame him, they blame each other — more cycles.

And what about what happens to our lives as individuals? We're not just parents and spouses, we're people, too, and our needs are often relegated even farther back on the burner than those of our marriage. This, too, is a self-fulfilling prophecy, since the less we do to replenish ourselves means the less we have to give to our families. We probably know this, but are so caught up in the merry-go-round of advocacy, intervention, and support that we have little time to think about it, let alone do anything about it. Our lowered self-esteem not only puts a strain on our relationships, but our LD kid is liable to pick up on the lowered self-esteem, and it's a bad message to be sending to someone with an already precarious sense of worth. The situation is dangerous, since it only fosters our resentment of our LD child, our spouse, and ourselves.

Research has shown that parents of children with any handicap go through similar phases of grief — from initial awareness through guilt, anger, blame, acceptance, and transcendence. At first, we may feel a sense of relief, but then we're bound to be struck by the enormity of the problem. Parents report anger toward themselves, their child, spouse, medical personnel, and God. The sense of helplessness and the immutability of the situation make a bitter pill to swallow.

Parents' anger toward themselves usually takes the form of guilt, which can last a long time and affect the way they go about getting help, or even whether they decide to get help. In this phase, many parents overcompensate and do so much for their LD kid that he never gets a chance to learn the necessary skills. Toward others, this guilt is manifested by helplessness, self-pity, loneliness, doubt, a loss of interpersonal warmth, and fatigue.

Blame is a particularly dangerous phase, since it can put additional strains on the marriage and family at a time when those relationships can ill afford the extra burden. The accompanying anger can damage relationships permanently at home, and adversely affect interactions with potentially helpful professionals in the field. If a doctor hands down a diagnosis of ADD, it may not be beneficial to the child to blame the doctor and storm out of the office, especially if you're going to need medical cooperation for the child's treatment.

Parents report that these emotions eventually fade in favor of a more practical acceptance, and some parents even learn to transcend the problem and gain strength from the ordeal. But most parents who have gone through the various stages report that the earlier, angry emotions tend to resurge at various points in their LD child's life, particularly at milestones such as graduation or puberty.

Again, it is essential that parents seek help in working through these phases, regardless of their degree and duration. Individual counseling, couples' counseling, or family therapy is helpful in some instances, but it may just be that exposure to other parents who are going through the same process will provide the strength and perspective necessary to see them through. Appendix A contains lists of various formal organizations that may provide a parent network, but sometimes the local, informal circle established in a community is most effective.

2. Families: All of these are strong emotions, and we're kidding ourselves if we don't admit that they take a toll on ourselves and our relationships — not just with our LD kids, but with the rest of our family as well, and beyond, with the rest of the world. Certainly our families are deeply affected by the presence of an LD child, and the dynamic works both ways — the child affects the family as well.

Several studies have been done on the families of LD children, and the results are inconclusive, but interesting. The sociologist Doreen Kronick, for example, has argued that LD kids seem more

175

often to come from unstable families where there are more conflict and more trauma. But she points out that LD children are also more vulnerable to family problems and tensions, and that their presence has a negative effect on family stability.

Another study, "The Social Life of LD Youngsters," by the educational psychologists James and Tanis Bryans, reveals that LD kids actually cause stress in their families, and may impact on the development of parental affection and aggression toward them. The difficult infant who develops into the LD child (or into a child with another type of problem) is going to make parenting harder for us, and it's only natural that we should react in this way. Our feelings, in turn, will affect the LD child's self-image, which affects his behavior . . . and yet another cycle is perpetrated. But remember, the establishment of affection is a two-way street, and the less guilty we feel about our ambivalence, the more effectively we will be able to manage it.

Moms more than dads feel the stress, according to the Bryanses, and dads are more likely to display their ambivalence as anger, while moms display more protective behavior — perhaps as a way to alleviate the guilt they feel about the ambivalence. But the Bryanses also found that, in the families they studied, there was no significant degree of increased conflict in families with LD children or in the parent–child interaction of those families, as opposed to families without LD children. Moms of LDs asked the LDs more questions, gave more instructions and more rewards, which, according to the Bryanses, could be seen as a positive family dynamic.

Still, our other children realize our ambivalence about their LD sibling, and are often quick to voice their own complaints. The LD kid takes up too much of our time; he is not living up to his share of the chores; he is sloppy, embarrassing, uncontrollable. Siblings may be feeling that they should be able to protect their LD brother, and feeling guilty because they can't do it.

Their own success may be a source of guilt to them, especially if they've been feeling anger toward him and secretly wishing he would fail. They may also be afraid that they'll turn out the same way, especially if they're younger. In any case, their own development, both inside and outside the house, is affected by him, and they blame both the LD kid and us for that.

3. Other Children: Our feelings about children outside our families may be just as complicated. We see their (seemingly) blithe progress through school, their effortless acquisition of physical and social skills, and we're jealous. Why can't it be that easy for our LD child? It's hard not to be angry at a child who comes over to play with ours and who says something like "Hey, why can't you do that? You dumb or something?" Even if it's not meant maliciously, it hurts our child, and it hurts us to the quick.

When it *is* malicious, we may feel the need to intervene, sailing into the middle of a conflict with all the stops pulled out on our accumulated rage. It may not be the best idea, from our child's point of view, and certainly not from the other child's. The question of intervention in our LD kid's conflicts is a huge one, and we have to establish fairly consistent measures by which we can judge when to step in and when to let the child handle it on his own. But anger is certainly what we feel, and, even if we control our tempers, the hostility may be apparent in our voices and our eyes.

4. Other Adults: That resentment we feel toward other children may carry over to other adults, especially to the parents of those children, regardless of whether their children are guilty of cruelty to our LD child or not. Parenting seems so simple for them (it's not!), and they appear to be fighting no constant private battles (they probably are). We feel alone as the parents of an LD child, and this isolation can magnify the degree of our difficulty.

We have an ambivalent relationship with our child's teachers at school. We are dependent on them for our child's academic progress, and yet we are protective of our child's emotional needs and anxious that they be met in the classroom (if there is a good IEP in place, they should be). We have to be able to advocate for our child without alienating those adults who will be providing him services, which means walking a fine line between accommodation and confrontation. For parents who are not satisfied with the results of their child's evaluation, and who are involved in the hearing process, this can be a particularly painful situation.

Our relatives can be yet another source of anxiety. Since LD was not routinely identified a generation ago, grandparents may not understand the source of the child's problems, and they may question our handling of our own child or, even worse, diagnose him as lazy or foolish and treat him as such. Even strangers can cause tension with an insensitive remark or attitude.

5. Adolescents: Dealing with our LD teenager is simply a magnification of all of the above. His burgeoning conflict between freedom and insecurity makes him impossible to deal with on a rational basis, and our fear that we will do something truly anti-social escalates as he gets older. He is rebelling doubly, against his own accumulated frustration as well as against the usual menu of teen complaints, and he seems to be sliding backward rather than making progress as he did in elementary school.

We see more than ever the limitations he may suffer as an adult, and that old pain we felt when we first found out about his LD is renewed and sharpened. In addition, he knows nothing about sex, drugs, or violence, yet is so hungry for approval that he may get involved with them just to gain acceptance with his peers, and so we fear for his safety as well as for his future. Our attempts to deal with sexuality and morality, man-to-man or woman-to-woman, are nearly impossible and can create tensions in our marriages besides.

Yet, at a time when he needs so much support from us, he is unable to ask for it, and often unwilling to endure it when it's offered. The more he needs us, the farther away he drifts and the more unendurable is his behavior toward us. Our efforts to educate him are met with disdain, and our attempts to exert some degree of control over his life are met with defiance. We feel both repelled and alarmed in the face of this emerging danger to our already precarious family life. Those studies linking LD and "JD" (juvenile delinquency) haunt us, and we feel helpless to stop the descent. It is truly a dangerous time for us all.

What can we do? We can get as much information as possible about the problem so that we are not taken unaware. We can provide our LD kid with a variety of support systems, both in school and at home, and make sure he knows that there is always someone (parent or professional) who will be willing to listen sympathetically to his concerns. We can bring our entire family into the process of coping with the LD child and work hard to share the burdens as well as the pleasures of family life. We can join support groups to help us cope with the additional stresses as they arise.

A diagnosis of LD, as devastating as it may be, is not a death sentence. Millions of people have survived and thrived, many never knowing they were any different from anybody else. Many have made the most of their strengths and been extremely successful in their chosen fields. The hardest part of being LD, my daughter points out, is going to school — a complaint that I counter by reminding her that she won't be in school forever.

Most important, we can remember that there is a lot we can do, here and now, to insure that the future is bright and the present not nearly as bad as it sometimes seems. In the next chapter, we'll examine some of the things we can do at home — for our children and for ourselves.

CHAPTER 7

Teaching Survival Strategies

Question: "How did you learn to feel better about yourself?"

Answers: "It took me a long time to be able to admit to myself that I wasn't just a failure. Somehow, it was easier to blame it on myself. But I'm learning that there are some things that I can do very well, and I'm starting to do them. Also, when I help younger kids who are LD, I can tell them, 'Hey, it isn't so bad; look at me!' That makes me feel terrific." (Age 16)

"When my mother first showed me the drawing that explained why I couldn't read as good as Hannah, I ran right out and showed it to her. Then she could see I wasn't stupid and that made me feel a lot better." (Age 6)

Question: "How do you manage to survive life with an LD kid?"

Answers: "Barely. Every day requires more patience than I ever thought I had. It seems as if every time Dennis learns something, he forgets it the next day — even something simple, like remembering to take out the garbage. I remind him and remind him, but sometimes it seems like I'm not helping at all."

"I was only able to take control when I decided to separate Laurie's learning disabilities from her behavior as an eight-year-old. When Laurie understood that we expected certain things from her — that being LD wasn't all she was, and she was also a contributing member of this family — well, life got a lot better around here quick."

Skills Can Be Taught

We can help the LD child and the LD teen to cope with and overcome their emotional conflicts. We can help them organize their feelings as well as their thoughts, learn social cues and coping mechanisms for dealing with the world on their own. We can help them develop their abilities and talents so that their self-image improves by their own hand, not by ours. We can teach them that human qualities count, and that these kids have those in abundance purely by virtue of having suffered themselves. We can teach them:

1. How to be a more functional member of the family
   • chores
   • relationships
2. How to take better care of themselves
   • hygiene
   • time management
3. How to boost academic skills and other talents
   • homework
   • language skills and reading
   • extracurricular activities
4. How to manage their own behavior
   • learning social cues
   • coping strategies

Information like this should, by rights, go into a chapter on remediation (in fact, much of this material is relevant to the information in chapter 8 and will be reiterated there). But I feel that helping our children — and ourselves — with emotional and behavioral coping strategies so they can develop a more positive self-image is so crucial to their success in school and the world at large that the topic should be considered before moving on to more formal academic and medical therapeutic techniques. To a large extent, the emotional life of LD children dictates their ability to absorb information effectively, and, as parents, the single most important thing we can do for them is to help them learn to love themselves.

Regardless of how we're trying to help — academically, socially, or emotionally — we have to remember a few rules. LD children need to succeed in order to rebuild their shattered self-esteem. To insure that they do, we need to follow a step-by-step strategy regardless of our goal. This may sound complicated and overly particular. For most children, there would be no need to break down tasks into minute components and offer constant repetition and support. But the LD child is different. Let's look at a few examples of how step-by-step strategies work in helping her acquire some basic skills while at the same time boosting her self-esteem.

1. *Provide a predictable environment, a safe haven in which the child can learn.* Make sure that she knows that her routine is going to take place at the same time, in the same place, each evening. Further reduce the anxiety level by letting her have a hand in establishing her own routine.

Let's say the goal is to establish a personal hygiene routine. What does she think she needs to do to keep clean?

2. *Break the task down to its simplest level and focus on only one element of a task at a time.* Divide the routine into very small steps. A checklist is especially helpful.

a. Remove and put away soiled clothes.
b. Check bathwater for proper temperature.
c. Remember soap and shampoo.
d. Don't forget behind ears, fingernails, genital areas, etc.
e. Dry off well before changing into nightclothes.
f. Brush and floss teeth.

3. *Simplify your presentation of the material, and give explicit instructions.* When establishing the routine, be sure you explain what you

mean by brushing the teeth (it's not just wiping the brush across the surface of the teeth). Let her watch you and then do it herself, so that several senses come into the learning operation.

4. *Make sure there are no distractions during instruction.* Kick out the baby brother and turn off the television in the other room while you're working.

5. *Be patient and repetitive with your information.* Be prepared to give the same instructions several times without appearing to be impatient with the child.

6. *Be consistent.* Point out that the same step-by-step procedures can stand her well in other situations. When she seems to have mastered the situation, praise her for her new skill. Point out that the same procedure could be applied to other tasks, like cleaning her room, for example. Give it a try, if she seems ready and willing.

THERE may be other ways to achieve the same goals, using the same principles but applying them differently. Several toy companies have developed colorful charts that are often effective in establishing home routines for children. The child, with the help of a parent, decides what tasks he wants to accomplish and lists them on the chart — doing homework, making the bed, clearing the table are good choices. The Good For Me kit (from Toys To Grow On, a mail-order company) comes with stickers, which the child affixes to the plasticized surface every time a task is completed. Then, when an agreed-upon number of stickers is reached, the child can redeem a reward or prize of some kind with a certificate that is part of the kit.

All of this should be done with parent and other sibling input, so that the child feels she is really becoming a productive part of the family. Rewards needn't — and probably shouldn't — be financial or material. A trip to the park with Mom or Dad, a story read at night, an extra television show are all good choices that don't depend on gift-giving. And you can make your own chart easily with an erasable blackboard and a bunch of stickers.

My daughter established her own version of the chart, which she calls the Love/Hate Chart (she says she has to do something she hates in order to get something she loves). Instead of stickers, each task has its own reward. For instance, if she is ready for bed by a certain time, she gets a story each night. If she cleans her room on Saturday morning, she can collect her allowance. If she remembers to feed the dog, she gets to watch television (if she doesn't, both she and the dog suffer, and an adult has to do the job, making it a three-way loss). She was instrumental in creating both the responsibilities and the privileges, and she seemed to delight in making the love fit the hate, so to speak.

Organizing the LD child's room can go a long way toward helping her to organize her life. Try labeling the contents of bureau drawers and storage spaces. Help her put her homework area in order so that everything is where she expects to find it every day. Time management is another problem with LD kids. Their temporal sense is often faulty and they have difficulty organizing their day into blocks of time. Even when given a specific time frame, such as "Be back in a half hour," the LD child can seldom gauge the passage of time.

Keeping a calendar, clock, timer, and daily schedule on the wall can give a child a tremendous sense of self-control, especially if checking off days and chores becomes a part of the daily schedule itself. These skills can be built into step-by-step programs, especially with the help of an alarm clock and a kitchen timer. If the child has trouble reading an analog clock, use one with a digital readout. Help the child set the clock each night until she becomes comfortable with setting it herself. Have her do her homework or her chores to a set period on a timer. Not only will doing this give her a sense of accomplishment, but it will help her improve her timekeeping skills. Reading for thirty minutes a day on the timer will eventually give the child a better idea of just how long a half hour really is.

A sample schedule might look like this:

7:30 — Wake up. Clean clothes are on the other bed (they have been laid out the night before, we hope). Put pajamas away and wash up in the bathroom.
7:50 — Come down to breakfast. (M/W/F make your own cereal, T/Th Mom or Dad cooks an egg.)
8:15 — Mom makes lunch and you pack it.

8:25 — Off to school. Pick up Lucy on the way.

3:00 — Home from school. T/Th dance class, W to doctor, F friend comes over.

5:30 — Feed the dog.

6:00 — Dinner. (M/W/F clear the table; T/Th take out the garbage.)

7:00 — Homework. (M/W/F with Mom, T/Th with Dad.)

8:00 — Get ready for bed (M/Th bath nights) — wash and get into pajamas, set out tomorrow's clothes.

8:30 — Story time.

A place to check off tasks is not necessary, as this might take more time than the chores themselves, especially in a large house. But it might be a good idea to start out that way, until the child gets a sense of what is expected.

Remember, though, that structure does not mean rigidity. Allow flexible time in the schedule and don't be ferocious if the schedule should break down once in a while. It's for the child's own peace of mind, not for punishment purposes, and the child will soon learn that even the best-laid plans often go awry in "real life."

The Principles of Behavior Management

All of these procedures are forms of behavioral management or behavioral modification. "Behavior mod" is familiar to many teachers and psychologists working with all sorts of problem situations. It is very effective in establishing guidelines for LD kids, especially if everything is arranged in small, doable increments and the environment is controlled so that success is virtually assured. It's up to you to make sure the controls insure that success, so don't be afraid to start very small.

Behavioral modification takes many forms, and can be a very complex process, so it won't be discussed at length here. There are several good books written about adopting such techniques for more effective parenting (see the Bibliography). Basically, behavior mod works by using positive reinforcement to encourage appropriate behaviors and by ignoring (not reinforcing) inappropriate ones. It involves keeping track of a child's patterns and focusing on specific aspects of them, rather than trying to reshape the entire pattern. It takes patience and consistency, but it can pay off.

In using behavioral modification strategies, it's important to remember that the payoff must be immediate and consistent, but that it need not be material. Rewards can take the form of reading time, a television show, special events with parents, or just pure praise. As a matter of fact, it's a good idea to decrease the material rewards gradually as the child internalizes the positive reinforcement. Slowly, she'll build up a repertoire of tasks at which she is successful. Her anxiety about these tasks will be reduced, and she may feel more competent about trying to achieve other, more complex goals.

It's important to make sure the goals stay realistic and to provide protection from failure or frustration. Clue other members of the family and allow them to participate, but treat the program as the child's special domain. Make sure, though, that she has already acquired the skills necessary to complete the task. If she can't pull her bed out from the wall, expecting her to make her bed is going to be more frustrating than rewarding to both of you. And be careful about falling into the trap of using candy or toys as rewards. The material payoff for a task completed should be secondary to the personal reward of accomplishing the task itself. This point shouldn't be difficult to establish, since LD kids want approval, success, and achievement more than anything else, which makes social reinforcements a potent source of satisfaction to them.

Perhaps most important, we must listen to our LD child and incorporate her input into our programs. Giving her a voice in her own destiny is perhaps the single most effective way of establishing a positive sense of worth. Show her that you respect her by letting her participate in controlling her behavior, and she will eventually be able to control it herself.

Building Family Relationships

Dealing with household chores, personal hygiene, and time management can all be handled with the step-by-step success strategy, but sometimes the goal is not as concrete as brushing teeth or getting dressed in twenty minutes. Behavioral management techniques can work with more abstract tasks as well. In establishing more positive relationships within the family, for instance, we can use the same kind of model to create more effective and satisfying interaction between parent and LD child or between siblings.

Let's say the child needs to work on controlling her anger toward a younger brother. First, parents need to assure the child that they are eager to work together to create a constructive alternative behavior. Reprimanding the LD child for her behavior is not going to do any good at this point. It's far more effective to accentuate the positiveness and attainability of the goal than to dwell on the inappropriateness of the behavior.

Keeping a record of situations in which certain unacceptable behaviors occur might be a good place to start. Choose a set period of time and list the time of day, the type of behavior and the alleged reason for it, as well as its outcome. A typical entry might read:

1. *Time:* 4:15 P.M.
2. *What:* Molly jumped off the couch and hit younger brother.
3. *Why:* Molly says Billy switched channels without asking; Billy says it's his turn to choose the show being watched.
4. *Outcome:* Billy reprimanded for not asking before switching channels; Molly finally sent to her room because of continued angry protests.

With a record like this, family members can isolate the specific situations under which tensions arise (playing with the sibling's toys, tagging along, upstaging during family mealtimes) and find ways to redirect behavior before it gets out of control. Help the child clarify exactly what it is about the behavior that needs to be changed, and help solicit from the child suggestions about how it might be changed. Help the child choose which are the most positive alternative behaviors for everyone involved, then decide what is to be gained from those new behaviors. Molly, for instance, could have reminded Billy that it was not yet his turn to choose, and she could have referred to a schedule that said so.

Make sure that these discussions are kept as simple as possible, and that no distractions, such as current family arguments, interrupt them. They might need to be conducted over a period of time before a strategy can be agreed upon. The cause-effect nature of the behavior patterns should be made very clear to the child so that she understands how and why the appropriate behavior model works. Be prepared to repeat the instructions to her often and without impatience, until she is better able to monitor herself. Hearty praise when a situation is resolved without a battle is paramount in making behavioral modifications effective in relationships, especially if siblings are not able to acknowledge the improvement themselves.

This sort of program won't work, however, if the LD child is the only one doing the work. Family dynamics are a two-way street, and all members must acknowledge their involvement and be willing to make an effort to change.

Although the step-by-step strategy may seem cumbersome, it can be translated into a fairly simple practical application. Let's look at a practical application again. The LD kid claims that she's constantly being teased and bested by her older sister, while the older sister feels the LD kid is too easily let off the hook. The issue, everyone decides, is not that there should be no fighting, but that the fighting should be fair. A list is drawn up of acceptable and unacceptable behaviors in specific situations.

SITUATION: Whose turn is it to walk the dog?
SISTER'S RESPONSE:
(*Unfair*): "It's your turn to walk the dog, dummy. Can't you ever remember anything?"
(*Fair*): "It's your turn to walk the dog. I know I did it yesterday, because it was raining and my coat is still wet."
LD KID'S RESPONSE:
(*Unfair*): "I can't walk the dog today! I've got too much to do already, and besides, you always get to do what you want. It's not fair!"
(*Fair*): "I still have homework to do. If you can help me out today, I'll walk the dog for two days, as long as you remind me or write it down so I can remember."

Sometimes actual contracts can be drawn up between family members to insure that behaviors are managed to mutual satisfaction. Parents can develop such contracts to make clear to the LD child what behaviors they expect when they are out of the house, offering alternative choices to unwanted activities and rewards for desirable results. Older siblings can draw them up with each other to maintain boundaries for privacy and to guard against intrusion into social situations. Entire families can work together to develop a family plan for mealtimes once or twice a week. Such contracts don't have to be all-inclusive, and they shouldn't overwhelm the natural rhythm of family life or become a burden to any member of the family. They do provide the LD kid with the structured system she needs to function successfully, and they offer the added advantage of slowly rebuilding weakened self-images through repeated success and the formation of positive loving relationships at home.

Acquiring Social Skills

All children live their lives as part of a peer group, even if it's a rejecting one, says Betty Osman in *No One to Play With: The Social Side of Learning Disabilities*. She points out that, in the case of the LD child, adults may have to help him gain access to individuals and groups that are right for him. She offers some good suggestions:

- Find local organizations that he can handle, and that seem appropriate, such as Scouts or YMCAs.
- Encourage the child to pursue what he is best at, to enhance his image with his peers as well as with himself.
- Arrange social contacts, even with "bait" if necessary. A well-stocked refrigerator, a trip to the mall or the movies may provide the necessary lure for initially reluctant playmates.
- Teach social games and skills such as dancing, bowling, or roller skating to facilitate peer-meeting opportunities.
- Affiliate with local church groups or form a group of your own choosing.

These excellent suggestions may work, but they ignore the basic element of peer interaction: how the child is going to relate to his peers once the connection has been made. Just as with learning bowling or dancing, a child must be taught interpersonal skills if he is to develop and maintain social relationships on his own.

Once again, behavioral management can be used to great advantage when helping LD children overcome their social inadequacies. It helps if the child has already had success inside the house and gained some confidence from improved relationships with parents and siblings. By helping our LD child evaluate and manipulate his environment, we can assist him with some important skills to help him deal with his peers outside the house.

In order to cope with predictable situations more appropriately, the LD kid has to be taught to read social cues. We have to help our LD child to understand what age-appropriate behavior really is. A five-year-old may need to be shown that tattling on his peers is going to backfire, and a nine-year-old may need to learn when to stop joking around in class, something his friends seem intuitively to understand.

Using a list or a chart, parent and child can itemize the kinds of behaviors that are exhibited by the child and his peers, and examine any differences. LD kids are often quite perceptive in establishing "proper" behavior codes, even if they cannot yet adhere to them. A third-grader, for instance, may see that boy-girl relationships are often taboo, although he may go unacceptably overboard in his teasing of the girls. A fifth-grader, on the other hand, may recognize budding male-female friendships and not yet be able to develop them.

In the safety of the home, it might be a good idea, especially with younger children, to rehearse some of these appropriate responses to certain situations. Have an agreeable older sibling play the part of a classmate and let the LD child explore ways to interact with him or her. What happens if the classmate is teased? If she is expected to go on playing a game when the teacher has asked for her attention several times? Siblings may appreciate this opportunity to help their brother or sister, and their own social sensibilities can be an invaluable help to the LD child.

Once behaviors are chosen, you and your child can decide on some appropriate role models. Have your child make a list of positive and negative behaviors and a list of children in his class. You can make a game of having him connect certain behaviors with certain classmates. Which children exhibit most of the positive behaviors? They might be good children to concentrate on as both role models and friends. Parents can help the child, arranging play dates for younger children and helping the older children decide on effective ways to approach such a child.

190

The game might also help the child to see where his behavior pattern falls in relationship to his peers. If he connects himself with only negative behaviors, try to point out his positives. Then let him come up with a few suggestions for changing those negatives.

Parents can help the child understand the parameters of acceptability and can provide support in dissecting the particulars of a chosen behavior pattern. When she was in the second grade, my daughter and I spent a lot of time discussing the use of baby talk, which had been socially acceptable the year before, but was no longer considered "cool." Once she understood that it was her peers, and not the adults, who disliked the behavior, she started to monitor herself to break the pattern.

Self-monitoring techniques are important in helping a child establish appropriate behavior, since we can't (and don't want to) be by his side all the time to do the monitoring for him. Establishing internal problem-solving strategies and applying them to specific tasks can be done through "cognitive behavioral modification." Cognitive behavioral modification (CBM) refers to the self-instruction, self-control, and self-monitoring techniques applied by a person to specific situations in order to come up with a more positive choice of actions. Because the individual is actively involved in the teaching process, he or she is more likely to cooperate and benefit from the techniques. CBM has only recently been applied to children in a methodical manner, but it is being used successfully in both school, home, and clinical environments.

While formal CBM techniques require some training to employ (see chapter 8), they can be done on an informal basis. Try using a word or phrase that the child chooses and adopts to remind himself of appropriate behavior patterns when the situation arises. A privately muttered "secret code" can be used as a reminder or a trigger until the child is able to respond without it.

This can work well, not only with learning appropriate behaviors, but with limiting inappropriate ones as well. Talk with your LD child and help him understand that teasing his best friend, for instance, is only going to make him more unhappy: his best friend will be angry and not want to play with him, leaving him without a playmate. Let him understand that he needs to think about his own interests in the friendship as well as his friend's. Once he's expressed a desire to change that situation, he can look at some alternative behavior choices and find a trigger word to remind him

191

to use the alternative instead of the negative behavior. If his best friend objects to his teasing, he can say "best friend" to himself, and that might help him remember to stop teasing before it's too late.

Remember, though, that your child will need your patience and support in sorting out acceptable behaviors, since he may not have the skill to do it alone. And he'll certainly need your moral input in order to establish which behaviors are acceptable in the larger world outside his social circle. LD children, who are often targets of cruelty and teasing themselves, are certainly capable of developing strong moral codes, but not always able to control their behavior in their desire to be accepted by the group. If a child your son admires is stealing, for instance, you can help him to understand that stealing is not acceptable behavior from anyone, regardless of his or her social status in the neighborhood.

Implementing the newly chosen behaviors, however, is something you can't do for your LD child. It's largely a matter of trial and error, and you simply cannot be there to supervise him when he's "in the field." You can, however, explain to your child that his attempts to fit in won't always work, that they take practice, just as reading and writing do. Your comfort and support will certainly be necessary at times, until the child can establish his own defense mechanisms.

The LD child has to learn that, while some other children are pleasant and fun, others are cruel or unpleasant and should simply be avoided. Unfortunately, trial and error will also be needed to establish who is who, and the pain of rejection or failure is hard to bear for both parent and child. Train yourself to resist the urge to intervene (unless it's absolutely necessary); the child's sense of self-sufficiency will only be reduced if you attempt to live his life for him.

While the child is learning socially acceptable behaviors, he must also learn coping skills for dealing with unpredictable situations. Doing this is a little trickier, since LD kids so often have trouble dealing with the unexpected. As he establishes social connections, however, he is going to become more independent, more involved with classmates and friends. What if he is in a group of children who throw a baseball through a store window? What if he and a friend get lost? What if another child challenges him in some way?

Obviously, the best thing we can do is to discuss all the possibilities beforehand so that the child can get a sense of where such situations might lead. Often it is the unknown aspect itself that is most frightening about such situations. In the case of the broken window, for instance, the child may not be so much afraid of the reprimand itself as he is of not knowing what to expect at all. Will he be yelled at or attacked? Thrown in jail, killed? LD children often have an inadequate sense of proportion, so they have no way of judging a stranger's response, or even a friend's response in a strange situation.

Let the child hypothesize possible situations and various alternative outcomes. That way, he can get a sense of control and mastery over the environment, and realize that he does have the skills necessary to make sense out of them and to cope with them. Have him imagine how he might feel, and how he might be able to behave in order to have the most positive effect on the situation. Let him discuss his fears about the situation, and help him see that the fears, too, are manageable once they are dissected and understood.

The LD child, like any other child, can learn to know his limitations as well as his capabilities, and with our help can develop a strong sense of what he can or cannot deal with. He can learn that there are situations that no one is able to deal with effectively, and that this inability is not a sign of personal failure but of life's capriciousness. Obviously, this sort of behavioral management requires an older child with well-developed abstract skills. But you can help a younger child by discussing such situations and having him pretend to be there and act out his responses.

The important lesson to be learned from all this is one of independence. The child's LD is not going to go away, but it can be managed and, as she grows older, it is the child herself who is going to have to do the managing.

Providing Academic and Extracurricular Support

Perhaps the area in which parents are most eager to intervene is in the LD child's academic progress. Regardless of the quality of the child's school program, it's only natural that we should want to keep actively involved in gauging our child's skill acquisition and, if possible, helping it along.

193

As we have seen, intervention provides a tremendous boost for an LD child, and the parent who continues to take an active involvement in the child's academic progress is doing the right thing. But, when that involvement occurs at home, we have to distinguish between supporting the classroom efforts and insisting on extra hours of hard work. We can monitor our child's work at home, but we cannot play the role of teacher or tutor very well — not if we expect to continue being supportive as parents.

All children have to do homework, and the LD child is no exception. A time and place should be set aside for it, and a parent should be available for providing help in organizing the material and answering questions. But most experts agree that doing homework with the child is not a good idea, and attempting to teach the child is even worse.

We've all tried teaching our children, and, LD or not, we usually find that it doesn't work well. There's too much emotional baggage brought to the lessons; there are too many opportunities for other issues to arise that might interfere with the teaching. As we have seen, that precarious emotional situation is even more delicate with an LD child.

Not only can we do damage to the child's psyche, and to our own, but we can undermine the success of the classroom academic program. When one is working with LD kids, who require a very specific cumulatively designed learning program, any small deviation in the program can be disastrous. Except for clearly delineated home assignments, it's a good idea to maintain a low profile in the actual execution of the child's schoolwork.

This doesn't mean home teaching is never successful. Some parents have undertaken to educate their LD children at home, with remarkable results. Helen Ginandes Weiss and Martin S. Weiss have written an intriguing book, *Home Is a Learning Place,* in which they outline their successful efforts to educate their three LD sons. The Weisses felt that the school system was not able to adapt to the personal learning styles of their sons — and other LD kids — and so they developed a series of home activities designed to work with each child individually, using small skill units and games.

If it is part of your child's school program for you to work closely with him at home, there are a few principles to follow,

with his teacher's awareness and direction, of course (note the similarities between these and our step-by-step strategies for building a more successful home environment).

- Make sure you have clear goals and strategies organized in conjunction with the teacher before involving your child in the activity.
- Simplify the presentation of the material by breaking it into small components.
- Focus on the text with no distractions for a short period of time, and let the child know how long that time will be.
- Don't push the material on the child, and be patient with the rate of progress — accentuate the positive and play down the negative.
- Repeat experiences that will reinforce the skill.

Although we may not want to teach our child at home, we can boost her academic progress in other ways. Most important, we can continue to monitor the schoolwork closely and keep in touch with the child's specialists. We can make sure that our child's emotional needs are being met in school, that she is not being pushed too fast or held back, that issues with her peers are being handled appropriately, that her program is geared toward future success and not limited by her disability. If the IEP team agrees, we can even arrange for tutorial services or homework support at home — as long as we're not the ones doing it.

Perhaps even more important, we can foster a sense of accomplishment in our LD child by encouraging the growth of nonacademic talents. As Howard Gardner says in *Frames of Mind,* there are other forms of intelligence than those that are exploited by our American school system. Artistic, mathematical, interpretive, physical, and interpersonal skills are all skills in which the LD child might excel, regardless of her educational abilities. In particular, LD children seem to exhibit unusual creative talents in music, art, dancing, and drama.

It's up to us to encourage the development of these skills in order to build our LD child's self-image and sense of worth. We can point out that academic progress, while it might seem all-important during school, is not the end-all and be-all of life. People have gone on to successful careers in the arts, sports, science,

195

and government in spite of (some say because of) the LD. This is probably a good time to bring up that standard list of Famous LD Kids Who Have Made It: Albert Einstein (science), Nelson Rockefeller (government), Cher (acting), Chuck Close (art), Wayne Gretsky (sports). You can probably add to it by looking for local heroes, too.

The question is how to help your child choose which talent is right for her. This is often a matter of trial and error, and may take several years of classes and workshops that amount to nothing. Don't lose heart. The experience of trying various expressive media can't hurt, especially if you're careful to pick noncompetitive, nonthreatening environments in which the child can do some exploring. Often the child will gravitate to a particular natural ability, although many LD kids seem to drift in and out of a number of interests. Don't lose heart if your child seems to be an extracurricular dilettante. Sooner or later (and probably not before she's gained the attentional skills necessary), she will find something that's very important to her, something at which she can excel in spite of (or because of) her LD.

Sports are a bit harder to manage for the LD child who is eager to be an athlete. Although coordination is a problem for some LD kids, others are quite agile and able to handle themselves well physically. Learning to play by a complicated set of rules and thriving in the often cutthroat competitive environment of many organized sports is another matter. This is where some of those social skills may come into play and where you can help by being supportive without entering into the competitive spirit yourself. Be encouraging but not pushy, and look hard for a setting that will maximize your child's success in whatever she endeavors. And encourage your child's participation in noncompetitive sports such as swimming, gymnastics, track, skating, skiing, and cycling. These activities are rewarding on their own, and can be done in a group on a more formal level if the child indicates the desire.

The Question of Therapy

All the best efforts in the world may not be enough to help your child overcome a self-image problem. Just when you think you've done everything possible to foster self-confidence and self-worth, something comes along to make you realize that your child is still feeling like a failure, blaming herself for all her problems and putting down all the good news to dumb luck.

The brighter the child, the more likely it is that she'll be able to see the discrepancy between her ability and her performance. Sometimes it can be very painful to watch a child suffering from her own self-awareness, especially if our pain is compounded by a very real sense of helplessness. We have to be able to recognize when the time is right to call in outside help.

Doing this should not make us feel like failures any more than our child's LD should make her feel like a failure. If our child breaks an arm, we have no problem with finding a doctor to realign the bones. We should look at therapy with the same pragmatic eye: we want to fix what's wrong with our child, regardless of whether the hurt is visible or not. But we often feel that unseen hurts should be kept private and dealt with in our own homes. Unfortunately, we're not always equipped to deal with them. In order to be successful at anything, one needs to have the necessary skills. Our LD child may not have the decoding skills necessary to read, and we may not have the professional skills necessary to provide support strategies.

Don't wait for a crisis to seek help. If a demonstrable emotional or psychological problem has developed as a result of your child's LD, your local school system is legally responsible for seeing that it is treated. Usually some sort of psychological counseling or therapy program is included in the IEP — if not, you can certainly demand that it be revised to include one. Unfortunately, many public schools do not provide adequate therapeutic treatment for the severe self-image problems suffered by many LD kids. School psychologists are usually trained to deal with classroom intervention for behavioral situations and offer counseling for home crises. A child who is struggling with a poor self-image may need more help than can be offered by a guidance counselor or a school adjustment counselor during twenty-minute weekly visits.

You would be within your rights to demand outside intervention from a professional psychologist, psychiatrist, or social worker who specializes in helping children who have learning disorders. You would have to prove that although your child's problems are emotional in nature, they are involved with his LD problem, and they are not being remediated through the school's channels. Such an undertaking can be time-consuming and frustrating, especially if your school system decides to dig in and refuse to authorize payment for independent treatment.

As long as you have the documentation, you should be able to persevere, even through the hearing and appeal level. But, in the meantime, you may want to find qualified help right away. (Whether you can get the state to reimburse you for that treatment after a legal decision has been made is a matter for your advocate to determine.) If you are a member of a comprehensive health plan, such as an HMO, your insurance may cover a limited amount of treatment. Traditional health policies sometimes cover outpatient treatment, but rarely more than $500 or $1,000 worth of visits per year, which doesn't go very far with today's rates.

In either case, you'll still need documentation such as testing results and recommendations from both teachers and pediatricians. If you can't get help through your insurance carrier or HMO, there are mental health clinics that will accept sliding-scale payments. If you live in a city with a good teaching hospital, look into training programs, which can sometimes provide excellent and highly motivated doctors-in-residence.

You may be able to overcome your feelings of embarrassment or weakness about seeking out professional guidance, but your LD child might have a harder time. Your attitude is pivotal in determining your child's willingness to work with a therapist. Like you, she may see therapy as more evidence of her own failure and inadequacy, which will only make the therapeutic process more difficult. It's up to you to convince her that there is no stigma attached to seeing a therapist, and that you fully expect it to provide relief for her. Sometimes just hearing that someone recognizes the problem and is going out of his or her way to help can reduce a child's sense of dead-end isolation, making her more amenable to getting that help.

Some children are proud of the extra help they're getting, and take comfort in announcing their support network to anyone who cares to listen. Although we may fear social reprisals on their behalf, it's surprising how many children respond with a wistful "I wish I had my own talking doctor." Still, if there is a problem with the child's embarrassment, there's no reason why therapy sessions have to be made a matter of public knowledge. The child's attitude should be respected by the family, and visits to the doctor can be kept private if she wishes.

What kind of therapy is right? There are as many therapeutic models for dealing with the emotional problems of LD kids as there are educational models for dealing with academic problems. A more effective way to deal with the question would be to determine what kind of help we want to get out of the sessions. Do we want to uncover the underlying personal issues or establish a positive family dynamic? Do we want our child to feel better about her schoolwork or to discover her other strengths so that schoolwork does not assume such an unbalanced importance in her life?

The goals of any therapy, whether it's one-on-one with the LD kid and a therapist, group therapy for several LD kids, or family therapy, should be the same:

- to repair or rebuild the child's self-esteem
- to develop a set of behavioral goals and a system for managing those goals
- to restore a sense of discipline and self-discipline at home or in school
- to repair a significant adult-child relationship, thus rebuilding trust
- to help a child or family through a crisis situation, and teach them strategies for coping with future crises

All LD kids have a few basic questions they want answered. They want to know what their learning disability means, whether it's going to go away, and how it's going to affect their lives. These are legitimate concerns, and a good therapist should be able to address them in a straightforward manner. For this reason, it's often a good idea to start out with individual sessions. The LD child must build up trust in the therapist, and the therapist can learn to read the child as well. In these private sessions, the child can be honest about her feelings, and the therapist, using discussions, games, and imagery, can help her to sort them out, enabling her to admit her pain, let go of her anger, and, one hopes, recognize her strengths.

Group therapy can also be important, especially if the child is feeling isolated by her LD. Finding other children with the same or similar difficulties often goes a long way toward alleviating the sense of guilt and abandonment that many LD kids express. They can also learn practical and effective social skills from one another.

Parents can also benefit from therapy, both as individuals and as a unit, as suggested in chapter 6. Sometimes a therapist can act as an outside mediator to help parents decide on effective compromises that they might not have been able to come up with on their own. And parent groups such as schoolwide special needs councils and local informational networks can also function as informal group therapy sessions. In the company of adults with similar issues, mothers and fathers can work out their own parenting conflicts in order to gain more perspective on their situation. By talking with a counselor, pastor, or close friend, individuals can resolve some of the personal issues that are bound to arise. And, of course, open lines of communication between spouses are essential to a successful marriage and parenting experience.

Perhaps most important, though, is family therapy. The mere fact that parents and siblings are willing to become involved in a therapy program tells the LD child that she is loved and valued in her home. In family sessions, with active mediation from a professional, parents and children can let go of some old thoughts and attitudes, stop blaming one another, and realign themselves to form more positive and loving relationships. The entire family can work on management techniques designed to help the family function more smoothly. If a crisis does develop, professional therapists are equipped to deal with it (either individually or within the family model) and then to go on to offer long-term remedial therapy, helping LD children and their families come up with their own creative solutions to the problems of being an LD family.

Remembering the Child

In the end, we must remember that the LD child is still a child, and that, for the most part, her responses are dictated by her developmental stage. We must not ask too much of our children, nor must we ask too little. All children want to be loved, accepted, respected, praised, protected, and disciplined, and the LD child is no different. She needs to be accepted for what she is, for her differences as well as for her similarities to other children.

Doing this requires some willingness on our part to go the extra mile, to be flexible in our approaches to parenting, to understand the special issues of LD child encounters. But we also need to stop feeling guilty, and to remind ourselves that, regardless of how much time and energy we spend on our children, they are still who they are. Our time is more wisely spent in learning to love who they are — and helping them to love who they are — than in trying to change that.

Nevertheless, progress can be made, and it is well worth the effort to make it. When the LD child learns that it is her learning disability that is making her life more difficult, she can stop blaming herself and taking out her anger on her family. When she learns to manage her own behavior, she can begin to feel better about herself and go out into the world with more confidence and skill. My daughter's favorite saying, which she read in an LD handbook, says it all:

"I have met the enemy, and she isn't me."

CHAPTER 8

What Can We Do about LD?

NOW for the nitty-gritty: what kinds of help can we get for our LD child and where can we get it? We've already discussed what I think is the single most important aspect of remediation — helping a child to rebuild a weakened self-image and to learn how to get along within the family and without. But providing emotional support and socialization instruction will not solve an LD kid's problems. Regardless of how we may feel about the overemphasis on certain academic skills in our society, the fact remains that our children *do* need to learn how to read, write, and conduct basic mathematical operations. They need to be able to perform cognitive tasks that require memorization, sequencing, fine motor coordination, and organization. They need to be able to function adequately as adults regardless of the kinds of careers they will ultimately choose for themselves.

In this chapter, we will examine some of the ways in which they can be helped to acquire those skills. We'll approach it three ways: *instructionally,* by examining methods for teaching the child specific skills; *developmentally,* by examining methods for bringing the child to the level where those skills can be learned; and *biologically,* by looking at medical, physical, dietary, or environmental remediations. These are arbitrary distinctions, of course, and the difference between the first two is particularly hard to define. Instructional intervention makes use of developmental theory, and

202

developmental theory is instructional in nature. There are so many therapies, quite a few of which overlap in both theory and practice, that it would be impossible to list them all, or to separate them from one another. And all of them, we must remember, are not effective without the behavioral component we discussed in chapter 7. As a matter of fact, an emphasis on behavioral and emotional issues is integral to many of the therapies mentioned below, regardless of their orientation.

In any case, the choice is not all in your hands. You will (we hope) be guided by experts who have thoroughly evaluated your child and chosen the best possible intervention methods for him. The chances are good that your child's IEP will offer him the most effective and comprehensive remedial system, incorporating several types of programs to cover the specific nature of his LD.

But you should be aware that there are alternatives to the programs offered by the school, where choices may be limited by budgetary constraint or lack of expertise. In that case, if and when the school's program does not seem to be working, you will want to know that there are other possibilities that might be more effective. I've chosen what I feel to be a representative cross-section of both mainstream and alternative theories so that you can get a good idea of the *range* of possibilities for getting help for your child. The division into instructional, developmental, and biological is my own, devised purely for reasons of simplicity.

However, there are two important things to remember. Just because it's not listed here doesn't mean a particular remedial therapy is not worth looking into for your child. Every existing remediation could not possibly be given proper attention in one book, and new ones are being developed all the time. Naturally, there are highly recommended remediations that have stood the test of both time and scientific examination, just as there are theories that are generally regarded as unproven and ineffective.

In general, the most commonly used therapies are the most effective. But it is by no means always the case that the most popular technique is the best. There are parents and experts who swear by the most controversial of therapies, and children who have made remarkable gains with them, regardless of the therapies' low standing in the professional LD community.

Some of each have been included here, and I have indicated their status in the professional community and, to a certain extent, their level of acceptance by parents and practitioners in the field. But, while I think it's important to know the status of various therapies, I've tried to refrain from passing judgment on them myself. That's because it's important for you to make your own choice. Presumably, by now you've done your homework, listened to the theories, gotten all the evaluations, talked to the experts — and spent a lot of time with your kid. You know him best, and if a therapy model seems to be right for him, *pursue it,* regardless of how little known it is, or how well regarded.

Second point: don't expect any magic pills. Like most everything else in the world of the LD child, nothing comes easily and no one remedial therapy will work by itself. As a matter of fact, that may be the best way to spot a remedial poor risk — if it purports to do the job simply and quickly and without backup therapies in associated areas, it's probably not a legitimate choice. (Again, this may not be true for everyone; there are some therapies that make sweeping promises, and that have been extremely effective for a small number of children. Your child may or may not benefit, although the odds are higher that he won't.)

More commonly, remediation takes a great deal of both time and effort, and works best when accompanied by other changes in the child's environment. For instance, a series of visuomotor coordination tasks may have to accompany a new reading system; an alteration in diet may have to accompany repatterning techniques; or school counseling may have to accompany the change to a self-contained classroom. And again, *any* kind of remediation will almost certainly have to be accompanied by the behavioral and emotional therapies we discussed in chapter 7.

Goals: What We Can Expect

Let's look for a moment at the goals we want our child's remediation to accomplish. If we know in advance what we have in mind for our child, we'll have a better chance of judging the progress of the therapy we've chosen.

Suzanne Stevens, in her book *The Learning Disabled Child: Ways That Parents Can Help,* has outlined a precise series of both long- and short-term goals. Parents, she says, can

1. hope and expect that the child will learn to read at a fourth-grade level, which is the reading level considered minimal for survival in the adult world.

2. hope but not expect that the child will become a normal or even average reader, which means being able to read at a high school level.

3. not hope or expect that the child will ever be a good speller. [As Stevens says, she has never seen an LD child who is a good speller, but spelling is not all that important to most adults — unless they become writers or editors, and even then, dictionaries are always at hand.]

4. hope and expect that the child will learn to tell left from right and not suffer from any enduring spatial deficiencies as an adult. [However, many non-LD adults, particularly left-handers, report that they still have to think for a moment before telling left from right, and many use private mnemonic devices to help them. Your child will very likely be able to do the same.]

5. hope, and perhaps expect that the child will not always feel inferior as a result of his learning disability.

6. hope and expect that the child will be able to attend college or trade school. [Many colleges are now developing programs for LD students — see Appendix C — so this expectation is steadily rising.]

7. hope and definitely expect that the child will be able to live normally as an adult.

The list is not conclusive, but these goals seem both realistic and positive, and they put the scope of a child's LD into good perspective. Never becoming a good speller does not seem as important as becoming a confident and fully functional adult, does it? And, by differentiating between our hopes and our expectations, Stevens is reminding us that what we want for our children may not necessarily be what's needed for their happiness.

Unfortunately, the methods by which our children can arrive at these goals are not nearly so easily categorized. The different approaches to remediation are a lot like the different approaches to computer programming operations. Some computers use DOS, some use BASIC, others use a combination of both or another system entirely. To add to the metaphor, there's not necessarily anything wrong with the LD kids' hardware; it's the software that may be at fault. And the number of software programs, each with a slightly different function and set of commands, is endless. Much to the dismay of the end users, there is no standard operating system. That makes it difficult when computers are trying to talk to one another, and it makes it difficult when we are trying to talk to more than one computer.

The same is true of therapeutic systems. No two systems are alike, although many share some of the same techniques, language, and functions. That makes it hard for parents (the "end users" of a program, because they are making the final choice) to decide which program to choose. Having a trusted expert, preferably several experts, to evaluate the LD child's problem can certainly make the job of choosing a program easier. A good remedial program is always based on the needs of the particular child, and those needs will dictate the type of program we choose. And we must remember that we can always switch if, after a certain period of time, our child does not seem to be making progress. But the final choice — whether to stick with academic remediation, try a functional-deficit program, or look into medical intervention — is ours.

However, we can look at some basic therapeutic principles and come up with some common denominators. A good program should be

- based on a comprehensive evaluation of the child's needs;
- systematic in its approach;
- consistent in its methodology;
- repetitive in its presentation;
- accomplished in small groups or one-on-one;
- oriented toward treating the whole child by these and other methods.

How can these be accomplished? Jerome Rosner, in *Helping Children Overcome LD: A Handbook for Teachers,* has organized remedial tasks into a series of basic principles that reflect these elements. They work in most every therapeutic situation, even though Rosner is speaking specifically about classroom remediation. When you are looking for possible programs for your child, these principles could form a framework by which you can judge the effectiveness of any of them.

206

1. Analyze the exact nature of the problem.
2. Set a positive and specific goal. (That is, "The child will be able to read, write, and so on, as well as the other children in his group. His progress will be equal to that of the majority of his classmates, despite the fact that he may continue to be hard to teach.")
3. Organize material to insure greatest success.
4. Make sure the child has the factual knowledge needed to profit from the lesson.
5. Develop a clear strategy that will help the child retain new information, by linking up new information with information he already knows.
6. Encourage the child to use other senses (not just eyes and ears) to explore concrete and abstract aspects of the task at hand.
7. Provide enough repeated experiences so that the information is securely established in the child's long-term memory.

A Few Words about Reading

Before we differentiate and enumerate some types of programs, let's look for a moment at the one skill that seems to constitute the underpinning of most LD problems and their remediations: reading. Even though successful passage through school involves the acquisition of many skills, reading disorders represent the single major cause of school failure in our educational system. Without reading, higher levels of information cannot be acquired. What exactly is reading, and what does the task involve?

Although there are endless arguments on the topic, reading is most commonly defined as a visual symbol system, superimposed on auditory language and followed by written expression. But it's much more complicated than that. There is no one center in our brain that does the job of reading, just as there is no one location for the acquisition and use of language. Reading and language are inextricably intertwined, and their function depends on the inter-relationship of a great number of functional, cognitive, and physical abilities. Some of those factors involved in learning to read are

- biology (maturational, neurological, pathological, genetic);
- psychology (motivational, attentional, inhibitional);
- socializing (appropriate stimulation at critical ages);

- familial environment and style;
- educational opportunity (exposure);
- appropriateness and adequacy of teaching.

Jeanne S. Chall, dean of the Harvard Graduate School of Education and director of the school's renowned reading laboratory, has defined six stages involved in the acquisition and evolution of the ability to read. Not only are the stages linked to the child's developmental level, they are also connected to his evolving ability to integrate what is read with what is known about the world.

Stage 0: Prereading (birth to age six) — marked by a growing control over language skills

Stage 1: Initial reading or decoding (grades one to two) — mastery of the alphabetic principle, sound-letter relationships, and basic decoding skills

Stage 2: Confirmation, fluency, and ungluing from print (grades two to three) — consolidation of what has been learned and gaining of further insight into comprehension of familiar text

Stage 3: Learning the new (grades four to eight) — the beginning of reading as a tool for acquiring knowledge, feelings, insights, and so on, beyond the child's experience

Stage 4: Multiple viewpoints (high school) — requiring more complex language and cognitive ability to explore an advanced content area

Stage 5: Construction and reconstruction (college) — constructing knowledge for own use from reading what others say

During stages 1 and 2, reading can be taught in several ways. Entire books have been written on various methods of teaching reading, but, for the purposes of this book, we need only briefly explore the major methods. On one end of the continuum are the structured phonics methods, in which children are given symbols for parts of words and encouraged to put together whole words from what they know of their components. In these methods, the development of vocabulary is controlled by sound/symbol relationships.

On the other end are the language-experience and whole-word methods, in which children are saturated with a text and encouraged to draw conclusions about how words are structured from what they know about the words they've learned — in other words, the vocabulary is controlled by language experiences, and the child draws conclusions about language from what he knows.

The difference is much like that between inductive and deductive reasoning in scientific theory. The child learns to read by moving inductively, from the part to the whole (phonics), or deductively, from whole to part (whole-word). Depending on the school's curriculum and the prevailing winds of educational philosophy, one or the other of these methods or a variety of methods that incorporate elements of both are probably used in your child's school. Currently, the language-experience method, which incorporates pertinent and high-interest-level material with developing a sight vocabulary and writing skills, is enjoying the upper hand over the more phonetically inclined basal readers such as the Dick and Jane series and their descendants.

But what happens when neither of these methods seems to be working? LD kids are unable to develop their own consistent language theory simply by learning words, nor can they learn words simply by being given parts. It used to be a commonly held educational theory that if most students learned to read using one particular method of instruction and some students did not, there was something wrong with the latter students, not with the method. Fortunately, that philosophy seems to be less pervasive these days, although it certainly still exists. Unfortunately, many classroom teachers are still trained to use one method and not another, despite the proven fact that some children learn in different ways.

And LD children learn in different ways — not only differently from their non-LD classmates, but also differently from one another. To understand this, let's go back to our basic types. Instructional remediations teach the child certain skills and learning behaviors. They are goal-oriented, because they refer to any skill-based or behavior-based method that concerns itself with the acquisition of academic skill levels and the ability to learn effectively. Developmental therapies bring the child up to a certain cognitive, perceptual, or motor skill level so that he can acquire those skills and behaviors. This approach is more process-oriented, because it refers to developmentally based or brain-based therapies designed to improve the child's functional abilities so that he can perform learning tasks. Biological remediations are concerned with approaches imposed by medicine, by diet, or by altering either the child's five senses or his environment. They could be called externally oriented, since they are imposed by outside sources or manipulations.

Naturally, the success of one or the other of these techniques depends on the way in which the child learns, which should be determined by his evaluation. Many of the most effective remediations are combinations of goal- and process-oriented techniques, and the two types overlap so often that the only reason for differentiating between them is for purposes of clarity. At their most effective, all three approaches make integral use of the kinds of behavioral management techniques we discussed in chapter 7. Whether we are developing a child's reading skills, his visuomotor coordination, or his nutrition levels, we are modifying his behavior in an essential way. Furthermore, any remedial technique that is not coupled with a focus on the child's emotional state is very likely doomed to ineffectiveness. The child's heart must develop along with his mind!

Instruction-oriented Approaches

Common reading techniques (such as basal readers, whole-word or sight-reading and language experience) are examples of goal-oriented approaches. But we've seen that reading techniques alone are not sufficient for the child with dyslexia, information-processing deficits, visuomotor coordination problems, or any of the wide variety of specific learning disabilities. For these kids, the task of learning to read requires more complex intervention; they need to learn how to *learn,* not just how to read. Not only do we have to break the ineffective patterns of learning, and substitute more efficient ones, but we must also provide LD children with appropriate behaviors for effective learning. If they don't have those effective learning behaviors in their repertoire (such as paying attention, focusing on the appropriate stimuli, or controlling their motor functions) — and most don't — they can be taught those as well.

Instructionally oriented approaches assume that intervention in problematic learning behaviors is more important than investigation into the causes of such behaviors. This does not mean that etiology is ignored. Testing provides crucial information regard-

210

ing the nature of the disability, and the remedial program is carefully geared to that information. If an educational evaluation indicates that a child is an auditory learner who responds well to sight words, a structured phonics approach is not going to work.

According to the instructional theorists, LD problems are rooted in inadequate basic skills — information-processing skills — so those basic skills have to be retaught, rather than traced to their developmental source. Individual differences in learning are analyzed, and the teaching method is geared toward finding the one method that best suits the child's particular learning style.

Remediation takes place in the form of a pragmatic and task-oriented program that provides immediate rewards in the way of skills acquired and behaviors learned. It focuses on learning experiences rather than organic systems, and progress is judged by a child's educational achievement. In an instructionally oriented program, remediation should be geared to fit the academic situation in addition to attempting to resolve the abstract dysfunction that may be behind it.

But how does it work in a specific system? According to one LD expert, the methodology of the skill-oriented approach is fairly simple; unzip the code, take out the concept behind it, and make the concept concrete. If a child is having trouble with a math procedure — adding numbers taken from a word problem, for example — a skill-oriented program might assist by helping the child see the relationship between the numbers in sentence form and the way they are arranged graphically, one below the other with all the place values in the right position. Then, by repetition, the teacher could lead the child to understand that all word problems could be treated this way — that the concept worked no matter which numbers were used. Once the concept makes sense, the procedure becomes doable, and the child can make use of the material he has learned.

Some remedial systems of this type take their single-minded approach literally, and focus on very small increments of knowledge (the sound of the short vowel *e,* for instance), learned through one sensory mechanism. Step-by-step basal readers, which build on extensive repetition of small phonetic increments, are a good example of this approach.

But we have seen that LD kids need reinforcement in more than one sense mechanism or modality. And by far the best-known and most respected approach is the Orton-Gillingham system, which uses several senses to teach a child one concept. The system was not invented by either Samuel Orton or Anna Gillingham, however. A precursor was developed by Grace Fernald in the early 1940s. Fernald used a whole-word approach to teaching reading, but she used more than one modality. The child was instructed to hear the word, say it, trace it, even feel it (a small rubber dog, for instance, for the word *dog*), to watch his own hand create the word, to listen to himself saying it, and, finally, to recognize its resemblance to other similar words. Fernald was also a strong believer in what she called "reconditioning" in order to help her students manage the behavioral problems that resulted from their reading difficulties — and this was back in 1943, when very few people recognized the connection between behavioral problems and academic ones.

But it was Samuel T. Orton who developed the remedial learning system that is now most commonly used in American schools. He took the concept of small-task orientation and Fernald's multisensory approach and expanded both into a multidisciplinary approach that went far beyond reading skills.

Until the 1920s, dyslexics were taught in much the same way that everyone else was taught, just less effectively. Orton, a psychiatry professor at the University of Iowa, developed teaching methods for nonreading students that achieved much greater success by allowing the students to use their senses of touch, hearing, and speech to reinforce the material. Unlike Fernald, he concentrated on phonetic and syllable construction. He continued to refine his program while he was professor of neurology at Columbia University in the 1930s and 1940s. In the mid-forties, he asked Anna Gillingham, a psychologist and remedial teacher, to formalize the technique and organize procedures, which she did in a series of color-coded manuals that form the basis of nearly 80 percent of this country's remedial programs. The program she designed was geared toward third- to sixth-graders, a younger population than that of Orton's (and Fernald's) original work.

Orton's theory was that reading disorders were caused by a neurological and/or maturational lag, resulting in delayed lateral dominance for language and disturbances in perceptual functioning. He believed that there was a genetic etiology: in other words, that the problem was passed from one generation to the next.

The problems manifested themselves in a number of ways, and Orton hoped his remedial technique would address them all, rather than focusing on just one aspect of learning difficulties. According to the Orton Dyslexia Society, we all need to learn how to fill in the gaps between what we actually hear, see, and feel in the outer world and how we think about these things. The LD child needs more help than others to sort, recognize, and put this information into some kind of order. Thus the essentials of the approach are

1. Individualized: The curriculum is designed to meet specific learning needs of the student.
2. Multidisciplinary: It makes use of a variety of techniques.
3. Multisensory: It uses all the learning pathways — seeing, hearing, touching, feeling, even smelling (it is mostly visual, auditory, and kinesthetic, but it also makes use of other senses).
4. Alphabetic-phonic: The system uses an inductive method of word learning that builds words out of sounds put into a specific order.
5. Linguistic: It presumes that, since words and sentences are carriers of meaning, linguistic power comes from fluency in language patterns.
6. Systematic: The material is organized in a logical way, befitting the nature of our language.
7. Sequential: It moves step-by-step from the simplest to the most complex, not progressing to a more complicated skill until the underlying skill is mastered.
8. Cumulative: Each step is based upon those already learned.
9. Cognitive: The student is helped to understand the reasons for what he is learning, so that he can gain the confidence to think his own way through language problems.
10. Emotionally sound: A person's confidence about himself and about learning are vital to his successful education. Such confidence comes from mastery of the material.

How is it done? First, of course, the child must be carefully evaluated so that the exact nature of the problem is clear to the educator. Then each component of the problem must be dealt with separately, in small increments. Let's say the child has trouble with the short vowel sounds (*e* in *bed, a* in *bat, o* in *body*). Using a variety of techniques, the teacher would expose the child to those sounds — and only those sounds — in simple combination. Using multiple stimuli to enrich the message, a teacher might have the child read, say, hear, and see the written sounds. Tracing the written word with a finger, then with a pencil, and finally trying to write it alone would be another component of the learning experience.

Then the child would see pictures of words that have the sound in them, and possibly hold objects that the sound represents (a doll furniture bed, a plastic egg). Because they are more easily represented, the teacher would probably start with nouns. Once the concept has become familiar, the teacher can expand the child's familiarity with the sounds by introducing familiar-looking words from other forms of speech (*bet, Ben, beg*), thus increasing the child's understanding of the sound and broadening her grasp of its applicability.

All of this would be done in carefully cumulative steps, each one building on the already acquired skill. Constant repetition and simple explanations would accompany each presentation, and the teaching would be done in a patient and positive manner, concentrating on building the child's confidence in her ability to understand this particular concept and to learn in general.

Sound familiar? You've probably recognized many of the elements of the behavioral modification approaches we discussed in the previous chapter. That's because Orton believed that teaching an LD child to read meant modifying that child's behavior. The high success rate of the Orton-Gillingham technique is a result of this multidisciplinary focus — the child does not just learn how to decode sounds and words; he learns the concept behind decoding, and he learns how to complete the decoding process by himself, as well as how to relate it to similar skills.

The Orton-Gillingham technique is only the best known of a number of programs that employ those basic concepts. A number of others are briefly listed here so that you can recognize them if they are mentioned in your child's IEP (they may not be mentioned by name, but if you ask to see your child's instructional materials — as you certainly should — you will probably find the name of the program indicated there). You do not have the right to demand that a specific instructional method be used for your child, but if you're not happy with the way he's learning, you can suggest that an alternative program be used.

All of these programs — and others like them — are considered acceptable instructional methods with a good record of success.

Slingerland: Beth Slingerland adapted the Orton-Gillingham technique to a classroom situation so that it could be applied to larger groups of children. She made use primarily of the auditory and kinesthetic sensory channels for teaching language, and of the visual channels for teaching reading. According to Slingerland, the development of sensory channel associations would teach younger children to acquire "thought patterns" that would in turn guide their language performance skills.

Like Orton-Gillingham, she begins with the smallest units of sound, building several consonants and one vowel into a word. This process is called encoding, or blending, and both the Slingerland and the Orton-Gillingham techniques say that this must take place before decoding, or unlocking the meaning of words. Slingerland also developed excellent screening techniques, which are widely used in today's school systems.

Write-To-Read: John Martin has developed a system that concentrates on a child's ability to express himself in writing as a precursor to reading. Using and listening closely to their own idiomatic language, children begin to grasp the concept that letters are symbols for the sounds they make. Such a system is particularly useful in areas where black English and other idiomatic variations are spoken, since children can use their own language experience to form patterns about reading and writing. An experimental Write-To-Read project has been used with great success in a dozen southern states, using computers to enable the child to learn the alphabetic principle: that twenty-six letters of the alphabet and their combinations make it possible to write everything they can say.

Minnesota Reading Project (Project Read): The researcher Mary Lee Enfield created a multiphased language arts program to develop comprehension, writing, and decoding skills for LD children. She concentrated on a very structured language system, since she felt that LD kids were unable to develop inductively a language system from repetition of its components. After studying the reading technologies available in American classrooms, Enfield concluded that an instructional alternative to inductive, basal-reading approaches was needed for children who could not learn in that manner. She designed her program with those alternative learners in mind, and also designed a companion math program based on similar principles. The program is meant to be used by the classroom teacher and is therefore considered more of a preventive approach than a remedial one.

(If programs such as Enfield's, Martin's, or Slingerland's were used in the classroom, there would theoretically be far fewer children referred for LD evaluation, because fewer children would be failing to learn. Whether such systems actually solve the larger problem of learning disabilities is not yet known.)

The Writing Road to Reading: Similar to John Martin's program, this one, developed by Robert Spaulding and Doris Johnson, concentrates on developing the kinesthetic encoding abilities involved in writing before going on to actual decoding skills.

Color Phonics/Initial Teaching Alphabet: These systems attempt to teach children to read by substituting different symbol systems that are easier for them to grasp than the often complicated English alphabetic system. Color phonics uses color-coded symbols, while the controversial ITA uses a more phonetically consistent alphabet system to replace our own temporarily until the child becomes comfortable with decoding skills. The child is then transferred back over to a regular system. (This can be a problem, especially if the child is thrown back on conventional methods for learning the regular system.)

Creative Learning: Structured creative projects (in art, music, creative writing, poetry, games) can accompany the presentation of vowels, consonants, phonograms, and elementary grammar rules. Programs such as this are considered excellent supplements to methods of the Orton type, since they concentrate on the enrichment of the material as well as on developing creative skills that

216

may be a strength for the child, offsetting her weaknesses in academic skills.

Remember, the programs listed above are by no means the only such programs of their kind currently in use in American schools. There are many variations on them, and many good LD tutors will combine the best elements of several systems, depending on which seems to work best for a particular child. Others have come to depend on one system because they are most familiar with it and because it has been proven effective in their experience — which is fine if your child's progress is good. However, if an LD tutor swears by only one system, and your child doesn't seem to be making progress, it might be time to suggest that alternatives be considered.

Most instructional therapists believe that the effect of their work carries over to other areas of the child's life. It certainly creates the confidence to do other things more effectively, and may even help create alternative neuronal pathways. There is a strong behavioral management component to the above programs and others like them, because they are so highly structured and success-oriented. For that reason alone, they should also have a positive effect on the emotional life of the child.

Developmental Therapies

Developmentally oriented therapists also believe that their approach carries over and improves the child's academic progress. In fact, it may be hard to distinguish between the instructional and developmental approaches, since they so often overlap in methodology, if not in underlying theory. Once again, the division is largely arbitrary, and many of the researchers who developed these programs would argue with their placement in one category or the other. Certainly Samuel Orton was a strong believer in the developmental cause of LD, just as Marianne Frostig and Samuel Kirk believed their approaches to be educational as well as developmental in focus.

Like the instructional therapists, those in the developmental school believe that learning problems are symptomatic of a dysfunction in some underlying process. The difference between the two lies in the approach. Instruction-based programs tend to focus more on the content of the material and on the student's output ability — such a process assumes that remediating the child's ability to write, for example, will improve his underlying visuomotor deficit.

The latter group feels that the best way to get rid of a symptom is to go back and find what is causing it, then work on the cause. Developmental therapies are directed at remediating a specific function by working from the inside out — by working on the underlying deficit to improve the child's ability to perform tasks.

Such programs focus on the process of input and output more than on the content. They are primarily concerned with the ability of the child to overcome specific deficits in basic learning functions; for this reason, they are also called *function-deficit* remediations. With the exception of widely used speech and language therapy and occupational therapy, most programs that use the function-deficit model are clinical extensions of research theory, and they are usually conducted in limited experimental settings. While you may not find these programs in general use, however, the methods they employ are often adopted as part of other remedial programs, and knowing about them will give you a good idea of what the function-deficit approach is all about. And, as with the instructional approaches, none of these programs is meant to be used without complementary programs that address other areas of the child's LD.

Occupational Therapy: OT helps children to develop underlying skills that are prerequisites for learning and vocational training. OT therapy is an acknowledged component of most school intervention systems, and most children who are screened for an LD evaluation will be tested by an occupational therapist. Practitioners provide special equipment for developing balance, fine motor skills, motor coordination, handedness, and sensory development. They help develop muscle tone and movement patterns to decrease clumsiness. They tackle the skills behind writing ability, spatial planning, and perceptual organization. They can adapt home and school environments, too, for children who need assistance in self-help skills and in interacting with their environment.

Sensory Integration Therapy: Dr. Jean Ayres was a noted occupational therapist who believed that the child's brain was still plastic and adaptable, making it possible for work to be done on nonmajor neurological dysfunctions such as LD. Ayres's theory was that LD is caused by the brain stem's inability to organize sensations from the various sensory systems. She developed a program that provided gradual stimulation to those systems, such as the vestibular (which governs balance) and the somatosensory (which governs positional awareness in space) as well as the five "basic" sensory systems.

By exercising these systems, Ayres found that the brain's capacity for multisensory integration could be increased, and the child would be better equipped to handle tasks that require such integration, like speaking, reading, and writing, higher-level cognitive tasks, and physical awareness of the body in space. She also developed tests (the Southern California Figure-Ground Perception Test and the Ayres Space Test of spatial orientation) that are frequently used by OT evaluators. OT therapists need special training before they can be certified by Ayres's institute, Sensory Integration International. (Call the institute in Los Angeles at 213-533-8338 to find a local certified instructor.)

Physical Therapy: PT is used rarely with LD kids, and only when OT cannot provide enough support in terms of gross motor skill acquisition. It can, however, provide additional support for children with multiple handicaps who also have LD problems, by increasing their motor skill ability and their confidence.

Speech and Language Therapy: Speech therapy is often used for non-LD students, but many LD children have speech and language problems. Speech therapy addresses articulation and motor problems by working with the mechanics of the system — mouth, tongue, teeth, and jaw placement can all be affected. Language therapy is more involved with the expressive elements of speech: in what is said rather than how it is said. However, the two elements are most often addressed together, since they are often difficult to separate (except in the case of a child with a pure speech impairment such as a stutter or lisp).

Most speech and language therapies attempt to follow the model of normal language acquisition, and to help children acquire the natural rules of language. Most children seem to possess an innate ability to acquire this complex system of rules and exceptions, but children with LD often do not. In a carefully structured environment (which includes a quiet room and no distractions — something parents might want to look out for in this era of space crunches), they must be taken through the stages of acquisition:

- sound recognition
- short-term focus (remembering the rules about the sound)
- storage, categorization, and organization
- retrieval systems (finding the right words)
- motor production of the sounds

The goals of a good therapy program go beyond increasing a child's ability to use and comprehend language, whether it's simple word names or complex sentence structure and story organization. They should improve a child's listening skills, his attentional ability, and his ability to provide appropriate verbal feedback and to communicate nonverbally (with gestures, posture, and eye contact) as well.

Marianne Frostig's Visual Perception Training Program: If Samuel Orton's technique supposes that one must use language to gain language, the developmentalists like Frostig believe that one must go back to more basic skills in order to develop language ability. Her technique concentrates on developing eye-motor coordination, figure-ground and perceptual constancy, and spatial perceptions through nonacademic work such as block play, drawing, figure-reading, and other gamelike programs. Elements of Frostig's remedial approach are commonly found in occupational therapy, language therapy, and instruction-oriented approach.

Kirk and Kirk: Sam and Winifred Kirk believed that adequate testing for visuomotor problems was essential before a proper remediation program could be developed; their Illinois Test of Psycholinguistic Abilities is one of the most effective in the field. Like Frostig's program, the Kirks' remediation theory went behind the academic skill and concentrated on developing the tactile, kinesthetic, and motor skills of dyslexic children, depending on their particular disability as indicated by the ITPA.

Barry: Barry developed a motor skill instruction method that concentrated on training in body image as the goal for achieving language skills. The instruction included balance and movement skills such as walking, rolling, jumping rope, playing ball and hopscotch, and executing an obstacle course, as well as fine motor skills developed by folding paper, knitting, crocheting, cutting and pasting, buttoning, tying, and zipping, and identifying objects by touch. Other motor skills are oculomotor (following a moving target, making eyes hop), and vocomotor (whistling, inflating balloons, alliterating). Like Frostig's programs, Barry's instructional methods form the basis for many occupational therapy programs today (see above).

William Cruickshank: A noted researcher, Cruickshank also developed a modified classroom model to remediate learning problems by placing the child in a physical environment that reduced extraneous stimulation (such as outside noises, lots of posters or pictures on the walls, the presence of other students) while at the same time enriching the child's curricular stimuli (with a multisensory approach).

Jerome Rosner: Rosner's Perceptual Skill Project at the University of Pittsburgh is mostly a research model, but it is worth noting because it integrates the elements of developmental and academic remediation, designed to maximize the link between perceptual skills and academic performance. While it is developmental in nature because it concentrates on underlying perceptual skill development, the project is more connected to academic progress because it seeks to design a curriculum to teach these skills.

Movigenic Curriculum: Leo Barsch's movigenic curriculum concentrated on one area of the senses — the kinesthetic. He believed that humans lived in a primarily spatial world, and a child had to be instructed to strive toward more efficient motor skills before she could integrate higher skills. His instructional system was designed to teach a child how to operate in twelve dimensions through space, and he believed that such fluency helped develop the child's ability to function linguistically.

Ocular Training: Arnold Getman was an optometrist who worked closely with the researchers Newell Kephart and Arnold Gesell on the visuomotor aspect of development. He designed an ocular training program that would develop a child's perceptual abilities to the point where she could handle abstract language patterns. Getman believed that visual acuity was equivalent to perceptual ability, and he developed a "physiology of readiness," in which the individual moves from general coordination through balance, eye-hand coordination, eye movement control, form perception, and visual memory to the most advanced level, imagery ability. His theories have been questioned by many professionals, since they do not account for the visually impaired person who acquires such ability without sight.

Developmental Optometry: Taking Getman's ocular therapy as a basis, some researchers have examined the possibility that perceptual disorders are the result of peripheral eye defects unlikely to be spotted by a traditional eye examination. Unlike ophthalmologists, who treat eye diseases, and most optometrists, who treat vision problems, the developmental optometrists deal with kinetic vision — not just how well the child sees, but how her eye functions while she's seeing. Problems with peripheral vision, tracking (following words from one line to the next or looking from blackboard to paper, for example), and convergence (how the eyes move together) are treated by special prismatic lenses designed to strengthen eye muscles and a series of exercises for the same purpose.

Tinted Glasses: The researcher Helen Irlen has evidence that some LD children and adults are unable to "lift words from the page" when reading; they literally cannot distinguish the words from the background of the page. For such people, reading through variously colored tinted glasses may have a positive effect. Irlen cautions that not everyone with a reading disability will benefit, and agrees that tinted glasses are no substitute for learning how to decode words.

Cerebellar-vestibular Imbalances: Dr. Harold Levinson has conducted studies at his clinic that indicate that LD is caused by a dysfunction in nerve pathways of the inner ear, and that the resulting imbalances in the vestibular system lead to the various associated learning problems. According to Levinson, motion sickness medication will help, although there is little evidence beyond his own clinical case histories to support this theory. Still, those case histories are impressive, and the jury is still out on the scientific research to support the theory.

Patterning: Patterning programs (and there are several) have much in common with the developmental approach, but they take the concept much farther. A basic premise is that there are normal developmental patterns that evolve sequentially, and if these are interrupted, the result can cause problems in learning or perception. Advocates of patterning argue that, if we retrace the developmental sequence until we find the aberrant pattern, we can then restructure that particular pattern and move forward through subsequent phases, eliminating the problem.

Perhaps the best-known and most controversial advocates of this theory are Robert Doman and Carl Delacato, whose Institute for the Achievement of Human Potential is in Philadelphia. According to Doman and Delacato, patterning "reaches the brain itself by pouring into the afferent sensory system all of the stimuli normally provided by the child's environment, but with such intensity and frequency as to draw a response from the corresponding motor systems." In other words, impaired neurological systems can be repaired by manipulating and stimulating the damaged pathways.

Originally, the Doman and Delacato method was used for brain-damaged patients; eventually it was found that the technique could be used with LD kids, as well as to enhance the intellectual aptitude of non-LD students and to alleviate various behavioral disorders. Using the familiar biology epigram, "Ontogeny recapitulates phylogeny," Doman and Delacato theorized that just as the lower brain must be structured before the higher brain during development, so the more "primitive" developmental functions must be mastered before the more advanced ones.

Doman and Delacato advocates also believe that patterning can train for cerebral dominance, which would resolve the mixed-dominance problems that many believe are the root of LD problems. Since language and reading disabilities are faults in neurological organization (whether caused by dominance or other abnormal architecture), treatment must give the child a chance to reorganize her brain. In effect, we could actually correct the brain through exercises such as creeping, crawling, special breathing, and running.

Of course, this is a tremendous oversimplification. The exercises are quite specific and extensive, involving the use of specialized equipment and training for several facilitators. A Doman/ Delacato-trained therapist would first identify the level of the cortex on which the deficiency lay (for example, the spinal cord or the medulla), and then provide exercises to stimulate development in that particular area. In addition to the rigorous physical regime, there are passive exercises, sleep positions, and dietary restrictions.

It is an extremely rigid, rigorous, and demanding program, and that is one of the reasons why the Joint Association of Neurologists and Pediatricians has been critical of patterning programs. The association also states that the results claimed by the institute are inconclusive — and so they are — but there are many parents, teachers, and children who are willing to provide glowing testimonials to the remarkable achievements of patterning programs.

Biologically Oriented Remediations

While instructional and developmental interventions concentrate on helping the child to acquire skills and abilities, biological remediations work from without, in an attempt to provide the child with the necessary aids to functioning, or to remove obstacles to that functioning. While they are imposed externally by diet, medication, or restructuring techniques, these interventions are not like braces or crutches. Ideally, they are absorbed by the child, and thus become instructional (and developmental) as well, in that they improve the child's ability to function. Biological intervention can take several distinct forms.

Pharmacological Approaches: Perhaps the strongest and longest-running controversy in the field of LD has been the question of medication. Can drugs actually improve the performance of an LD child? At what cost? There is no question that in a number of cases, particularly those in which ADD and hyperactivity play a large role, medication has had a dramatic effect. But even when the results are overwhelmingly positive, the questions still remain: What are the possible side effects? How will the use of the drugs affect the child's self-image? What happens when the drug is discontinued?

The judicious use of medication has a clearly noticeable effect on some types of LD problems. Some of the symptomatic behaviors of ADD in particular (focusing ability, hyperactivity) seem to respond well to medication. Since many of these behaviors are triggered by a neurological dysfunction, a drug that can inhibit the dysfunction or stimulate a more functional neurological response will be effective. However, since the cause of so many LD problems is neurological, and since it is so difficult to pinpoint the source of the problem, medication is often useless and sometimes harmful. In addition, children are more likely than adults to have unpredictable responses to medication — which is why certain drugs, like Ritalin (methylphenidate hydrochloride) and phenobarbital, have effects on adults opposite to those on children.

But let's look at the instances in which they can be used effectively. Most of them alter the chemistry of the brain so that it responds in a different way. But, while the majority of pharmacological remediations fall into one category, other types of medications can have a beneficial effect on other symptoms. The numbers in parentheses after each drug indicate the expected incidence of control, as reported in a study by Gordon Millichap, "Drugs in the Management of MBD."

— **Psychostimulants:** They act on the central nervous system and are the most commonly used category of medication. Although they have been prescribed for other LD problems, they are used most commonly for children who have been diagnosed as having ADD.

- Ritalin (methylphenidate hydrochloride) (84%)
- Dexedrine (amphetamine) (69%)
- Deaner (deanol acetomidobenzoate) (47%)
- Cylert (pemoline) (not available)

— **Tranquilizers:** These have not been found effective in most LD cases, but they are sometimes prescribed by a child psychiatrist to counteract extreme anxiety and associated overactivity.

- Librium (chlordiazepoxide) (60%)
- Mellaril (thioridazine) (57%)
- Thorazine (chlorpromazine) (55%)
- Valium (diazepam) (not available)

— Sedatives/Antidepressants/Anticonvulsants: These are also rarely prescribed these days, usually only when there are additional problems that require medication. No statistical information is available on their effectiveness for this reason.

- Tofranil (imipramine; antidepressant)
- lithium carbonate (antimanic)
- phenobarbital (sedative)
- Dilantin (phenytoin; anticonvulsant)

Naturally, the decision to medicate is in itself a difficult one, and the choice of category and generic drug must be carefully examined. What are some of the pros and cons? On the plus side, there is ample evidence that medication does work wonders for a number of children suffering from attentional disorders and hyperactivity, and that the concentration levels of such children are often improved, particularly by the use of the psychostimulant drugs. Those medications, most notably Ritalin, act quickly and do not accumulate in the system. Judicious dosage allows the child a remarkable degree of control over her impulsive behavior and allows her to focus on the tasks at hand, in school and out.

But judicious dosage is a difficult thing to determine. The current line of thinking holds that the best way to approach it is to start with the absolute minimal dosage and to wait several days before increasing it by very small amounts until the minimal effective dose is achieved. The drug is often administered only in the morning (and sometimes at lunch) so that its effectiveness is limited to school hours, allowing the child drug-free time after school and on weekends.

Of course, the child must be willing to participate, and the parents must be willing to support the therapy. Drug-taking is a sensitive issue in our society, and without proper counseling and monitoring, drug therapy can do more harm than good. Assuming that the child and parents are cooperative, however, the conservative use of drug therapy can be an effective adjunct to other forms of remediation — not even the strongest advocate would consider using medication without academic tutoring or some other form of intervention. After all, attentional disorders are only a small part of a child's LD problem, and what good is being able to concentrate if one still cannot perceive the letters on the page properly?

The possible side effects of any medication can outweigh the benefits: decreased appetite, sleeplessness (often due to the rebound effect of being off the drug at night), dazedness, slower growth, and emotional instability are serious concerns to parents and physicians. Oddly enough, drug addiction does not seem to be a problem, although there are some researchers who claim that the lack of evidence is not conclusive. There certainly remains the issue of drug dependency, especially since most children are taken off the medication at puberty (when the drug may cause hormonal upsets), a time when many youngsters are emotionally fragile and susceptible.

Medications other than the psychostimulants do accumulate in the body and can cause more serious physiological repercussions. And there is some argument about the use of drug therapy during school hours only. It might create a physical rebound problem, and it can put a child on an uncomfortable emotional roller coaster, where she is in control between 8:30 and 2:30 and then falls apart the rest of the day, adversely affecting her home and social life.

There is a more pervasive argument against the use of drug therapy. Drugs may be a temporary stopgap, but children don't outgrow most of their LD problems; they just learn to manage them. With medication, they may not learn those skills until they stop taking it — and by then it may be much more difficult to learn coping strategies. Drug therapy can also be prescribed inappropriately, when there is no attentional problem or hyperactivity, simply because parents or teachers believe it will make the child easier to handle. In addition, there is evidence that medication is more routinely prescribed to the economically disadvantaged children who present behavior problems in the classroom, raising the specter that it is used more to suppress undesirable behavior than to correct any true attentional disorder.

Since no clear pathology for LD or ADD has ever been found,

drug therapy will continue to be a source of controversy, especially since the dynamics of dosage and administration have not yet been solved. Until they are, parents must make absolutely sure that medication therapy is closely monitored by a physician. Schools should be informed of any course of medication, even if the child is not being administered the medicine during school hours. If a school-time dose is to be administered, it should be done by a school nurse, and under closely supervised conditions.

Orthomolecular Approaches: Another biologically oriented theory holds that the functioning of the brain is affected by the molecular concentrations of many chemical substances that are naturally present. If the balance between these substances is off, the functioning of the brain will be adversely affected. Orthomolecular treatment of LD is accomplished by providing an optimal molecular environment for the brain. Such treatments fall into several categories.

— Diets: Dr. Benjamin Feingold created the famous K-P diet (named after California's Kaiser-Permanente Clinic, where he worked) to combat what he felt were the orthomolecular imbalances that resulted in hyperactivity and other learning problems. According to Feingold's theory, the low molecular weight of certain chemicals found in food caused the imbalances — food additives such as artificial dyes, preservatives, artificial flavors, and salicylates are the main culprits.

The K-P diet recommends that children eat or drink none of the following foods:

> artificially colored or flavored breakfast cereals
> bologna, ham, frozen fish, hot dogs, nitrate meats
> flavored yogurts, ice cream, instant breakfast drinks
> prepared cake mixes, bread doughs, flavored gelatins
> soft drinks except 7-Up
> aspirin compounds, cough drops, toothpaste, vitamins, and
>   pediatric medications
> all citrus and tomato products
> all berries
> peaches, plums, grapes, raisins, prunes
> cocoa, chocolate

pickles
mayonnaise, butter, margarine
mustard
colored cheeses
commercial soups
candy
almonds, apricots, cucumbers, apples

Perfumes and topical treatments with fragrance or artificial colors are also to be avoided.

Feingold's reports are based on his own ample clinical evidence. More precise "challenge" studies indicate that there is a subset of hyperactive children (particularly younger children) who benefit from diet restrictions. However, blind studies indicate that the results are not as dramatic as Feingold's proponents claim. For one thing, parents (who had a strong vested interest in the results of the study) noticed more change than teachers did (this is called an anticipatory bias); laboratory results showed an even lower indication of change as a result of the diet.

In addition, the diet is considered too high in carbohydrates and too low in vitamin C. Its rigidity can also work against the diet, making it extremely difficult to measure results, since Feingold claims that even a single bite can cause a severe behavioral reaction in children. And, because the diet is so extreme, it is difficult to determine which of the many restricted foods are to blame for the child's imbalance. Although there is little clinically substantiated evidence, the K-P diet continues to be a popular adjunct therapy, and many parents swear by the remarkable changes it has caused in their children even while they bemoan the extreme difficulty of adhering to the diet. However, even if one does not subscribe to Feingold's therapy, it makes sense to keep your child away from processed foods, high-sugar foods, and foods with artificial coloring, as these clearly have no benefit to young bodies.

— **Minerals and Trace Elements:** A deficiency (or overabundance) of zinc, copper, magnesium, potassium, chromium, or manganese might also be the cause of LD. Hair analysis shows altered levels in some children, and treatment with controlled doses of these minerals may have a positive effect on them. Again, the scientific proof of such a theory is lacking, although advocates have amassed a body of case histories to support their evidence that such a therapy can be effective.

— Allergies: Like Feingold, William Crook found central nervous system flare-ups in some LD kids who consumed sensitive foods. His theory is that some children have hidden allergies that might cause such a reaction and interfere with their cognitive functioning. Such allergies are difficult to spot by traditional methods, but can cause fatigue, hyperkinesis, LD, anemia, abdominal pain, headaches, and frequent colds.

Allergy therapy looks for the culprit food (or class of foods) and eliminates it by trial diets (called elimination diets) that are in effect much like the K-P diet. Crook is also the proponent of the "yeast theory," which holds that the common yeastlike fungus *Candida albicans,* normally found in the body, can cause illness when an oversupply of it weakens the immune system. Another doctor, Orian Truss, first developed a yeast-free diet (garlic, acidophilus milk) and antifungal medication (the antibiotic nystatin or caprylic acid products) to combat the oversupply of *Candida albicans,* but Crook applied it to LD kids. Most professionals see no merit to Crook's theories, and they do seem farfetched, but again, there are parents who swear by the positive effects of allergy therapy and the yeast theory.

Environmental Approaches: Exposure to high concentrations of lead and mercury in the environment can cause learning problems, and cleansing the body of such toxins can alleviate the symptoms. However, they cannot reverse the damage to the brain done by lead poisoning, and the child who has suffered from such an environmental insult will need plenty of help in school as a result.

Megavitamins: The researcher Humphrey Osmond worked with schizophrenics in the 1960s and was successful in treating some of them with large doses of natural vitamins to restore their bodies' chemical balance. In 1971, Dr. Allan Cott theorized that LD was caused by the breakdown of certain chemicals normally found in the brain, a situation that could be treated in a fashion similar to Osmond's. In particular, Cott found that certain B vitamins, when administered in large quantities, could stop this breakdown and reverse the imbalance. Cott also examined the connection between hypoglycemia (low blood sugar) and LD. Taking the statistically higher incidence of hypoglycemia in the LD population, this theory holds that those low glucose levels affect the functioning of the central nervous system, and can be reversed by medical and dietary treatment to raise the levels. Cott's theory has come under fire because of the potential dangers of vitamin overdose, and because Cott has not yet proven to the satisfaction of other researchers the connection between LD and those chemical breakdowns that the megavitamins are intended to redress.

Biofeedback: Alpha waves are electrical brain waves that control our higher cognitive functions. There is a strong body of evidence to support the theory that people can learn (by simple concentration techniques and exercises) to recognize and manage the rate and quality of their alpha waves and thus improve their ability to concentrate and perform mental tasks. An interesting new theory holds that, by learning to control the brain's alpha waves, LD kids can significantly affect their mental alertness. While it is as yet unproven by rigorous scientific methods, it is a theory that bears watching, since it is a relatively easy skill for children to acquire.

Intervention: When to Stop

Does it ever end? Can we ever stop playing policeman and guard, cheerleader and advocate for our child? Some of those roles are essential to being parents, and no, they don't stop. But we can hope and possibly expect that our child will someday be able to function on his own. Even if not, he will certainly need a break, and a time to test his skills without intervention. We can comfortably assume it's time to take a break or finish remediating when our child

- has more successes than failures;
- can do most schoolwork alone;
- can live comfortably with his weaknesses.

We have experts to help us decide when that moment (or moments) comes. And we have constant legally mandated evaluations to determine how close or how far away that moment is.

But, in the final analysis, we can't trust test scores to make decisions for us. We have to trust our LD kids to be able to tell us and show us how far they've come. And we have to trust our own knowledge of our child's confidence and accomplishment. As Suzanne Stevens concludes, it's time to stop when the child is basically happy.

Of course, happiness is not exactly an objective criterion. According to the law, we and our LD kids should be happy if they are reading within two years of grade level. But many parents and educators feel that achieving grade level is not good enough. The psychologist Roger Saunders, past president of the Orton Society, says: "A child with intact senses and reasonably adequate cultural opportunities should be able to acquire academic skills on a level commensurate with his intelligence, not merely his chronologic age or grade level."

Many parents (and LD kids) would agree — good enough is not really good enough. But that may reflect our middle-class attitudes about achievement more than it reflects the final outcome of LD remediation. If a child is truly comfortable with finally being able to perform adequately at grade level (and why shouldn't he be, after all that struggle?), then he should be left alone to enjoy his success.

In the end, there is more unanimity among the various remedial approaches than one would expect. After all, they do all agree that the child needs to be enabled to function more competently and appropriately in our society (although there are some interesting theories that oppose this view — see the next chapter). The goal and process-oriented approaches are both grounded in the proper development or realignment of the child's basic perceptual functions. Even the proponents of most of the external remediations agree that the whole child must be treated in context rather than as an isolated set of symptoms. Everyone acknowledges that cognitive skills must be built up along with motor abilities, and nothing will work unless the child's self-esteem is as carefully cultivated as his ability to read.

This brings us right back to what we talked about in chapter 7 — if nothing else can be done for the LD child, he should be helped to understand that he is not stupid, not to blame, and not alone. Fortunately, this is the area in which we, as parents, can exercise the greatest power and have the greatest effect.

The researcher Doreen Kronick says it well:

> The home environment has the power to undermine or reduce the effectiveness of the external remedial program, or conversely, to bolster and enhance the remedial process. We parents can "set our child up" for a productive day in school, or destroy that which the school has achieved within minutes of his return home. We are also capable of weaving knowledge and problem-solving experiences into the pattern of our family lives. There has been insufficient acknowledgment that parents are powerful vehicles of change, that we may be the decisive factor in our child's ability to cope with the life process.

CHAPTER 9

What Does the Future Hold?

Question: "What are some of the good things about being LD?"

Answers: "I was one of the first people to be diagnosed as having an LD, nearly thirty years ago. With help, by the time I got to college, I was amazed at how much easier it was for me than for the kids who had just coasted along through high school on their natural abilities. It was because I had learned, at a very young age, how to work, and how to work *hard*." (Age 38)

"Sometimes the disadvantages lead to strengths. If you grow up not being a natural at things, being able to do them at all requires a finer understanding of the process than it does for someone to whom it comes easily. It can lead to the accumulation of an eclectic but interesting body of knowledge with a better view of the big picture." (Age 30)

"Sometimes I wish I could wear braces or have crutches so people could see that I'm hurting inside. But my LD doesn't show that way, and I guess that's good. Because once I get better at certain things, I'll be all right, just like everybody else." (Age 9)

"I think I have a bigger heart than my friends. Sometimes it hurts more, but I can understand them and I don't know if they can understand me the same way. I don't know if that's good or not, though." (Age 7)

SO where does this all leave us? We know a lot now about our child's LD, about the symptoms she exhibits, the possible causes for her problems, and the ways we can get help for her. We're still left with a difficult job, though. As parents of an LD kid, we, too, have to work harder at everything. We have constantly to remember that we are dealing with another human being, and not just a product of two sets of genes, two sets of dreams for the future.

It may be true that nobody ever told us parenting was going to be easy, but many of us may have expected it to be a little easier than this. So it's all right to feel overwhelmed at times by the size and duration of the task of raising and teaching an LD kid (not to mention doing everything else that we have to do with our lives), and to feel disillusioned by the minute increments of progress that are made.

And it's all right to continue doing whatever else it is that we do with our lives, and not to become consumed by the job. Parents are people, too, and we have more power as parents if we keep our parenting in perspective and maintain our other roles as much as possible. Our children will have better models and feel better about themselves if they see us living fruitful lives.

But we are our children's most powerful allies and advocates, and we must prepare ourselves to look out for their best interests. With the right information and the right attitude of positive determination, we can work wonders. And we can look forward to a future full of possibilities that, while they may not be those we dreamed of at our child's birth, nevertheless hold out the promise of a rich and happy life for our children and ourselves.

In this chapter, we'll look at the future of LD research and at the ongoing debate it still generates. We'll listen to some dissenting voices in the field and talk about the positive aspects of LD. Then, with a sense of the future as well as the past, we can assess our options as parents and feel comfortable about the choices we — and our LD kids — will make.

Early Intervention

Why am I including information on early intervention in a chapter on the future? Simply because I believe, as do a growing number of experts, that it is the best hope for the future of any LD child. While our own children may not benefit directly from it, early intervention is becoming more and more important as a means to find and treat the LD child most successfully, and a growing awareness of this powerful concept will certainly benefit all LD families.

If you go back to chapter 2, you can see that the lists of symptoms include many that can be detected at an early age — certainly before a child begins her formal schooling. New federal regulations extend the age at which children are eligible for free evaluation and intervention from three to twenty-one, and some states extend that farther, from birth to age twenty-six. Through community outreach programs, many states are training day-care workers and nursery teachers to detect high-risk children and have them screened. Pediatricians are paying closer attention to warning signs described by parents or observed through well-child checkups.

Dr. Heidelise Als, a developmental psychologist at Children's Hospital in Boston, is working with even younger children. Dr. Als is one of those experts who feel that forecasting is the future of the field, and her work with newborns has made some fascinating inroads in that direction. Studying the behavior of pre- and full-term infants, Als has found strong connections between the nature of the behaviors that they exhibit and the kinds of brain-function patterns that those behaviors imply. Even at five or six days of age, it is possible to draw conclusions about later patterns.

She uses an expanded form of several fairly typical newborn evaluation systems, but, instead of just looking at the types of behavior, such as the infant's ability to focus, to follow a moving object, or the response to sound or touch, she tries to evaluate at what cost to the nervous system such skills are performed. An infant who can perform the required tasks but is exhausted or stressed by doing so is scored differently from a child who performs easily or a child who has trouble with the tasks themselves.

And Als has found that performance on such tests is a good indicator of performance on tests administered to older children. The children who perform adequately but appear to be stressed by their performance are children who, at age three and even at age five, will be sensitive, easily disorganized, and easily overloaded. While Dr. Als is not saying that such children are automatically LD, the strong degree of predictability holds much promise for future work in the field of predicting problems like LD.

Another researcher, Dr. Joseph Fagan of Case Western Reserve University, has developed a predictive intelligence test that can be used on infants to determine the likelihood of their having an above- or below-average intelligence at ages three to six. There is some controversy over the use of such a test, which might lead educators to focus on the above-average children and ignore the greater needs of the below-average — and even the average — population. However, Fagan is not alone in believing that such tests will someday be valuable tools by which we can determine if a child is at risk, and do something to prevent the risk from being fulfilled.

But such tests are not yet in common use, nor are they likely to be in the near future. Dr. Als believes that parents are usually the first to notice such behavior, even when pediatricians and others insist that there is nothing wrong. They must have confidence in their instincts and insist on getting help in learning how to parent such a child before the child develops a crippling history of failure in school. Such skills do not come naturally or easily to us, just as the simplest skills do not come naturally to our children. Both parent and child need to learn how to build positive self-images, and by building our own confidence we will be building our child's as well.

Aside from the LD parent support networks mentioned earlier, there are a number of support groups and agencies devoted to helping parents of all infants and young children maximize their parenting skills so that raising a family is easier on them and more beneficial for their children. Organizations such as Parents Anonymous have local branches with groups that get together regularly to discuss parenting skills and problems. Many have hot-line numbers that parents can call for on-the-spot relief. (See Appendix A for a listing of major groups.) If you feel your needs are more specific because of your child's problems, don't hesitate to get in touch with your pediatrician and have her recommend a therapist or counselor who can help you out. There *are* things you can do to make it more manageable!

PARENTS have legal support for looking to early intervention as a source of assistance in raising their LD child. The 1986 amendments to PL 94-142 — known as 99-457 — specifically address the needs of very young children with handicaps (including possible learning disabilities). The U.S. Department of Education must now disseminate to all public schools and community programs information on early intervention programs for children from birth to age five. The law provides for special preschool grants, which mandate a broader spectrum of remedial service for three- to five-year-olds, and also make provisions for further research into the issues of early childhood.

Most important, an entire new section of the law (Part H) was developed specifically for handicapped infants and toddlers from birth to two years, and it provides for extensive family services in addition to direct services for the child. These services include family training, counseling, and home visits, special instruction, and annual reviews via a special IEP written for the family; it's called the Individual Family Service Plan. (Appendix A provides names of resources for more information.)

This is not an altogether altruistic move; the government has finally realized what special educators have known for years: that early intervention is actually cheaper in the long run. Such early intervention for both child and family, according to the law, will actually reduce the costs of eventual educational services once the child reaches school age.

As early as 1969, the National Advisory Committee on Dyslexia of the Department of Health, Education and Welfare had recognized the potential fiscal damage of LD.

Within the existing educational system across the nation, an estimated 15% of otherwise able students experience difficulty in learning. This difficulty is of sufficient severity to impair seriously

. . . their ultimate usefulness and adaptability to modern society. Among the underprivileged, the problem is even more pervasive. A student's initial failure in learning to read can have enormous consequences in terms of emotional maladjustment, tendency toward delinquency, likelihood of becoming a dropout and difficulty in obtaining employment. The economic loss to the nation as a result of these failures is incalculable.

Unfortunately, many of the children most in need of early intervention are not in programs where they can be screened, or not from homes where they are likely to be spotted. Cultural and ethnic biases often work against these children, making it difficult to distinguish the LD child from the child who simply cannot comprehend unfamiliar information. More work needs to be done in picking up such children at an early age, when they are most likely to benefit from help.

The law does not only look at the preschool side of the problem. Earlier may be better, but research has shown that it is never too late to intervene on behalf of the LD child — even after that child becomes an adult. PL 99-457 also covers postsecondary education programs for adults identified as LD.

We must acknowledge the limitations of such a law. We can't realistically deal with primary prevention of LD (that is, treating the problem before it begins) any more than we can "cure" it once it's established. But early intervention, in which we can target children who are likely to fail, is much more doable. And the growing number of adult literacy and adult LD support programs aimed at those who fell through the cracks a generation ago is encouraging, if only because it gives the adult LD sufferer a forum for regaining his or her self-esteem.

New Directions for Research

Aside from the work of Als and others in supporting the growing interest in early identification and intervention, there are other promising new directions in LD research that bode well for the future. Drs. Herbert Lubs and Karen Gross-Glenn, geneticists at the University of Miami Medical School, have done remarkable work isolating the precise gene that, they believe, causes the genetic predisposition to dyslexia in families. By using a painstaking method of trail and error in looking at marker genes in families with a proven history of dyslexia, they have determined that it's probably a gene on chromosome 15. "We're not there yet, but we're terribly close and getting closer all the time," says Dr. Lubs, and his information could have tremendous repercussions for the entire field of LD.

For one thing, it may someday allow us to predict at a very early age, and solely on the basis of genetic markers, which infants may be at risk for later learning problems. These children could be provided with an enriched environment to stimulate and strengthen areas of weakness before they even got to first grade.

In addition, since Dr. Lubs believes that we can correlate certain types of behavior with certain genetic configurations, we may be able to provide different types of remediation for children with different types of dyslexia, as indicated by the genetic pattern. Lubs's associate, Dr. Gross-Glenn, has already found significant differences, not only between the brain patterns of dyslexics and nondyslexics, but also among dyslexics.

The Quantitative Electrophysiological Battery (QB) developed at the Brain Research Laboratory of New York Medical College is another cutting-edge research tool. A painless brain-wave-emission measurement device, the QB can provide more accurate data about the nature of a child's LD than an entire battery of psychological tests. Someday it may be possible for us to get a complete picture of our brain's physiological health as simply as we now get a blood-pressure reading.

All of this is very promising for both identification and remediation. So is the ongoing work of researchers like Albert Galaburda, who is also getting closer and closer to finding genetic markers for the source of variations in brain architecture that cause learning disabilities, among other things. "We have to find as many biological markers as we can," he says, "and then correlate them with all our empirical research on the behavioral indices of LD. It's a long story, still being written. But, even as we are struggling to establish these essential links between brain and behavior, we are disclosing the beauty of the human system."

Mel Levine's elegant research into attentional deficit disorders has led to a far more precise and revealing classification system, which will lead to more accurate diagnoses and interventions. But Levine, like so many other current researchers, recognizes that, in spite of the inroads being made in identification, the value of children's differences must not be ignored. "I hope that adults who find themselves immersed in the lives of struggling children will accept and respect developmental variations, trying to change only what must be changed, and recognizing that, in dealing with such children, we ourselves intrude upon the pages of a biography of a new generation."

Other aspects of current LD research focus on emphasizing the strengths of children with differences along with remediating their weaknesses. Therapies that construct a curriculum around a child's particular learning style, which draw on an LD kid's creative abilities, which work with whole families rather than just the LD child, and which recognize that there is no such thing as an isolated learning problem are gaining credence and popularity. But they are by no means the norm for intervention. And the field is still under fire, not only from those who feel it is a waste of time and money to concentrate so many resources on "lazy" kids, but also from within the field itself.

Dissenting Voices

The future of LD research is bright. But so is the future of the debate on the subject. Is it fair to remediate the child and not the system? Can we define a problem merely by its deviation from the norm? Is there such a thing as LD? Many experts would argue that there is not, that all the current theories are a lame attempt to fix something that is merely believed to be defective, not necessarily so. It's like the old fallacy of arguing backward from the evidence: just because there's a body doesn't mean there was a murder. Let's look at the current debates regarding the definitions, limitations, and cultural questions surrounding the concept and treatment of LD.

The first question is the most basic one: Is there such a thing as LD? Gerald Coles, author of the controversial book *The Learning Mystique,* argues that there is not. He proposes instead "an alternative theory of learning disabilities that attempts to understand them within the context of the child's social life. It is society which must change, not the child who just happens to have differences in his intellectual abilities and predilections." This ties in with Howard Gardner's alternative types of intelligence (see chapter 3). But, while Gardner points no fingers and concentrates on examining those differences, Coles lays the blame squarely at the feet of the family and the society.

He begins with the family, looking closely at the nature of family interactions as a cause of LD: "Numerous combinations of both subtle and overt mediations, interactions and activities will be found that adversely affect the child's cognitive development and strongly contribute to the creation of LDs. Parents play a major role, and the child is an active participant." Then he goes on to look toward broader social influences that shape this kind of family.

Coles does not dismiss biological functioning as unimportant, but suggests that LD develops, not within the individual, but from his or her unsatisfactory interaction with society. Broad social, economic, political, and cultural influences, he believes, are fundamental to the creation of and prevention of LD. He argues against the current methods of identifying LD kids, because he feels that tests designed to measure neurological impairment assume impairment before they are even administered. The theory itself — that LD has a neurological cause — has disabled the research.

Another researcher, Doreen Kronick, has also looked at family interaction and parenting styles as a source of LD, blaming the vicious cycle created by missed connections and unfulfilled demands made by both parent and child. But neither theory explains why one child in a family is LD and others are not, or why LD runs in families from generation to generation without regard for social or economic status and the dilution of family styles through marriage.

Coles believes that it does no good to ameliorate the problem without demanding any structural changes in society, and advocates sweeping changes in our school systems, not just in LD classrooms. He feels that current efforts at remediation are addressing only the product, not the process that led to the product. This is a radical and disturbing view for parents, but not without validity, although there is little practical value in advocating a major social reconstruction when we are struggling with such small steps.

Other researchers advocate similar views: Barry M. Franklin warns against the lack of warranted scientific evidence to support LD as a handicapping condition. LD, he believes, is an emotionally laden concept rather than a scientific construct — children suffer from an externally applied standard rather than from an internal dysfunction. "The source of the problem is not a defect in these children. On the contrary, it is because they are unable to meet the demands of schools for behavioral conformity." All our current theories can be traced back to Werner and Strauss, who concentrated on brain-damaged patients, not intelligent children. Franklin says we need to replace those antiquated studies with more updated theories and provide more adequate foundations for study.

Likewise, Allan Buss contends that LD research is not a body of objective knowledge but an ideology that reflects current attitudes of society. Differential psychology — the study of individual differences — is an emerging field that may offer more help and answers in the future.

Some researchers eschew societal explanations and look at the definition of LD itself as the source of concern: Patricia Myers and Donald Hammill argue that the definition of LD in PL 94-142 is inherently wrong. The concepts of "basic psychological processes," "perceptual handicap," and "minimal brain damage" are totally ambiguous, and other phrases in the definition equally misleading. In addition, Myers and Hammill argue that 94-142 never identifies whether learning disabilities are a primary or a secondary handicap, and that the definition that results when one removes all the ambiguities could easily include "all children with all problems."

Some researchers say that the problem lies with the term itself. Anne Bennison charges that the phrase *learning disability,* like the turn-of-the-century phrase *feebleminded,* is used to control deviancy and assume biological determinism. And James Carrier says that the current definitions reflect nothing more than changing social attitudes. In the 1960s, the negative term *brain-injured* absolved adults of responsibility, whereas the more aggressive 1970s spawned the term *LD,* which is hopeful and accentuates a positive image of the child who suffers from it. In any case, says Carrier, neither is based on sound scientific evidence, but both have been shaped by prevailing social and political forces.

Some dissenting voices look at our educational system as the villain. Christine Sleeter argues that "all this controversy is beside the point. What really and only concerns schools is whether the kid is underachieving in reading and writing, because students who don't are a bother." Ball and Werner say that LD classrooms exacerbate the problem because they are run exactly like the regular classrooms in which LD kids have failed. They use standardized procedures, predetermined goals, and a competitive environment — a bureaucratic approach guaranteed to produce failures.

Furthermore, argues Pugach, special education only increases an LD kid's isolation, accentuating her differences. And Alan Ross, perhaps the best-known voice in the field, argues eloquently that we infer LD from any child's learning difficulty, regardless of cause. "What about blaming the teaching method? If I taught you how to drive a car by showing you how to saddle a horse, who would be to blame for your inability to drive a car properly?"

The researcher Russell Snyder has the most radical approach of all. In an article entitled "The Right NOT to Read," he argues that skill in reading is desirable, but its importance may be overemphasized by schools. Reading skills are determined relatively, not absolutely, he says, and thus relatively poor readers will always exist. Time will heal many poor reading problems, and besides, most poor readers read well enough. Like Pugach, Snyder believes that some remediation techniques may be more traumatic than not reading itself, and defends "the right not to read. Although reading should be encouraged, it should not be insisted upon."

In many cases, say the dissenters, LD is simply defined by what it's not, and that's a valid criticism. Even more important is the point that any definition of LD will suffer when subjected to cross-cultural or economic scrutiny. Ross (and many others) believes that there is a cultural bias built into the identification system. That is, children who are identified as LD are all too often only those who are in a position to be screened — they're more likely to be middle-class, white, with educated parents.

Why are the disadvantaged left out of the definition in PL 94–142? So they can be put in less demanding programs because their parents demand less for them or their schools care less about their performance? Is it because their cultural and economic limitations are more important than the educational limitations that they cause? Is the only LD child one who has no other problems but LD? If that were the case, how many children would qualify?

More likely, the exclusion of the economically, socially, or culturally disadvantaged from the legally accepted definition is a means of further excluding them from the system, despite the broad protections of the law. Go elsewhere for help, these children are told; we don't want you here.

Research has made it clear that, regardless of label being used, similarities in dyslexics cut across boundaries of language and culture. All have a difficulty in mastering the skills their culture expects of them in their mother tongue. It is our responsibility to see that all LD children are given the opportunity for a "free, appropriate education," regardless of their background. We would expect no less for any child.

A Gentler View

All of this can be somewhat disturbing to parents who have worked so hard to come to terms with a child's difficulty. It's very hard for us to hear that there is no such thing as LD, or that society is — or we ourselves are — a contributing factor. Certainly we have to face our own limitations as parents, and work hard to redirect our parenting skills to meet the special needs of our LD child. But there is little sense in casting blame, and no sense at all for us to spend our limited energy in looking backward. While the dissenting voices raise legitimate concerns for the field cf LD research, we must maintain a much more practical stance. Examining the possible causes of LD is a fascinating pursuit, but it doesn't do much for our kids. And what we want to do is look forward, and move forward, and prepare for the future with them.

When I think about my daughter's LD, I like to think about Marcel Kinsbourne's views on the subject, because they seem to put everything in a gentler, but much more realistic, perspective: "A deficit in math or reading doesn't differ in principle from an inability to carry a tune. The only difference is practical — no one cares greatly about humming a tune, and reading is one of those areas in which society insists that children do well."

This concept fits in quite well with Howard Gardner's idea that there are many different kinds of intelligence, and that our LD kids are measurably superior in areas that do not require the kinds of logical and linguistic skills known as "IQ." The LD is also the creative child, and often the gifted child. That may make her harder to teach, and harder to parent, and it certainly makes life more difficult for her, but there are definite advantages, although they may not appear obvious now.

Says Richard Masland, "You can't have it both ways — the development of superior language skills is at the expense of other skills. A reversed or non-dominant pattern in the brain may cause an increase in creativity, imagination, and adaptive skills — which would explain why so many dyslexics enjoy such a remarkable degree of mastery over their difficulties."

If we accept the premise that there are other important things besides reading well, and that our LD kids are special in some ways, we can begin to look for other proficiencies to emphasize. Let's look at Priscilla Vail's list of the strengths of LD kids again and see if we can recognize our children in some of them:

- rapid grasp of concepts
- awareness of patterns
- energy
- curiosity
- concentration on applied tasks
- exceptional memory for certain details
- empathy
- vulnerability/openness
- heightened perceptions
- divergent thinking

How can we help our child apply these strengths to make up for her weaknesses? It takes some doing, and there will be a lot of trial and error, but we must remain confident that there are areas in which our children can succeed and excel. The future for our

LD kids may lie in their ability to acknowledge and make the most of these very real gifts. Just look at Einstein, who didn't speak until he was three, and who failed math.

This doesn't mean that we're going to abandon rigorous efforts to help our children succeed in the real world. There is no question that a practical education (including reading, writing, basic calculation skills, and organized thinking skills) is essential for functioning in modern society. Regardless of other gifts, all children must learn these basic skills. But there are also computers for poor spellers, calculators for poor mathematicians, and methods of self-management to help the poorly organized.

"Unlike some other exceptionalities," says Doreen Kronick, "the prognosis for LD is favorable. Once LD persons have completed their schooling, they have often left behind them the most formidable demands of the life process. One can successfully pursue some of the most sophisticated vocations, professions, and social lives without having to face chemistry, physics, algebra, geometry, foreign languages or sports. Adults are not expected to write neatly and can avoid most spelling demands. They have far greater leeway in choosing their vocational and recreational lifestyles than do children and adolescents, and, by avoiding their deficits and maximizing their strengths, they may well be able to 'cross over' from disabled to intact.

"If the LD adult is literate, has a grasp of basic mathematics, is flexible, somewhat organized, and has some degree of interactional effectiveness, he is no longer disabled in terms of his ability to meet cultural expectations. Therefore, parents can anticipate a hopeful outcome, which should facilitate emotional adjustment."

There is also a degree of benefit to be gained from the stress itself of being LD. The college graduate quoted at the beginning of this chapter is a perfect example. Children who struggle with LD often become more self-reliant at an earlier age, are better able to express their feelings, are able to turn to others for support, and are more aware of processes (thinking, decision-making). They also understand the importance of a sense of humor, are far more tolerant of others' weaknesses, more empathic, and more independent. They've learned the meaning of real work, and they often grow up to have an understanding of the vagaries of the real world far beyond that of other people their age.

In short, our LD kids end up being pretty spectacular people. We have to try to remember this during the hard times, and maintain our perspective — and help our children maintain theirs. As my daughter says to me whenever things get rough with her schoolwork: "Only nine more years and I won't have to worry about this ever again!"

Parent Power

What does all this mean about our future? Certainly our job as parents of LD kids is far from over. Sometimes it may feel as if it will never be over. But we can look forward to an increasing sense of strength and power if we continue to focus on the choices we and our children have, rather than on the limitations.

We can be more effective if we reach out to other parents who may be in the same position. Naturally, we can get a tremendous amount of support from these parent networks. We can find

- acceptance, friendship, compassion;
- new approaches to solving problems;
- practical ideas for working with children;
- an awareness of common needs and strengths;
- greater self-understanding and insight;
- reactions and advice;
- opportunities to express emotions;
- less isolation.

But, perhaps even more important, we have a social responsibility to reach out to the parents of other LD children who might not have the wherewithal to get as far as we have come — who may still be struggling to understand their child, or who may have stopped struggling. Parent action groups and advocacy agencies are making an effort at community outreach, but they all agree that the most important outreach is word of mouth.

I'm not talking about conducting your own LD kid search — you don't have the credentials. But, as organized parents, you can see that your school is keeping tabs on low-performance children and not just writing them off. Make sure that explanatory information is easily available, in several languages. Speak up at parent-teacher meetings. Publicize your support group.

Involvement can even be more active. Some parent-operated programs can fill in the gaps in the spectrum of services provided to children and parents, be catalysts for improved services. Parents are invaluable information resources. A number of newsletters published by national parent networks are listed in the Bibliography. Find the one closest to you and get in touch.

We can also work more effectively from a position of confidence, knowing that we do make a difference, and that the difference, while it may be difficult to perceive, is measurable and real. In building our confidence, we will of course be building our child's self-esteem as well. Bill Mitchell, who works for the Association for Retarded Citizens, puts it beautifully: "The importance of receiving the message that those who care about you have faith in your ability, not only to succeed, but to survive failure, cannot be overstated. To know that failure is a normal part of life, and that people will still care for you and believe in you can encourage you to get up and try again. Another effect is a sense of feeling more in control of your own destiny."

There are obstacles that we can work on overcoming to increase our effectiveness in building this sense of confidence. We must guard against overprotecting our LD kids so that they do not learn how to function as independent people. We must guard against expectations that are unnaturally low or high, and we must foster a stable support system to give our kids a sense of belonging and a feeling of security. Since they are possessors of unique gifts as well as limitations, we must help them to feel more comfortable in taking risks, to be able to assess their own strengths against no other measure than themselves.

It takes time, and nothing will change overnight. But the concept of the family as the crucible of values — the repository of moral and social training and the safe-deposit vault for a child's self-esteem — cannot be overstated. That, more than anything else, is our mandate for the future.

We can accomplish this by helping our child achieve self-determination. Bud Fredericks lists some ways we can do it:

1. Treat your child as a capable human being and support efforts to explore, take healthy risks, try new situations.
2. Provide opportunities for self-awareness by focusing on strengths and special qualities

3. Let your child know you enjoy spending time with him.

4. Share family stories and traditions to strengthen a sense of family and permanent place in the larger scheme of things.

5. Provide opportunities to help your child with social confidence.

6. Acknowledge efforts towards a goal, not just final product.

7. Help your child experience success by building on strengths.

8. Have realistic expectations.

9. Let your child take responsibility for his or her actions.

Our Future: Hopes and Expectations

So, what does the future hold for us and our LD child? On the national scene, certainly we can hope for and expect new information about the causes and treatments. We can expect new longitudinal studies about the effectiveness of various interventions, giving us new insights into the long-range effects of LD. We can look for more concentrated efforts to be made in early remediation and postsecondary follow-through, and welcome a new emphasis on whole family intervention rather than just treating the LD child. We can hope that more research will lead to more funding and to the expanded availability of programs.

And what about on a personal level? What can we see for our kids? We hope that the future will bring a much broader acceptance of alternative definitions of intelligence, providing our kids with more opportunities to shine as we know they can. We can hope for a greater emphasis on the strengths of LD kids, on their abilities to contribute to society in ways that those of us who are not LD cannot begin to imagine. And, on a very practical level, perhaps we can see a future in which our LD kids will be well-adjusted and fully functioning adults, pursuing their chosen careers with clarity and confidence. Quite simply, we hope, like parents of all children, that they will be happy. And, with our help, they probably will be.

National and Local Resources

(The names, addresses, and telephone numbers in this Appendix are up-to-date as the book goes to press.)

I. National Special Needs and Advocacy Organizations

Association for Children with
  Learning Disabilities (national
  HQ)
4156 Library Rd.
Pittsburgh, PA 15234
(412) 341-1515

Center for Law and Education
236 Massachusetts Ave. NE
Suite 504
Washington, DC 20002
(202) 546-5300

Children's Defense Fund
122 C St. NW
Washington, DC 20001
(202) 628-8787

Children's Foundation
1028 Connecticut Ave. NW
Washington, DC 20036

Closer Look/Parents' Campaign
  for Handicapped Children and
  Youth
1201 Sixteenth St. NW
Washington, DC 20036
(202) 833-4160
(202) 822-7900

Council for Exceptional
  Children
1920 Association Dr.
Reston, VA 22091
(703) 620-3660

Council for Learning Disabilities
P.O. Box 40303
Overland Park, KS 66204
(913) 492-8755

Disability Rights Education and
  Defense Fund
2032 San Pablo Ave.
Berkeley, CA 94702
(415) 644-2555

Federation for Children with
  Special Needs (National
  Network of Parents)
312 Stuart St.
Boston, MA 02116
(617) 482-2915

Foundation for Children with
  Learning Disabilities (National
  Foundation for Learning
  Disabilities)
99 Park Ave.
New York, NY 10016

Mental Health Law Project
2021 L St. NW
Eighth Floor
Washington, DC 20036
(202) 467-5730

National Association for the
Education of Young Children
1834 Connecticut Ave. NW
Washington, DC 20009

National Coalition of Advocates
for Students
76 Summer St.
Boston, MA 02110
(617) 357-8507

National Committee for Citizens
in Education
10840 Little Patuxent Pkwy.,
Suite 301
Columbia, MD 21044
(301) 997-9300

National Head Start Association
1029 31st St. NW
Washington, DC 20007
(202) 337-6650

National Information Center for
Handicapped Children
and Youth
P.O. Box 1492
Washington, DC 20013
or
1555 North Wilson Blvd.,
Suite 508
Rosslyn, VA 22209

Orton Dyslexia Society (national
HQ)
724 York Rd.
Baltimore, MD 21204
(301) 296-0232

U.S. Department of Education,
Office for Civil Rights (OCR)
400 Maryland Ave. SW
Room 5000, Switzer Bldg.
Washington, DC 20202

U.S. Department of Education,
Office of Special Education
and Rehabilitative Services
330 C St. SW
Room 3006
Washington, DC 20202

II. General Parenting Support and Information Agencies

American Academy of Child
and Adolescent Psychiatrists
3615 Wisconsin Ave. NW
Washington, DC 20016
(202) 966-7300
(3,300 child psychiatrists and 19
advocacy organizations that
legislate for the handicapped)

Center for Parent Education
55 Chapel St.
Newton, MA 02160
(617) 964-2442

Center for Parenting Studies
Wheelock College
200 The Riverway
Boston, MA 02215
(617) 734-5200

Child Welfare League of America
440 First St. NW
Washington, DC 20001
New York: (212) 254-7410
DC: (202) 638-2952
(400 affiliated child welfare
agencies; for families, too)

Families Anonymous
P.O. Box 528
Van Nuys, CA 91408
(818) 989-7841
(307 chapters to help families
   with problem kids)

Family Service America
44 East 23rd St.
New York, NY 10010
(212) 674-6100
(provides family services,
   advocacy and referrals)

Other FSA Regional Offices:
14 Jackson Blvd.
Chicago, IL 60604
(312) 922-4748, 4749

1100 Navaho Dr.
Raleigh, NC 29609
(919) 878-9203

445 30th St.
Oakland, CA 94609
(415) 836-2448

Governmental Affairs Office
1346 Connecticut Ave. NW
Washington, DC 20036
(202) 822-8390

National Congress of Parents
   and Teachers
700 N. Rush St.
Chicago, IL 60611
(312) 787-0977
(8 regional offices, 52 state
   groups, and 26,000 local
   PTA/PTOs)

National Parent Center
   (National Coalition of Title I/
   Chapter I Parents)
1314 14th St. NW, Suite 6
Washington, DC 20005
(202) 483-8822
(9 regional groups working for
   total community participation
   in the education of the
   disadvantaged)

National Partnership for Parents'
   Choice (Institute for
   Responsive Education)
605 Commonwealth Ave.
Boston, MA 02215
(617) 353-3309
(citizen's participation in
   education — resource
   directory)

Parents Anonymous (stress
   hotline)
6733 South Sepulveda, Suite 270
Los Angeles, CA 90045
(800) 421-0353

Parents' Rights Organization
12571 Northwinds Dr.
St. Louis, MO 63146
(314) 434-4171
(alternatives to public school
   programs)

Stepfamily Association
   of America
602 E. Joppa Rd.
Baltimore, MD 21204

Toughlove
P.O. Box 1069
Doylestown, PA 18901
(215) 348-7090

(200 local parent support groups
focusing on minimal standards
for acceptable behavior from
children)

III. Regional Offices, Department of Education: Offices for Civil Rights

Region I (CT, ME, MA, NH, RI, VT)

Dept. of Education — OCR
John W. McCormack Bldg.
Post Office Square, Room 222
Boston, MA 02109
(617) 223-9662

Region II (NJ, NY, PR, VI)

Dept. of Education — OCR
26 Federal Plaza, 33rd Floor
New York, NY 10278
(212) 264-4633

Region III (DE, DC, MD, PA, VA, WV)

Dept. of Eduction — OCR
Gateway Bldg.
3535 Market St., Room 6300
Philadelphia, PA 19104-3326
(215) 596-6791

Region IV (AL, FL, GA, KY, MS, NC, SC, TN)

Dept. of Education — OCR
101 Marietta Tower, 27th Floor
P.O. Box 1705
Atlanta, GA 30301
(404) 331-2959

Region V (IL, IN, MI, MN, OH, WI)

Dept. of Education — OCR
401 S. State St., 7th Floor
Chicago, IL 60605
(312) 353-2520

Region VI (AR, LA, NM, OK, TX)

Dept. of Education — OCR
1200 Main Tower Bldg., Suite
2260
Dallas, TX 75202
(214) 767-3936

Region VII (IA, KS, MO, NE)

Dept. of Education — OCR
10220 N. Executive Hills Blvd.,
8th Floor
Kansas City, MO 64190-1381
(816) 891-8026

Region VIII (CO, MT, ND, SD, UT, WY)

Dept. of Education — OCR
Federal Office Bldg.
1961 Stout St., Room 342
Denver, CO 80294
(303) 844-5695

Region IX (AZ, CA, HI, NV, American Samoa, Guam, Marianas)

Dept. of Education — OCR
50 United Nations Plaza
San Francisco, CA 94102
(obtain phone number from
   Directory Assistance)

Region X (AK, ID, OR, WA)

Dept. of Education — OCR
Mail Code 10-9010
915 Second Ave.
Seattle, WA 98173-1099
(206) 442-6811

IV. State-by-State Listing of Organizations Serving LD Children and Their Families

Includes separate state offices for
(1) Protection and Advocacy Services
(2) Special Education
(3) The Orton Society (*note:* listed only by branch and community. Anyone wishing to reach a specific branch should call the Orton Society at its international headquarters. The toll-free number is 1-800-222-3123.)
(4) Association for Children with Learning Disabilities (ACLD)

ALABAMA

(1) Protection and Advocacy

Alabama Disabilities Advocacy
   Program
University of Alabama
P.O. Box 870395
Tuscaloosa, AL 35487-0395
(205) 384-4928

(2) State Office for Special Education

Student Instructional Services
Dept. of Education
1020 Monticello Ct.
Montgomery, AL 36117-1901
(205) 261-5099

(4) ACLD

P.O. Box 11588
Montgomery, AL 36111
(205) 277-9151

ALASKA

(1) Protection and Advocacy

Advocacy Services of Alaska
325 E. 3rd Ave., 2nd Floor
Anchorage, AK 99501
(907) 274-3658

(2) State Office for Special Education

Special Services, Dept. of
   Education
P.O. Box F
Juneau, AK 99811
(907) 465-2970

(4) ACLD

3823 Lunar Dr.
Anchorage, AK 99504
(907) 786-1771

ARIZONA

(1) Protection and Advocacy

Arizona Center for Law in the
    Public Interest
363 N. First Ave., Suite 100
Phoenix, AZ 85003
(602) 252-4904

*(2) State Office for Special
Education*

Special Education Section
Dept. of Education
1535 W. Jefferson
Phoenix, AZ 85007-3280
(602) 255-3183

(4) ACLD

P.O. Box 15525
Phoenix, AZ 85060
(602) 949-7112

ARKANSAS

(1) Protection and Advocacy

Advocacy Services, Inc.
1120 Marshall St., Suite 311
Little Rock, AR 72202
(501) 371-2171

*(2) State Office for Special
Education*

Dept. of Education
Education Bldg., Room 105-C
#4 Capitol Mall
Little Rock, AR 72201
(501) 682-4221

(4) ACLD

P.O. Box 7316
Little Rock, AR 72217
(501) 666-8777

CALIFORNIA

(1) Protection and Advocacy

California Protection and
    Advocacy, Inc.
100 Howe St., Suite 185N
Sacramento, CA 95825
(916) 488-9950
(800) 952-5746 (in CA)

*(2) State Office for Special
Education*

Special Education Division,
    Dept. of Education
P.O. Box 944272
Sacramento, CA 94244-2720
(916) 323-4768

*(3) The Orton Society Branch
Offices*

California Tri-County Branch
Santa Barbara

Central California Branch
Monterey

Inland Empire Branch
Riverside

Los Angeles County Branch
Woodland Hills

Northern California Branch
Palo Alto

Orange County Branch
Costa Mesa

San Diego Branch
San Diego

(4) ACLD

17 Buena Vista Ave.
Mill Valley, CA 94941
(415) 383-5242

COLORADO

(1) Protection and Advocacy

The Legal Center
455 Sherman St., Suite 130
Denver, CO 80203
(303) 722-0300

*(2) State Office for Special
Education*

Special Education Services Unit
Dept. of Education
201 E. Colfax Ave.
Denver, CO 80203
(303) 866-6694

*(3) The Orton Society Branch
Office*

Colorado Branch
Avon

(4) ACLD

P.O. Box 32188
Aurora, CO 80041
(303) 740-9638

CONNECTICUT

(1) Protection and Advocacy

Office of Protection and
  Advocacy for the
  Handicapped and DD
90 Washington St., Lower Level
Hartford, CT 06106
(203) 566-7616
(800) 842-7303 (in CT)

*(2) State Office for Special
Education*

Bureau of Special Education and
  Pupil Personnel Services
Dept. of Education
25 Industrial Park Rd.
Middletown, CT 06457
(203) 638-4265

*(3) The Orton Society Branch
Office*

New England Branch
Northfield, MA

(4) ACLD

139 Main Street
W. Hartford, CT 06107
(203) 236-3953

DELAWARE

(1) Protection and Advocacy

Disabilities Law Program
144 E. Market St.
Georgetown, DE 19947
(302) 856-0038

*(2) State Office for Special
Education*

Exceptional Children/Special
   Programs Division
Dept. of Public Instruction
P.O. Box 1402
Dover, DE 19903
(302) 736-5471

(4) ACLD

117 E. Sutton Pl.
Wilmington, DE 19810
(302) 994-0707

DISTRICT OF COLUMBIA

(1) Protection and Advocacy

Information Protection and
   Advocacy Center for
   Handicapped Individuals, Inc.
300 I St., NE, Suite 202
Washington, DC 20002
(202) 547-8081

*(2) State Office for Special
Education*

Division of Special Education
DC Public Schools
Tenth and H Sts., NW
Washington, DC 20001
(202) 724-4018

*(3) The Orton Society Branch
Office*

D.C. Capitol Branch
McLean, VA

(4) ACLD

P.O. Box 6350
Washington, DC 20015

FLORIDA

(1) Protection and Advocacy

Advocacy Center for Persons
   with Disabilities
2661 Executive Center Circle,
   W.
Clifton Bldg., Suite 209
Tallahassee, FL 32301
(904) 488-9070

*(2) State Office for Special
Education*

Bureau of Education for
   Exceptional Students
Dept. of Education
Knott Bldg.
Tallahassee, FL 32399
(904) 488-1570

*(3) The Orton Society Branch
Office*

Florida Branch
Tampa

(4) ACLD

331 E. Henry St.
Punta Gorda, FL 33950
(813) 637-8957

GEORGIA

(1) Protection and Advocacy

Georgia Advocacy Office, Inc.
1708 Peachtree St., NW, Suite
   505
Atlanta, GA 30309
(404) 885-1234
(800) 537-2329

*(2) State Office for Special
Education*

Division of Exceptional Students
Dept. of Education
1970 Twin Towers East
205 Butler St.
Atlanta, GA 30334-1601
(404) 656-2425

(4) ACLD

P.O. Box 29492
Atlanta, GA 30359
(404) 633-1326

HAWAII

(1) Protection and Advocacy

Protection and Advocacy
   Agency
1580 Makaloa St., Suite 1060
Honolulu, HI 96814
(808) 949-2922

*(2) State Office for Special
Education*

Special Education Section
Dept. of Education
3430 Leahi Ave.
Honolulu, HI 96815
(808) 737-3720

*(3) The Orton Society Branch
Office*

Hawaii Branch
Kailua

(4) ACLD

200 N. Vineyard Blvd., Suite
   402
Honolulu, HI 96817
(808) 536-9684

IDAHO

(1) Protection and Advocacy

Idaho's Coalition of Advocates
   for the Disabled, Inc.
1409 W. Washington St.
Boise, ID 83702
(208) 336-5353

*(2) State Office for Special
Education*

Special Education Section
Dept. of Education
650 W. State St.
Boise, ID 83720-0001
(208) 334-3940

*(3) The Orton Society Branch
Office*

Puget Sound Branch
Seattle, WA

ILLINOIS

(1) Protection and Advocacy

Protection and Advocacy, Inc.
175 W. Jackson, Suite A-2103
Chicago, IL 60604
(312) 341-0022

(2) State Office for Special Education

Special Education
State Board of Education
Mail Code E-216
100 N. First St.
Springfield, IL 62777-0001
(217) 782-6601

(3) The Orton Society Branch Office

Illinois Branch
Lake Forest

(4) ACLD

P.O. Box A-3239
Chicago, IL 60690
(312) 663-9535

INDIANA

(1) Protection and Advocacy

Indiana Advocacy Services
850 N. Meridian St., Suite 2C
Indianapolis, IN 46204
(317) 232-1150
(800) 622-4845 (in IN)

(2) State Office for Special Education

Division of Special Education
Dept. of Education
Room 229 State House
Indianapolis, IN 46204
(317) 269-9462

(3) The Orton Society Branch Office

Indiana Branch
Indianapolis

(4) ACLD

1604 Cranbrook Rd.
Kokomo, IN 46902
(317) 452-9897

IOWA

(1) Protection and Advocacy

Iowa Protection and Advocacy
  Services, Inc.
3015 Merle Hay Rd., Suite 6
Des Moines, IA 50310
(515) 278-2502

(2) State Office for Special Education

Division of Special Education
Dept. of Public Instruction
Grimes State Office Bldg.
Des Moines, IA 50319-0146
(515) 281-3176

(3) The Orton Society Branch Office

Iowa Branch
Mt. Auburn

(4) ACLD

2819 48th St.
Des Moines, IA 50310
(515) 277-4266

KANSAS

(1) Protection and Advocacy

Kansas Advocacy and Protection
  Services
513 Leavenworth St., Suite 2
Manhattan, KS 66502
(913) 776-1541
(800) 432-8276

*(2) State Office for Special
Education*

Special Education Division
Dept. of Education
120 E. Tenth St.
Topeka, KS 66612
(913) 296-4945

(4) ACLD

P.O. Box 4424
Topeka, KS 66604

KENTUCKY

(1) Protection and Advocacy

Office for Public Advocacy
1264 Louisville Rd.
Frankfort, KY 40601
(502) 564-2967
(800) 372-2988 (in KY)

*(2) State Office for Special
Education*

Office of Education for
  Exceptional Children
Dept. of Education
Capitol Plaza Tower, Room 820
Frankfort, KY 40601
(502) 564-4970

(4) ACLD

2233 Alta Ave.
Louisville, KY 40205
(502) 451-8011

LOUISIANA

(1) Protection and Advocacy

Advocacy Center for the Elderly
  and Disabled
210 O'Keefe, Suite 700
New Orleans, LA 70112
(504) 522-2337
(800) 662-7705 (in LA)

*(2) State Office for Special
Education*

Special Educational Services
Dept. of Education
P.O. Box 94064, 9th Floor
Baton Rouge, LA 70804-9064
(504) 342-3633

*(3) The Orton Society Branch
Office*

Louisiana Branch
Baton Rouge

(4) ACLD

500 Pine Lake Dr.
Pineville, LA 71360
(318) 442-1034

261

MAINE

(1) Protection and Advocacy

Maine Advocacy Services
One Grand View Pl., Suite 1
P.O. Box 445
Winthrop, ME 04364
(207) 377-6202
(800) 452-1948 (in ME)

*(2) State Office for Special
Education*

Division of Special Education
Dept. of Education and Cultural
 Services
State House Station 23
Augusta, ME 04333
(207) 289-5953

*(3) The Orton Society Branch
Office*

New England Branch
Northfield, MA

(4) ACLD

P.O. Box 394
Topsham, ME 04086

MARYLAND

(1) Protection and Advocacy

Maryland Disability Law Center
2510 St. Paul St.
Baltimore, MD 21218
(301) 333-7600

*(2) State Office for Special
Education*

Division of Special Education
Dept. of Education
200 W. Baltimore St.
Baltimore, MD 21201-2595
(301) 333-2400

*(3) The Orton Society Branch
Office*

Maryland Branch
Baltimore

(4) ACLD

320 Maryland National Bank
 Bldg.
Baltimore, MD 21202

MASSACHUSETTS

(1) Protection and Advocacy

DD Law Center for
 Massachusetts
11 Beacon St., Suite 925
Boston, MA 02108
(617) 723-8455

*(2) State Office for Special
Education*

Division of Special Education
Dept. of Education
1385 Hancock St., 3rd Floor
Quincy, MA 02169-5183
(617) 770-7468

*(3) The Orton Society Branch
Office*

New England Branch
Northfield

(4) ACLD

Field School
99 School St., Room 23
Weston, MA 02193
(508) 891-5009

MICHIGAN

(1) Protection and Advocacy

Michigan Protection and
 Advocacy Service
109 W. Michigan Ave., Suite 900
Lansing, MI 48933
(517) 487-1755

*(2) State Office for Special
Education*

Special Education Services
Dept. of Education
P.O. Box 30008
Lansing, MI 48909-7508
(517) 373-9433

*(3) The Orton Society Branch
Office*

Michigan Branch
Kalamazoo

(4) ACLD

20777 Randall
Farmington Hills, MI 48024
(313) 471-0790

MINNESOTA

(1) Protection and Advocacy

Legal Aid Society of
 Minneapolis
222 Grain Exchange Bldg.
323 Fourth Ave. South
Minneapolis, MN 55415
(612) 332-7301

*(2) State Office for Special
Education*

Special Education Section
Dept. of Education
812 Capitol Square Bldg.
550 Cedar St.
St. Paul, MN 55101-2233
(612) 296-1793

*(3) The Orton Society Branch
Office*

Upper Midwest Branch
St. Paul

(4) ACLD

1821 University Ave., Room
 494-N
St. Paul, MN 55104
(612) 646-6136

MISSISSIPPI

(1) Protection and Advocacy

Miss. Protection and Advocacy
 System for DD, Inc.
4793 B McWillie Dr.
Jackson, MS 39206
(601) 981-8207

263

(2) State Office for Special Education

Bureau of Special Services
Dept. of Education
P.O. Box 771
Jackson, MS 39205-0771
(601) 359-3490

(4) ACLD

P.O. Box 9387
Jackson, MS 39206
(601) 982-2812

MISSOURI

(1) Protection and Advocacy

Missouri Protection and
  Advocacy Service
925 S. Country Club Dr.,
  Unit B
Jefferson City, MO 65109
(314) 893-3333
(800) 392-8667 (in MO)

(2) State Office for Special Education

Coordinator of Special
  Education
Dept. of Elementary and
  Secondary Education
P.O. Box 480
Jefferson City, MO 65102
(314) 751-4909

(4) ACLD

P.O. Box 3303
2740 S. Glenstone
Springfield, MO 65803
(417) 864-5110

MONTANA

(1) Protection and Advocacy

Montana Advocacy Program
1410 Eighth Ave.
Helena, MT 59601
(406) 444-3889
(800) 245-4743 (in MT)

(2) State Office for Special Education

Special Education
Office of Public Instruction
State Capitol Room 106
Helena, MT 59620
(406) 444-4429

(4) ACLD

2535 35th St., SE
Havre, MT 59101
(406) 265-5633

NEBRASKA

(1) Protection and Advocacy

Nebraska Advocacy Services
  Inc.
522 Lincoln Center Bldg.
215 Centennial Mall South
Lincoln, NE 68508
(402) 474-3183

(2) State Office for Special Education

Special Education
Dept. of Education
P.O. Box 94987
Lincoln, NE 68509-4987
(402) 471-2471

(3) The Orton Society Branch Office

Nebraska Branch
Wayne

(4) ACLD

11118 N. 62nd St.
Omaha, NE 68152
(402) 571-7771

NEVADA

(1) Protection and Advocacy

Office of Protection and
    Advocacy, Inc.
2105 Capurro Way, Suite B
Sparks, NV 89431
(702) 789-0233
(800) 992-5715

(2) State Office for Special Education

Special Education Branch
Dept. of Education
400 W. King St. — Capitol
    Complex
Carson City, NV 89710-0004
(702) 885-3140

(3) The Orton Society Branch Office

Northern Nevada Branch
Reno

NEW HAMPSHIRE

(1) Protection and Advocacy

Disabilities Rights Center
P.O. Box 19
Concord, NH 03302-0019
(603) 228-0432

(2) State Office for Special Education

Special Education Bureau
Dept. of Education
101 Pleasant St.
Concord, NH 03301-3860
(603) 271-3741

(3) The Orton Society Branch Office

New England Branch
Northfield, MA

(4) ACLD

20 Wedgewood Dr.
Concord, NH 03307
(603) 224-5872

NEW JERSEY

(1) Protection and Advocacy

Office of Advocacy for the DD
Hughes Justice Complex CN-
    850
Trenton, NJ 08625
(609) 292-9742
(800) 792-8600 (in NJ)

(2) State Office for Special Education

Division of Special Education
Dept. of Education
225 W. State St.
P.O. Box CN 500
Trenton, NJ 08625-0001
(609) 633-6833

(3) The Orton Society Branch Office

New Jersey Branch
S. Orange

(4) ACLD

640 Ocean Ave.
West End, NJ 07740
(201) 229-1919

NEW MEXICO

(1) Protection and Advocacy

Protection and Advocacy
  System, Inc.
2201 San Pedro NE, Bldg. 4,
  Suite 140
Albuquerque, NM 87110
(505) 888-0111
(800) 432-4682 (in NM)

(2) State Office for Special Education

Division of Special Education
Dept. of Education
State Educational Bldg.
300 Don Gaspar Ave.
Santa Fe, NM 87501-2786
(505) 827-6541

(3) The Orton Society Branch Office

New Mexico Branch
Albuquerque

NEW YORK

(1) Protection and Advocacy

NY Commission on Quality of
  Care for the Disabled
99 Washington Ave.
Albany, NY 12210
(518) 473-4057

(2) State Office for Special Education

Office for Education of Children
  with Handicapping Conditions
Dept. of Education
Education Bldg. Annex, Room
  1073
Albany, NY 12234-0001
(518) 474-5548

(3) The Orton Society Branch Offices

Buffalo Branch
Orchard Park

New York City Branch
New York

Suffolk (Long Island Branch)
Northport

(4) ACLD

155 Washington Ave., 3rd Floor
Albany, NY 12210
(518) 436-4633

NORTH CAROLINA

(1) Protection and Advocacy

Governor's Advocacy Council
1318 Dale St., Suite 100
Raleigh, NC 27605
(919) 733-9250

*(2) State Office for Special
Education*

Division for Exceptional
   Children
Dept. of Public Instruction
Education Bldg., Room 442
116 W. Edenton St.
Raleigh, NC 27603-1712
(919) 733-3921

(4) ACLD

Box 3542
Chapel Hill, NC 27515
(919) 967-9537

NORTH DAKOTA

(1) Protection and Advocacy

Protection and Advocacy Project
Governor's Council on Human
   Resources
Judicial Wing, State Capitol
   Bldg.
Bismarck, ND 58505
(701) 224-2972
(800) 472-2670 (in ND)

*(2) State Office for Special
Education*

Special Education
Dept. of Public Instruction
State Capitol
Bismarck, ND 58505-0440
(701) 224-2277

*(3) The Orton Society Branch
Office*

Upper Midwest Branch
St. Paul, MN

(4) ACLD

7 E. Central, #202
Minot, ND 58701
(701) 852-5255

OHIO

(1) Protection and Advocacy

Ohio Legal Rights Services
8 E. Long St., 6th Floor
Columbus, OH 43215
(614) 466-7264
(800) 282-9181 (in OH)

*(2) State Office for Special
Education*

Division of Special Education
State Dept. of Education
933 High St.
Worthington, OH 43085-4017
(614) 466-2650

(3) The Orton Society Branch Offices

Ohio Valley Branch
Cincinnati

Central Ohio Branch
Worthington

(4) ACLD

2800 Euclid Ave., Suite 125
Cleveland, OH 44115
(216) 861-6665

OKLAHOMA

(1) Protection and Advocacy

Protection and Advocacy
  Agency for DD
9726 E. 42nd St.
Osage Bldg., Room 133
Tulsa, OK 74146
(918) 664-5883

(2) State Office for Special Education

Special Education Section
Dept. of Education
Oliver Hodge Memorial Bldg.,
  Room 215
Oklahoma City, OK 73105-4599
(405) 521-3352

(3) The Orton Society Branch Office

Oklahoma Branch
Oklahoma City

(4) ACLD

3701 NW 62nd St.
Oklahoma City, OK 73112
(405) 943-9434

OREGON

(1) Protection and Advocacy

Oregon Advocacy Center
400 Board of Trade Bldg.
310 SW Fourth Ave., Suite 625
Portland, OR 97204-2309
(503) 243-2081

(2) State Office for Special Education

Special Education and Student
  Services
Dept. of Education
700 Pringle Pkwy. SE
Salem, OR 97310-0290
(503) 378-2677

(3) The Orton Society Branch Office

Oregon Branch
Portland

PENNSYLVANIA

(1) Protection and Advocacy

Pennsylvania Protection and
  Advocacy, Inc.
116 Pine St.
Harrisburg, PA 17101
(717) 236-8110
(800) 692-7443 (in PA)

(2) State Office for Special Education

Bureau of Special Education
Dept. of Education
333 Market St.
Harrisburg, PA 17126-0333
(717) 783-6913

(3) The Orton Society Branch Office

Philadelphia Branch
Swarthmore

(4) ACLD

Toomey Bldg., Suites 2 & 3
Uwchland, PA 19480
(215) 458-8193
(800) 692-6200 (in PA)

PUERTO RICO

(1) Protection and Advocacy

Ombudsman for the Disabled,
Governor's Office
Chardon Ave. #916
Hato Rey, PR 00936
(809) 766-2333, 766-2388

(2) State Office for Special Education

Special Education
Dept. of Education
P.O. Box 759
Hato Rey, PR 00919-0759
(809) 764-8059

(4) ACLD

G.P.O. Box 1905
San Juan, PR 00936
(809) 761-0816, 788-6052

RHODE ISLAND

(1) Protection and Advocacy

Rhode Island P&A System
   (RIPAS), Inc.
55 Bradford St., 2nd Floor
Providence, RI 02903
(401) 831-3150

(2) State Office for Special Education

Special Education Program
   Services Unit
Dept. of Education
Roger Williams Bldg., Room
   209
22 Hayes St.
Providence, RI 02908-5025
(401) 277-3505

(3) The Orton Society Branch Office

New England Branch
Northfield, MA

(4) ACLD

103 Harris Ave.
Johnston, RI 02919
(401) 231-0914

SOUTH CAROLINA

(1) Protection and Advocacy

SC Protection and Advocacy
 System for the Handicapped,
 Inc.
3710 Landmark Dr., Suite 208
Columbia, SC 29204
(803) 782-0639
(800) 922-5225 (in SC)

*(2) State Office for Special
Education*

Office of Programs for
 Handicapped
Dept. of Education
100 Executive Center Dr.
Santee Bldg. A-24
Columbia, SC 29201
(803) 737-8710

(4) ACLD

1792 Sharonwood Lane
Rock Hill, SC 29730
(803) 366-5042

SOUTH DAKOTA

(1) Protection and Advocacy

South Dakota Advocacy Project,
 Inc.
221 S. Central Ave.
Pierre, SD 57501
(605) 224-8294
(800) 742-8108 (in SD)

*(2) State Office for Special
Education*

Section for Special Education
Dept. of Education

Richard F. Kneip Bldg.
700 N. Illinois St.
Pierre, SD 57501-2293
(605) 773-3315

*(3) The Orton Society Branch
Office*

Upper Midwest Branch
St. Paul, MN

(4) ACLD

4022 Helen Ct.
Rapid City, SD 57701
(605) 342-4320

TENNESSEE

(1) Protection and Advocacy

EACH, Inc.
P.O. Box 121257
Nashville, TN 37212
(615) 298-1080
(800) 342-1660 (in TN)

*(2) State Office for Special
Education*

Special Education Programs
Dept. of Education
132 Cordell Hull Bldg.
Nashville, TN 37219
(615) 741-2851

*(3) The Orton Society Branch
Offices*

West/Middle Branch
Memphis

East Tennessee Branch
Johnson City

(4) ACLD

P.O. Box 281028
Memphis, TN 39128
(901) 323-1430

TEXAS

(1) Protection and Advocacy

Advocacy, Inc.
7800 Shoal Creek Blvd., Suite
    171-E
Austin, TX 78752
(512) 454-4816
(800) 252-9018 (in TX)

*(2) State Office for Special
Education*

Special Education Programs
Texas Education Agency
William B. Travis Bldg., Room
    5-120
1701 N. Congress Ave.
Austin, TX 78701-2486
(512) 463-9414

*(3) The Orton Society Branch
Offices*

Austin Branch
Austin

Dallas Branch
Dallas

Houston Branch
Houston

(4) ACLD

1011 W. 31st St.
Austin, TX 78705
(512) 458-8234

UTAH

(1) Protection and Advocacy

Legal Center for the
    Handicapped
455 E. 400 South, Suite 201
Salt Lake City, UT 84111
(801) 363-1347
(800) 662-9080 (in UT)

*(2) State Office for Special
Education*

AT-RISK Students
State Office of Education
250 E. 500 South
Salt Lake City, UT 84111-3204
(801) 538-7706

(4) ACLD

P.O. Box 112
Salt Lake City, UT 84110
(801) 364-0126

VERMONT

(1) Protection and Advocacy

Vermont DD Law Project
12 North St.
Burlington, VT 05401
(802) 863-2881

Citizen Advocacy, Inc.
Champlain Mill, Box 37
Winooski, VT 05404
(802) 655-0329

(2) State Office for Special Education

Division of Special Education
Dept. of Education
120 State St.
State Office Bldg.
Montpelier, VT 05602-3403
(802) 828-3141

(3) The Orton Society Branch Office

New England Branch
Northfield, MA

(4) ACLD

9 Heaton St.
Montpelier, VT 05602
(802) 223-5480

VIRGINIA

(1) Protection and Advocacy

Rights for the Disabled
James Monroe Bldg.
101 N. 14th St., 17th Floor
Richmond, VA 23219
(804) 225-2042
(800) 552-3962 (in VA)

(2) State Office for Special Education

Office of Special and
   Compensatory Education
Dept. of Education
P.O. Box 6Q
Richmond, VA 23216-2060
(804) 225-2402

(3) The Orton Society Branch Office

Virginia Branch
Roanoke

(4) ACLD

5312 Balfour Dr.
Virginia Beach, VA 23464
(804) 424-4113

VIRGIN ISLANDS

(1) Protection and Advocacy

Committee on Advocacy for the
   DD, Inc.
31A New St., Apt. No. 2
Fredericksted
St. Croix, VI 00840
(809) 772-1200

(2) State Office for Special Education

Director of Special Education
P.O. Box 6640
Charlotte Amalie
St. Thomas, VI 00801
(809) 776-5802

WASHINGTON

(1) Protection and Advocacy

Washington Protection and
   Advocacy System
1401 E. Jefferson
Seattle, WA 98122
(206) 324-1521

(2) State Office for Special Education

Special Education Section
Supt. of Public Instruction
Old Capitol Bldg.
Olympia, WA 98504-0001
(206) 753-6733

(3) The Orton Society Branch Office

Puget Sound Branch
Seattle

(4) ACLD

17530 NE Union Hill Rd., Suite 100
Redmond, WA 98052
(206) 882-0792

WEST VIRGINIA

(1) Protection and Advocacy

West Virginia Advocates
1524 Kanawha Blvd., East
Charleston, WV 25311
(304) 346-0847
(800) 950-5250 (in WV)

(2) State Office for Special Education

Office of Special Education
Dept. of Education
Capitol Complex, Bldg. 6, Room B-346
Charleston, WV 25305
(304) 348-2696

(4) ACLD

2069 Enslow Blvd.
Huntington, WV 25701
(304) 529-1493

WISCONSIN

(1) Protection and Advocacy

Wisconsin Coalition for Advocacy, Inc.
16 N. Carroll, Suite 400
Madison, WI 53703
(608) 251-9600

(2) State Office for Special Education

Division of Handicapped Children and Pupil Services
Dept. of Public Instruction
125 S. Webster St.
P.O. Box 7841
Madison, WI 53702-7841
(608) 266-1649

(3) The Orton Society Branch Office

Wisconsin Branch
Milwaukee

(4) ACLD

6213 Middleton Springs Dr.
Middleton, WI 53562
(608) 238-8588

WYOMING

(1) Protection and Advocacy

Wyoming Protection and
    Advocacy System, Inc.
2424 Pioneer Ave., #101
Cheyenne, WY 82001
(307) 632-3496
(800) 328-1110
(800) 632-3496 (in WY)

*(2) State Office for Special
Education*

Federal Programs Unit
Dept. of Education
Hathaway Bldg., 2nd Floor
2300 Capitol Ave.
Cheyenne, WY 82002-0050
(307) 777-7414

(4) ACLD

1407 Palmer
Laramie, WY 82070
(307) 742-3973

AMERICAN SAMOA

(1) Protection and Advocacy

Client Assistance and Protection
    and Advocacy Program
P.O. Box 3407
Pago Pago, AS 96799
011 (684) 633-2418

(2) Office for Special Education

Special Education
Dept. of Education
Pago Pago, AS 96799
011 (684) 633-1323

GUAM

(1) Protection and Advocacy

The Advocacy Office
P.O. Box 8830
Tamuning, GU 96911
011 (671) 646-9026

(2) Office for Special Education

Special Education
Dept. of Education
P.O. Box DE
Agana, GU 96910
011 (671) 472-8901

NORTHERN MARIANA ISLANDS

(1) Protection and Advocacy

Catholic Social Services
P.O. Box 745
Commonwealth of the Northern
    Mariana Islands
Saipan, Mariana Islands 96950
011 (670) 234-6981

(2) Office of Special Education

Special Education Program
P.O. Box 1370
Commonwealth of the Northern
    Mariana Islands
Saipan, Mariana Islands 96950
011 (670) 322-9956; 322-9256

The ANSER System

FORM 2P
PARENT QUESTIONNAIRE

TODAY'S DATE _____

CHILD'S NAME _____ DATE OF BIRTH _____

YOUR NAME _____ TELEPHONE (HOME) _____

RELATIONSHIP TO CHILD _____ (WORK) _____

HOME ADDRESS _____

NAME OF SCHOOL _____ GRADE _____

SCHOOL ADDRESS _____

TEACHER(S) _____

A. Please list the problems with which you want help for this child:

1. _____

2. _____

3. _____

4. _____

5. _____

6. _____

7. _____

8. _____

B. What have you said to the child about this evaluation?

_____

_____

_____

_____

C. Whose idea was it that this child have an evaluation?

_____

_____

_____

_____

D. Has this child had previous evaluations outside of school?

☐ Yes ☐ No

If so, where and when? It might be helpful to attach any available report(s). _____

_____

_____

_____

E. Has this child received any special treatments (diets, medications, psychological counseling, psychiatric help, etc.) outside of school?

☐ Yes ☐ No

If so, please describe below:

APPROXIMATE DATE(S)	TYPE(S) OF TREATMENT (include name of any medicine you remember)

F. Please attach a recent photograph of the child, if available, in the space below. This will help us remember him or her if there is an inquiry from you after the evaluation. It is not essential, but it can be very useful. Any size is acceptable. This is not usually necessary for evaluations taking place within a school.

The ANSER System

The following checklists help us to decide whether there are any early medical factors that might be important. The checklist entitled "Possible Pregnancy Problems" concerns the pregnancy *with this child*, except for items 1.12 and 1.13, which refer to previous pregnancies. The "Newborn Infant Problems" checklist is about the baby's *first month of life*. Please read each list; then put an X in the appropriate column following each item.

1.0	POSSIBLE PREGNANCY PROBLEMS	TRUE	NOT TRUE	CANNOT SAY
1.1	Had bleeding during first three months			
1.2	Had bleeding during second three months			
1.3	Had bleeding during last three months			
1.4	Gained 30 or more lbs. (14 kgs.) (specify _____)			
1.5	Had toxemia			
1.6	Had to take medications*			
1.7	Vomited often			
1.8	Got hurt or injured			
1.9	Gained less than 15 lbs. (7 kgs.) (specify _____)			
1.10	Took narcotic drugs			
1.11	Drank much alcohol			
1.12	Had previous miscarriages			
1.13	Had previous premature baby(ies)			
1.14	Had an infection			
1.15	Smoked one pack (or more) of cigarettes a day			
1.16	Labor lasted longer than 12 hours			
1.17	Had a cesarean section			
1.18	Had a difficult delivery			
1.19	Was put to sleep for delivery			
1.20	Labor lasted less than two hours			
1.21	Length of pregnancy _____ months			

*Specify any medications:

1. _____
2. _____
3. _____

Other pregnancy problems/illnesses:

1. _____
2. _____
3. _____

Help Me to Help My Child

2.0	NEWBORN INFANT PROBLEMS	TRUE	NOT TRUE	CANNOT SAY
2.1	Born with cord around neck			
2.2	Injured during birth			
2.3	Had trouble breathing			
2.4	Got yellow (jaundice)			
2.5	Turned blue (cyanosis)			
2.6	Was a twin or triplet			
2.7	Had an infection			
2.8	Was given medications			
2.9	Had seizures (fits, convulsions)			
2.10	Had diarrhea			
2.11	Needed oxygen			
2.12	Was in hospital more than seven days			
2.13	Gagged often			
2.14	Vomited often			
2.15	Born with heart defect			
2.16	Born with other defect(s)			
2.17	Had trouble sucking			
2.18	Had skin problems			
2.19	Was very jittery			
2.20	Baby's birth weight _____ lbs. ☐ kgs. ☐			

Please list any other problems:

1. _____
2. _____
3. _____
4. _____

278

The ANSER System

Following are two checklists about problems parents sometimes have with young children. The checklist entitled "Health Problems" is about any medical problems the child may have had. The "Functional Problems" checklist includes personality or behavioral problems the child may have had. In both lists, if the child has had any of these problems, please put an X in the column under the age at which the problem(s) occurred. If a problem occurred over a long period, or over and over again, please check in the columns for each age during which the problem existed. If the child has never had the problem, put an X in the "Never" column.

3.0	HEALTH PROBLEMS	Never	0 - 3 months	4 - 6 months	7 - 12 months	13 - 18 months	19 - 24 months	2 - 3 years	3 - 4 years	4 - 5 years	5 - 7 years	Since 7 years
3.1	Ear infection(s)											
3.2	Rashes or skin problems											
3.3	Meningitis											
3.4	Seizures (convulsions) or spells											
3.5	High fevers (over 103° F. or 39° C.)											
3.6	Pneumonia											
3.7	Asthma											
3.8	Slow weight gain											
3.9	Trouble with ears or hearing											
3.10	Trouble with eyes or vision											
3.11	Bowel problems											
3.12	Hospitalization(s)*											
3.13	Surgery (operations)*											
3.14	Serious injury(ies)											
3.15	Food allergies											
3.16	Other allergies											
3.17	Anemia (low blood count)											
3.18	Lead poisoning											
3.19	Other poisoning or overdose											
3.20	Heart problems											
3.21	Kidney or urinary problems											

*Please give reasons for hospitalizations or surgery:

_____

_____

279

3.0	HEALTH PROBLEMS (continued)	Never	0 - 3 months	4 - 6 months	7 - 12 months	13 - 18 months	19 - 24 months	2 - 3 years	3 - 4 years	4 - 5 years	5 - 7 years	Since 7 years
3.22	Got sick after a shot (immunization)											
3.23	Other important illnesses (specify):											
	a.											
	b.											
3.24	Medications used over a long period (specify):											
	a.											
	b.											

4.0	FUNCTIONAL PROBLEMS	Never	0 - 3 months	4 - 6 months	7 - 12 months	13 - 18 months	19 - 24 months	2 - 3 years	3 - 4 years	4 - 5 years	5 - 7 years	Since 7 years
4.1	Feeding difficulty											
4.2	Poor appetite											
4.3	Unwillingness to try new foods											
4.4	Very unpredictable appetite											
4.5	Extreme hunger											
4.6	Colic											
4.7	Constipation											
4.8	Stomach aches											
4.9	Trouble falling asleep											
4.10	Trouble staying asleep											
4.11	Very unpredictable length of sleep											
4.12	Very heavy sleeping											
4.13	Overactivity											
4.14	Head banging											
4.15	Rocking in bed											

4.0	FUNCTIONAL PROBLEMS (continued)	Never	0 - 3 months	4 - 6 months	7 - 12 months	13 - 18 months	19 - 24 months	2 - 3 years	3 - 4 years	4 - 5 years	5 - 7 years	Since 7 years
4.16	Temper tantrums											
4.17	Self-destructive behavior											
4.18	Difficulty in being comforted or consoled											
4.19	Stiffness or rigidity											
4.20	Looseness or floppiness											
4.21	Crying often and easily											
4.22	Shyness with strangers											
4.23	Bashfulness with new children											
4.24	Irritability											
4.25	Extreme reaction to noise or sudden movement											
4.26	Difficulty in keeping to a schedule											
4.27	Trouble getting satisfied											
4.28	Desire to be held too often											
4.29·	Failure to be affectionate toward parents											
4.30	Unwillingness to go along with change in daily routine											
4.31	Tendency to make odd sounds, grunts, or snorts											
4.32	Tendency to twitch or jerk arm(s) or head often											

4.33   Was child breast-fed?   ☐ Yes (until age _____ months)   ☐ No

Help Me to Help My Child

Following is a checklist of early accomplishments of children. Please put an X next to each item under the column giving the age at which this "milestone" first occurred. If there are items the child still cannot do, please leave all the columns blank.

5.0	EARLY DEVELOPMENT	0 - 3 months	4 - 6 months	7 - 12 months	13 - 18 months	19 - 24 months	2 - 3 years	3 - 4 years	4 - 5 years	5 - 6 years
5.1	Sat up without help									
5.2	Crawled									
5.3	Walked alone (10-15 steps)									
5.4	Walked up stairs									
5.5	Rode a tricycle									
5.6	Caught a big ball									
5.7	Spoke first words (Mama, Dada, etc.)									
5.8	Put words together (Daddy bye-bye, Mama home, etc.)									
5.9	Spoke 2-3 word sentences									
5.10	Spoke clearly so strangers understood									
5.11	Used fingers to feed self									
5.12	Used a spoon									
5.13	Fully bowel trained									
5.14	Fully bladder trained									
5.15	Able to dress self									
5.16	Able to tie shoelaces									
5.17	Able to separate easily from mother (for school, play, etc.)									

5.18   Did this child attend a preschool/nursery school?   ☐ Yes   ☐ No

If so, were any problems with behavior noted?   ☐ Yes   ☐ No

Were any problems with learning noted?   ☐ Yes   ☐ No

5.19   Was this child ever retained in a grade?   ☐ Yes   ☐ No

If so, when? _____

5.20   What is the principal language spoken at home? _____

Indicate others that are used sometimes _____

282

The ANSER System

Following is a series of eleven problems that sometimes run in families. We are interested in whether anyone in the family *other than this child* has or has had any of these. Please put an X in the column of the family member(s) who have or have had each problem. If more than one brother or sister has or has had one of these difficulties, put an X for each one in the appropriate column. (For example, if there were two brothers who had trouble learning how to read, you would put two X's next to item 6.2 under the column "Child's Brothers.") The "Others" column (for family members such as cousins, aunts, uncles, grandparents) should be used in the same way.

6.0	FAMILY HISTORY	Child's Mother	Child's Father	Child's Brother(s)	Child's Sister(s)	Others (specify)
6.1	Hyperactive as a child					
6.2	Trouble learning to read					
6.3	Trouble with arithmetic					
6.4	Trouble with writing					
6.5	Kept back in school					
6.6	Speech problems					
6.7	Behavior problems in childhood					
6.8	In trouble as a teenager					
6.9	Depression					
6.10	Other mental illness					
6.11	Drinking problem or drug abuse					

6.12 Father's present age _____ School level completed _____

Present occupation _____

General health _____

6.13 Mother's present age _____ School level completed _____

Present occupation _____

General health _____

6.14 Brother(s): Age(s) _____

_____

6.15 Sister(s): Age(s) _____

_____

6.16 Please check any of the following that are true of this child:
☐ Was adopted   ☐ Is a foster child

6.17 Parents are ☐ separated or ☐ divorced. ☐ One or ☐ both parent(s) are deceased.
If so, child lives mainly with (check one or more):
☐ Mother   ☐ Stepmother   ☐ Grandparent(s)
☐ Father   ☐ Stepfather   ☐ Other _____

283

Help Me to Help My Child

Following is a list of abilities or skills (page 10) and a list of interests (page 11). Please put an X next to each item in the column that best describes this child's current ability or interest. If the child has had no experience with a particular item, leave it blank.

7.0	SPECIFIC SKILLS (OR ABILITIES)	Has great difficulty	Has some difficulty	Does pretty well	Does very well
7.1	Catching and throwing a ball				
7.2	Running fast				
7.3	Playing most sports				
7.4	Balancing/dancing				
7.5	Drawing/art work				
7.6	Building things				
7.7	Understanding spoken directions				
7.8	Understanding jokes and stories				
7.9	Speaking clearly				
7.10	Telling stories/describing things				
7.11	Remembering where to find things				
7.12	Remembering telephone numbers				
7.13	Telling time				
7.14	Telling left from right				
7.15	Using his/her imagination				
7.16	Understanding what he/she reads				
7.17	Reading fast enough				
7.18	Figuring out new reading words				
7.19	Handwriting				
7.20	Writing sentences or paragraphs				
7.21	Writing fast enough				
7.22	Spelling accurately				
7.23	Learning new math skills				
7.24	Doing well on math tests				
7.25	Using a computer in school				
7.26	Completing homework				
7.27	Remembering assignments				
7.28	Knowing what and how to study				
7.29	Learning new words (vocabulary)				
7.30	Memorizing things for school				
7.31	Please list any other *strong* or *poor* skills:				

7.32 On average, how many hours per week does this child watch television? _____ hours

7.0	SPECIFIC INTERESTS	Has little or no interest	Has moderate interest	Has strong interest
7.33	Playing a sport after school			
7.34	Dancing			
7.35	Building models			
7.36	Drawing or painting			
7.37	Other art or craft work/sewing			
7.38	Listening to music			
7.39	Playing a musical instrument/singing			
7.40	Using a computer			
7.41	Fishing or hunting			
7.42	Boy or Girl Scouts (or other clubs)			
7.43	Writing stories/poems			
7.44	Bicycle riding			
7.45	Cars/motorcycles			
7.46	Reading magazines/newspapers			
7.47	Pets/animals			
7.48	Schoolwork (in general)			
7.49	Reading schoolbooks			
7.50	Doing homework			
7.51	Writing reports/stories			
7.52	Learning new things in math			
7.53	Doing math problems			
7.54	Learning new spelling words			
7.55	Learning about science			
7.56	Learning about health			
7.57	Learning history/social studies			
7.58	Art in school			
7.59	Music in school			
7.60	Gym/physical education			
7.61	Talking about school at home			
7.62	Working on school projects at home			
7.63	Please list other *strong* interests:			

Help Me to Help My Child

Pages 12 and 13 list phrases and sentences that parents use to describe their children as they see them *at home*. All children act in these ways some of the time. Please read each item and check the appropriate square in the right-hand columns based on what you think is true of this child compared to most others of the same age. Use the key on page 13.

8.0		SELECTIVE ATTENTION–ACTIVITY	Definitely applies	Applies somewhat	Does not apply	Cannot say
8.1	FSQ	Notices things that no one else does				
8.2	FSQ	Can concentrate for only a short time unless things are very interesting				
8.3	FSQ	Understands the main ideas of things but misses important details				
8.4	SAB	Gets tired or seems to "burn out" too easily when expected to concentrate				
8.5	SAB	Has trouble getting started in the morning				
8.6	SAB	Has difficulty falling asleep or staying asleep at night and/or is a restless sleeper				
8.7	RIM	Does work or performs many tasks carelessly without thinking				
8.8	RIM	Doesn't seem to plan or organize *before* doing things				
8.9	RIM	Is in a hurry to get work or chores over quickly instead of doing them well				
8.10	AMP	Is able to remember minor or unimportant details better than most others can				
8.11	AMP	Learns a new skill well one day and then can't seem to do it a few days later				
8.12	AMP	Shows a great ability to recall things that happened a long time ago				
8.13	PCN	Does the same job or task very well sometimes and extremely poorly at other times				
8.14	PCN	Receives very unpredictable (inconsistent) grades or test scores in school				
8.15	PCN	Can work well *only* on things he/she really enjoys doing or thinking about				
8.16	FBR	Often doesn't notice when he/she makes mistakes				
8.17	FBR	Seems not to realize when he/she is disturbing someone				
8.18	FBR	Doesn't do much better after punishment or correction				

286

The ANSER System

			Definitely applies	Applies somewhat	Does not apply	Cannot say
KEY Definitely applies = *Much more* frequent and/or extreme than in others of the same age Applies somewhat = A little more frequent and/or extreme than in others of the same age Does not apply = Not different from others of the same age						
8.0	**SELECTIVE ATTENTION–ACTIVITY (continued)**					
8.19	SEC	Is a poor listener				
8.20	SEC	Seems to be looking around or staring a lot				
8.21	SEC	Makes comments about or is distracted by background noises or unimportant things				
8.22	ASC	Has an excellent imagination; keeps having original or unusual ideas				
8.23	ASC	Says things that have little or no connection to what others are saying or what is going on				
8.24	ASC	Daydreams often; seems to be in his/her own world				
8.25	APC	Is restless; gets bored too easily				
8.26	APC	Seems to want things right away and/or is hard to satisfy				
8.27	APC	Keeps thinking ahead (about what's coming next or later)				
8.28	SOC	Has trouble concentrating in a large group of children, such as at school				
8.29	SOC	Annoys or bothers other children				
8.30	SOC	Has problems getting along with other children and doesn't understand why				
8.31	MOC	Seems to have too much energy				
8.32	MOC	Body is in motion much of the time				
8.33	MOC	Is fidgety; keeps doing things with hands and/or feet				
8.34	BEC	Behavior is variable and hard to predict				
8.35	BEC	Gets into trouble without really meaning to				
8.36	BEC	Is a troublemaker; stirs things up				

Help Me to Help My Child

Following is a list of behaviors and characteristics. All children show some of these at some time during their lives. To the right of each item, please put an X in the column which best describes this child during the past six months. If a particular item does not describe the child, put an X in the column "Do not know or cannot say."

KEY
Definitely applies = Is *much more* frequent and/or extreme than in others of the same age
Applies somewhat = Is sometimes more extreme than in others of the same age
Does not apply = Is usually appropriate or better than average for his or her age

9.0	ASSOCIATED BEHAVIORS	Definitely applies	Applies somewhat	Does not apply	Do not know or cannot say
9.1	Is moody				
9.2	Has a bad temper				
9.3	Cries easily				
9.4	Is a worrier				
9.5	Has bad dreams				
9.6	Is often sad				
9.7	Is often very quiet				
9.8	Is fearful of new situations, people, places				
9.9	Is fearful of being alone				
9.10	Is often "down" on himself/herself				
9.11	Sleeps or tries to sleep with parent(s)				
9.12	Is often tired				
9.13	Speaks unclearly, stutters, or stammers				
9.14	Has stomach aches often				
9.15	Wets bed or pants often				
9.16	Soils underwear or has accidents with bowel movements				
9.17	Often has headaches				
9.18	Overeats often				
9.19	Bites nails				
9.20	Often complains of pains in arms or legs				
9.21	Has nervous twitches				

KEY
Definitely applies   = Is *much more* frequent and/or extreme than in others of the same age
Applies somewhat = Is sometimes more extreme than in others of the same age
Does not apply   = Is usually appropriate or better than average for his or her age

9.0	ASSOCIATED BEHAVIORS (continued)	Definitely applies	Applies somewhat	Does not apply	Do not know or cannot say
9.22	Complains of feeling ill often				
9.23	Has constipation				
9.24	Is often too neat or orderly				
9.25	Is often too concerned about cleanliness				
9.26	Tells lies				
9.27	Steals things at home				
9.28	Often plays with matches				
9.29	Bullies other children				
9.30	Is fresh, sassy to grownups				
9.31	Destroys objects at home				
9.32	Destroys objects away from home				
9.33	Is fearless				
9.34	Is mean				
9.35	Deliberately tries to make parents angry				
9.36	Gets in trouble with neighbors				
9.37	Is cruel to animals				
9.38	Is a "loner"				
9.39	Has no real friends				
9.40	Loses friends easily				
9.41	Has mostly younger friends				
9.42	Has mostly older friends				

```
┌─────────────────────────────────────────────────────────────────────┐
│                              KEY                                      │
│ Definitely applies  = Is much more frequent and/or extreme than in others of the same age │
│ Applies somewhat    = Is sometimes more extreme than in others of the same age │
│ Does not apply      = Is usually appropriate or better than average for his or her age │
└─────────────────────────────────────────────────────────────────────┘
```

9.0	ASSOCIATED BEHAVIORS (continued)	Definitely applies	Applies somewhat	Does not apply	Do not know or cannot say
9.43	Gets bossed by other children				
9.44	Prefers to play alone				
9.45	Is slow to trust adults				
9.46	Gets picked on				
9.47	Is not liked by other children				
9.48	Is slow to make friends				
9.49	Will not follow a leader in games				
9.50	Fights with brothers and/or sisters				

The ANSER System

Below is a list of positive or good behaviors. Please indicate which of these pertain to your child by putting an X in the appropriate column to the right of each item.

10.0	ASSOCIATED STRENGTHS	Often true	Occasionally true	Seldom true	Cannot say
10.1	Has an even disposition, is easy to live with				
10.2	Usually seems happy				
10.3	Enjoys new experiences				
10.4	Easily becomes involved in many activities				
10.5	Takes pleasure in many activities				
10.6	Is affectionate				
10.7	Is kind or sympathetic if someone else is sad or hurt				
10.8	Is friendly and outgoing				
10.9	Plays well with other children				
10.10	Shares or cooperates with others				
10.11	Accepts rules easily				
10.12	Plays gently with smaller children or animals				
10.13	Makes friends easily				
10.14	Enjoys playing with other children				
10.15	Has many friends				
10.16	Takes turns well				
10.17	Tolerates minor bumps and scratches without much complaint				
10.18	Tolerates criticism well				
10.19	Confides in others about worries				
10.20	Is forgiving (doesn't "hold a grudge")				
10.21	Doesn't take himself/herself too seriously				
10.22	Doesn't complain much when ill				
10.23	Compromises easily				
10.24	Stands up for himself/herself when necessary				
10.25	Recovers easily after disappointments				

Guides and Directories

Advisory Services on Private
Schools and Camps
171 Madison Ave.
New York, NY 10016
(212) 696-0499

*BOSC Directory for Facilities for
Learning Disabled* ($20.00)
Dept. F, Box 305
Congers, NY 10920

CALLED, Inc. (College
Association for Language
Learning and Educational
Disability)
P.O. Box 2, ET Station
Commerce, TX 75428
(214) 886-5937, 5932
(resource and support group for
college students)

*Campus Access for LD Students:
Handbook for Success for Post-
Secondary Programs*
Barbara Scheiber and
Jeanne Talpers.
Washington, D.C.: Closer Look,
1985.

*Colleges/Universities That Accept
Students with LD* ($3.00)
ACLD
4156 Library Rd.
Pittsburgh, PA 15234

*Directory of College Facilities and
Services for the Disabled*
($95.00)
Oryx Press
2214 North Central at Encanto
Phoenix, AZ 85004

*Guide to College Programs for LD
Students* (1985) ($5.00 plus
$1.00 postage)
National Association of College
Admissions Counsellors
9933 Lawler Ave., Suite 500
Skokie, IL 60077

*Guide to Postsecondary Educational
Opportunities for the Learning
Disabled* ($12.00)
Time Out to Enjoy
715 Lake St., Suite 100
Oak Park, IL 60301

*Guide to Summer Camps and
    Summer Schools* ($15.00 plus
    $1.50 postage)
Porter Sargent Publications
11 Beacon St.
Boston, MA 02108

Handbook of Private Schools
    ($35.00 plus $1.50 postage)
Porter Sargent Publications
11 Beacon St.
Boston, MA 02108

*Lovejoy's College Guide for the
    Learning Disabled* ($10.95)
Attention: Order Department
Simon & Schuster Publishers
1230 Avenue of the Americas
New York, NY 10020

*National Association of Private
    Schools for Exceptional Children:
    Membership Directory* ($16.00)
NAPSEC
2021 K St., Suite 315
Washington, DC 20006

*National Directory of Four-Year
    Colleges, Two-Year Colleges,
    and High School Training
    Programs for Young People with
    LD* ($15.95 plus $1.00
    postage)
Partners in Publishing
P.O. Box 503
Tulsa, OK 74150

*Peterson's Guide to Colleges with
    Programs for LD Students*
    ($13.95)
Peterson's Guide,
    Dept. 5710
166 Bunn Dr.
P.O. Box 2123
Princeton, NJ 08540

*Schooling for the Learning
    Disabled: A Selective Guide to
    LD Programs in Elementary and
    Secondary Schools in the U.S.*
    ($9.95 plus $1.05 postage)
Raegene Pernecke and
    Sara M. Schreiner
SMS Publishing Corp.
P.O. Box 2276
Glenview, IL 60025

GLOSSARY OF
USEFUL TERMS

(This list of terms is by no means comprehensive.)

Advocacy: the process of mediating and intervening on behalf of a child in need of special services

Affect: the subjective but conscious aspect of an emotion; the emotional aspect of a mental state

Age-appropriate: equivalent to behavior displayed by the majority of "normal" children within a particular age range

Agnosia: the loss or impairment of ability to recognize objects

Alexia: the loss or impairment of ability to read

Anomia: the loss or impairment of ability to remember words or names

Aphasia: the inability to express language, either spoken (receptive) or used (expressive)

Apraxia: the inability to reproduce oral or written language

Assessment: an official evaluation based on a variety of testing instruments

Attention deficit disorder (ADD): the chronic inability to focus on pertinent stimuli for an enduring period of time

Auditory discrimination: the ability to differentiate speech sounds

Auditory memory: the ability to retain or reproduce what is heard

Behavior modification: a technique of behavior control involving the alteration of undesirable behavior through a reward system

Central nervous system: the brain and the spinal cord, through the latter of which sensory impulses are transmitted

Cerebral dominance: the development of one side of the brain as more active than and dominant over the other, causing handed- and footedness and a tendency toward a particular kind of intelligence

Closure: the ability to complete an abstract idea from incomplete information; inferring a triangle from three lines that meet at both sides; hearing the phrase "yester-" and inferring "yesterday"

Cognition: perception, conception, reasoning, judging — skills by which knowledge is acquired

Conceptualization: the highest level of cognition, involving the abstraction of ideas

Congenital: present in an individual at birth

Decoding: the ability to decipher meaning from symbols

Development: the hierarchy of expected performance related to chronological age

Developmental disabilities: a group of handicapping conditions resulting from a breakdown in the expected hierarchy

Discrepancy theory: a theory that defines learning disabilities in terms of the distance between a child's aptitude and performance — the higher the discrepancy, the greater the likelihood of a learning problem

Distractibility: the inability to focus on specific input due to interference by insignificant stimuli

Due process: the legal procedures that, for example, protect a child's right to a free education

Dyscalculia: disturbances in arithmetic ability resulting from disorders in quantitative reasoning, due to neurological dysfunction

Dysfunction: disorder or impairment of a body system

Dysgraphia: a disorder of written language in which the child is unable to transfer visual patterns to motor patterns; inability to write properly

Dyslexia: impairment in the ability to read, due to neurological dysfunction

Early intervention: the introduction of support services for children from birth to age five who have been designated as LD or at risk for LD

Encoding: the ability to put symbols into meaningful units

Etiology: the cause of any dysfunction

Evaluation: the (written) results of a series of tests administered to determine the nature and extent of a child's learning problems

Expressive language: speaking and writing; skills that enable communication

Eye-hand coordination: the ability to synchronize the working of the eyes and the hands in motor activities

Figure-ground perception: the ability to attend to one part of a stimulus in relation to the rest of the field

Fine motor skills: the use of the hands necessary to perform precision tasks such as writing or object manipulation

Genetic: pertaining to hereditary characteristics passed from one generation to the next through genes

Grade equivalent: the level of school performance expected of a student in a certain grade

Gross motor skills: the skills, such as running, jumping, hopping, related to the use of large muscle groups

Hyperactivity: increased or excessive muscular activity resulting from a neurological disorder; not always related to learning problems

Hyperkinesis: restless behavior syndrome, usually connected to learning problems

Impulsivity: sudden, uncontrollable inclinations to activity

Individualized education plan (IEP): a precise curricular and extra-curricular program set up to meet the specific requirements of a child

Integration: the ability to coalesce information from various senses

Intelligence: the aggregate capacity to act purposefully, think rationally, and deal effectively with the environment

Inversion: confusing or turning upside down the direction of single letters or groups of letters, in either reading or writing

Kinesthetic: pertaining to the perception of motion and body awareness of motion

Language: learned behavior involving the use of symbols (words and numbers) via spelling, reading, writing, listening, and speaking

Least restrictive environment (LRE): the classroom situation that allows the special needs student minimal intervention while still addressing the needs of his or her disabilities

Linguistic disability: an impairment of those language systems needed for communication

Local education agency (LEA): the group of professionals responsible for administering and monitoring the needs of an LD student

Mainstreaming: the placement, to the greatest degree possible, of special needs students into educational programs along with normally functioning students

Maturational lag: a delay in the normal process of full development in character and mental capacity

Memory span: the length of time during which a person can remember something, whether long- or short-term

Minimal brain dysfunction: a neurological disturbance in children of average or above-average intelligence who display no major neurological or psychological defects

Modality: one of the five sensory processes through which learning occurs

Multisensory: resulting from two or more combined modalities; sometimes known as interneurosensory

Neurological: dealing with the nervous system

Ocular: referring to the eyes, in the context of this book applied particularly to eye movement

Organic brain syndrome: any mental disorder associated with or caused by disturbances in the function of brain tissue

Orientation: the awareness of self in time and space

Perception: the process of receiving, comprehending, and organizing sensory impressions for transmittal to the central nervous system

Perseveration: the tendency to repeat words or actions continuously; difficulty in shifting to a new activity

Phoneme: the smallest unit of sound in any language; the sound of the letter *b,* for example, is a phoneme

Phonetics: the study of the production of sounds used to symbolize language

Phonics: the study of sounds

PL 94–142: the federal legislation that mandates a free and appropriate education for all children

PL 99–457: the federal legislation that extends the benefits of PL 94–142 to infants, younger children, and adults, and mandates vocational training, research, and resource centers for the handicapped

Projective testing: the use of diagnostic instruments to measure a child's underlying emotional structure and basic responses to the world

Psychological evaluation: the use of diagnostic instruments (tests, interviews) to measure a child's native intelligence, perceptual and cognitive ability, and emotional maturity

Receptive language: language spoken or written by others and received by the individual; language absorbed through listening or reading

Remediation: the process of using a modified or alternative method of teaching in order to help a child learn most effectively; any therapeutic technique that helps an LD child to function more effectively

Resource room: a separate schoolroom to which the LD child can go for part of a day or week in order to receive special instruction or tutoring

Reversal: reversing letters, the order of letters within a word, or the order of words within a sentence, back to front

Section 508: the civil rights legislation that decrees it unlawful to discriminate against people on the basis of a handicapping condition

Self-contained classroom: a separate classroom where an LD child spends part of each day or the entire day being taught by special methods, along with other LD children

Sensorimotor: combining neural transmission of messages from a sensory organ to the muscles and the muscular response; examples of sensorimotor action are puckering after a bitter taste or squinting into the sun

Sequencing: the act of organizing and structuring information into a meaningful order

Spatial orientation: locating oneself in space — e.g., above the rug, to the left of the door

Speech: the articulation of sounds of language, using the mouth, jaw, and vocal cords

Strephosymbolia: an early term for dyslexia, meaning, literally, twisting symbols

Syndrome: a set of symptoms that occur together and create a discernible pattern

Tactile: relating to the sense of touch, or kinesthetic awareness

Temporal orientation: ability to relate in terms of time periods, such as hours or weeks

Tic: an intermittent, involuntary movement of a group of muscles, often without external stimulus; usually the sign of a neurological dysfunction

Vestibular: pertaining to the organ in the ear that controls the perception of balance

Visual discrimination: ability to distinguish shapes or figure-ground relationships

Visual perception: the ability to identify, organize, and interpret what is received by the eye

Visuomotor coordination: the coordination of visual stimuli with the movements of the body

Vocabulary: the level of knowledge of word symbols and their meanings or usage

BIBLIOGRAPHY

I. Books

Academic Therapy Publications. *Directory of Facilities and Services for the Learning Disabled* (annual editions). 28 Commercial Blvd., Novato, CA 94947.

Arena, John. *How to Write an IEP*. Novato, CA: Academic Therapy Publications, 1979.

Arent, Ruth P. *Stress and Your Child: A Parent's Guide to Symptoms, Strategies and Benefits*. Englewood Cliffs, NJ: Prentice Hall, 1984.

Baren, Martin, Lendon Smith, and Robert Leibl. *Overcoming Learning Disabilities: A Team Approach: Parent/Teacher/Child/Psychologist*. Reston, VA: Reston Publishing, 1978.

Barkley, Russell. *The Hyperactive Child: A Handbook for Diagnosis and Treatment*. Guilford, CT: Guilford Press, 1981.

Benton, Arthur, and David Pearl. *Dyslexia: An Appraisal of Current Knowledge*. New York: Oxford University Press, 1978.

Canadian Association for Children with Learning Disabilities. *Learning Disabilities: Information Please*. 1181 Rue de la Montagne, Montreal, Quebec H3G 1Z2.

Chall, Jeanne S. *Learning to Read: The Great Debate*. New York: McGraw-Hill, 1966.

Clarke, Louise. *Can't Read, Can't Write, Can't Talk Too Good Either*. New York: Penguin Books, 1974.

Coles, Gerald. *The Learning Mystique*. New York: Pantheon Books, 1987.

Consiglia, Sister Mary. *The Non-Coping Child*. Novato, CA: Academic Therapy Publications, 1978.

Cruickshank, William. *Learning Disabilities in Home, School, and Community*. Syracuse, NY: Syracuse University Press, 1977.

Cummings, Rhoda Woods, and Cleborne D. Maddox. *Parenting the Learning Disabled Child.* Springfield, IL: C. C. Thomas, 1985.

DesJardines, Charlotte. *How to Organize an Effective Parent Advocacy Group and Move Bureaucracies.* Chicago: Coordinating Council for Handicapped Children, 1980.

Duane, Drake D., and Che Kan Leong. *Understanding Learning Disabilities: International and Multi-Disciplinary Views.* New York: Plenum Press, 1985.

Farnham-Diggory, Sylvia. *Learning Disabilities: A Psychological Perspective.* Cambridge, MA: Harvard University Press, 1978.

Fisher, Johanna. *A Parent's Guide to Learning Disabilities.* New York: Scribner's, 1978.

Foundation for Children with Learning Disabilities. *FCLD Resource Guide: A State-by-State Directory of Special Programs, Schools and Services,* 5th ed. New York: Foundation for Children with Specific Learning Disabilities, 1985.

Franklin, Barry M. *Learning Disabilities: Dissenting Views.* Philadelphia: The Palmer Press, 1987.

Gardner, Howard. *Frames of Mind: The Theory of Multiple Intelligences.* New York: Basic Books, 1983.

Geschwind, Norman. *Selected Papers on Language and the Brain.* Boston: D. Reidl, 1974.

Geschwind, Norman, and Albert Galaburda. *Cerebral Dominance.* Cambridge, MA: Harvard University Press, 1984.

Gottlieb, Marvin, Peter Zinkus, and Larry Bradford. *Current Issues in Developmental Pediatrics: The Learning Disabled Child.* New York: Grune & Stratton, 1979.

Hallahan, Daniel P., and James M. Kauffman. *Introduction to Learning Disabilities: A Psychobehavioral Approach.* Englewood Cliffs, NJ: Prentice Hall, 1976.

Johnson, Stanley W., and Robert L. Morasky. *Learning Disabilities.* Boston: Allyn & Bacon, 1980.

Kavale, Kenneth A., Steven R. Forness, and Michael Bender. *Handbook of Learning Disabilities: Dimensions and Diagnosis.* Boston: College Hill Publications, 1987.

Kirk, Samuel, ed. *Learning Disabilities: Selected ACLD Papers.* Boston: Houghton Mifflin, 1975.

Lerner, Janet. *Children with Learning Disabilities: Theory, Diagnoses, Teaching Strategies.* Boston: Houghton Mifflin, 1976.

Levine, Melvin. *Developmental Variation and Learning Disabilities.* Cambridge, MA: Educators Publishing, 1987.

Levinson, Harold N. *Smart But Feeling Dumb*. New York: Warner Books, 1984.

Long, Kate. *Johnny's Such a Bright Boy, It's a Shame He's Retarded: In Support of Mainstreaming in Public Schools*. Boston: Houghton Mifflin, 1977.

Lyman, Donal E. *Making the Words Stand Still*. Boston: Houghton Mifflin, 1986.

MacCracken, Mary. *Turnabout Children*. Boston: Little, Brown, 1986.

McKinney, James, and Lynne Feagan. *Current Topics in Learning Disabilities*. Norwood, NY: Ablex Publishing, 1983.

Oettinger, Leon, ed. *The Psychologist, the School, and the Child with MBD/LD*. New York: Grune & Stratton, 1978.

Osman, Betty, *Learning Disabilities: A Family Affair*. New York: Random House, 1979.

———. *The Social Side of Learning Disabilities*. New York: Random House, 1982.

Painting, Donald H. *Helping Children with Specific Learning Disabilities: A Practical Guide for Parents and Teachers*. Englewood Cliffs, NJ: Prentice Hall, 1983.

Pavlidis, George, and Dennis Fisher, eds. *Dyslexia: Its Neuropsychology and Treatment*. New York: John Wiley & Sons, 1986.

Roberts, Joseph, and Bonnie Hawks. *Legal Rights Primer for the Handicapped: In and Out of the Classroom*. Novato, CA: Academic Therapy Publications, 1980.

Rosner, Jerome. *Helping Children Overcome Learning Disabilities*. New York: Walker & Co., 1975.

Ross, Alan O. *Learning Disabilities: The Unrealized Potential*. New York: McGraw-Hill, 1977.

Schoonover, Robert J. *Handbook for Parents of Children with Learning Disabilities*. Danville, IL: Interstate Printers and Publishers, 1983.

Silver, Larry. *Attention Deficit Disorders: A Booklet for Parents*. Summit, NJ: CIBA Pharmaceutical Co., 1987.

———. *The Misunderstood Child*. New York: McGraw-Hill, 1984.

Smith, Sally. *No Easy Answers: The LD Child at Home and at School*. New York: Winthrop Publications, 1979.

Special Learning Corporation. *Learning Disabilities: A Reference Book*. Guilford, CT: Special Learning Corporation, 1980.

Stevens, Suzanne. *The LD Child: Ways That Parents Can Help*. Winston-Salem, NC: John F. Blair Publications, 1980.

Vail, Priscilla. *Smart Kids with School Problems*. New York: Dutton, 1987.

Velten, Emmett, and Carlene T. Sampson. *Rx For Learning Disabilities*. Chicago: Nelson-Hall, 1978.

Weiss, Helen Ginandes and Martin S. *Home Is a Learning Place: A Parent's Guide to LD*. Boston: Little, Brown, 1976.

II. Articles

Brooks, Robert. "Learning Disabilities from the Perspective of a Clinical Psychologist." New England Joint Conference on Specific Learning Disabilities, 1987.

Chall, Jeanne S. "Reading and Early Childhood Education: The Critical Issues," *Principal* (May 1987).

Children's Defense Fund. "94–142 and 504: Numbers That Add Up to Educational Rights." Washington, DC, 1984.

Claycomb, Mary. "Brain Research and Learning." NEA Publications, 1978.

Duane, Drake. "Learning Disabilities: Medical Considerations," *Pediatric Annals,* vol. 16, no. 2 (February 1987).

———, and Paula Dozier Rome, eds. "The Dyslexic Child," *Pediatric Annals* (September 1977).

Enfield, Mary Lee. "An Alternate Classroom Approach to Meeting Special Learning Needs of Children with Reading Problems." Doctoral dissertation, University of Minnesota, 1976.

Kistner, Janet, and Mary Osborne. "A Longitudinal Study of LD Children's Self-Esteem," *Journal of Learning Disabilities,* vol. 4 (Fall 1987).

Levine, Mel. "Attention Deficit Disorders: The Diverse Effects of Weak Control Systems in Childhood." Educators Publishing Service, 1986.

Martin, John Henry. "The Writing to Read System and Reading Difficulties." JHM Corporation, 1986.

III. Journals and Newsletters

Closer Look (newsletter of Parents' Campaign for Handicapped Children and Youth)
Box 1492
Washington, DC 20013
(202) 822-7900

Education Daily
1101 King St., P.O. Box 1453
Alexandria, VA 22313
(703) 683-4100

Journal of Learning Disabilities
633 Third Ave.
New York, NY 10017
(212) 741-5986

LD Focus and *LD Research*
Council for Exceptional
Children
Division for Learning
Disabilities
1920 Association Dr.
Reston, VA 22091
(703) 620-3660

LD Quarterly (journal of the
Council for LD)
P.O. Box 40303
Overland Park, KS 66204
(913) 492-8755

OSER News in Print (newsletter
of Office of Special Education)
Switzer Bldg., Room 3018
330 C St. SW
Washington, DC 20202
(202) 732-1723

IV. Sources for Educational Materials

California Association for
Neurologically Handicapped
Children
Literature Distribution Center
P.O. Box 1526
Vista, CA 92083

DIALOG Information Services
340 Hillview Ave.
Palo Alto, CA 94304
(Ask for File 70: special
education computer material.)

LINC Resources, Inc. (special
education software center)
3857 N. High St.
Columbus, OH 43214
(614) 263-5462

National Committee for Citizens
in Education (newsletters and
pamphlets)
Columbia, MD 21044

National Information Center for
Handicapped Children and
Youth (news digests)
Box 1492
Washington, DC 20013

National Information Center for
Special Education Materials
P.O. Box 40130
Albuquerque, NM 87196
(Funded by the OSE.
Computerized bibliographic
information-retrieval system
of commercially available
materials.)

V. Interviews

Dr. Heidelise Als, pediatric
neurologist, Harvard Medical
School and Children's
Hospital, Boston, MA

Mary Briggs, LD specialist,
Graham and Parks School,
Cambridge, MA

Dr. Robert Brooks, child psychiatrist, McLean Hospital, Belmont, MA

Dr. Lois Carra, psychologist and educator, Cambridge, MA

Dr. Jeanne S. Chall, Graduate School of Education, Harvard University, Cambridge, MA

Dr. David Drake, headmaster, The Landmark School, Beverly, MA

Dr. Albert Galaburda, neurobiologist, Harvard Medical School and Beth Israel Hospital, Boston, MA

Dr. Mel Levine, University of North Carolina Medical School, Chapel Hill, NC

Dr. Herbert Lubs, geneticist, University of Miami Medical School, Miami, FL

Dr. William Singer, neurologist, Cambridge City Hospital, Cambridge, MA

Dr. Len Solo, headmaster, Graham & Parks School, Cambridge, MA

Dr. David K. Urion, neurologist, Children's Hospital, Boston, MA

Many teachers, parents, and children.

INDEX

Abstraction, visual and auditory, 26, 27
Academic "retardation," 41–42
Academic skills: developmental therapies and, 217–224; importance of, 42, 202, 246, 247; instruction-oriented approaches to, 202, 210–217; parental intervention and, 181, 193–196; and types of intelligence, 130
Achievement tests. See Tests
ACLD. See Association for Children with Learning Disabilities
AD (anomalous dominance). See Hemispheric (cerebral) dominance
ADD (attention deficit disorder), 21, 51, 53, 60–64, 240; causes of, 61, 87; and concentration, 87; defined, 23, 29, 295; incidence of, and male-female ratio, 61; medication and, 224, 225, 227; symptoms and diagnosis of, 61–64; and tests, 105, 106
Administrative appeal. See Legal rights
Adolescents. See LD children
Adult LD, 239, 247
Advocacy, defined, 295. See also Legal rights; Parents, intervention by; Protection and advocacy groups
Affect, defined, 295
Affective control, lack of, 64. See also Emotional disorders

Age: and appropriate behavior, 45–47, 86, 190, 295; chronological pattern, 57–58; and disorder symptoms, 48–50; and intervention, 236–238
Aggression. See Behavior
Agnosia: defined, 23, 295; visual or motor (as "soft sign"), 43
Alexia: congenital (as category), 21; defined, 23, 295
Allergies, 49, 72, 80; allergens and, 90; elimination diets and, 230
Alphabetic-phonic approach (to remedial reading), 213
Alpha waves, 231
Als, Heidelise, 236–237, 239
Ambidexterity, 43. See also Hemispheric (cerebral) dominance
American Psychiatric Association, 62
Anderson, C. M., 172
Anger: of LD child, 98, 165–167, 201; of parents, 172, 174, 175, 176, 177
Anomia, defined, 23, 295
ANSER (Aggregate Neurobehavioral Student Health and Educational Review) System, 64, 106, 275–292
Anticonvulsants, antidepressants, 226
Antisocial behavior, 52
Anxiety, 50, 52, 186
Aphasia, 69; defined, 23, 295; developmental, under PL 94–142, 138
Appeal process. See Legal rights

Appetite control, lack of, 63

Apraxia, defined, 23, 295

Aptitude tests. *See* Tests

Articulation defects (as "soft sign"), 43. *See also* Speech problems

Assessment, defined, 295. *See also* Evaluation; Tests

Assessment of Children's Language Comprehension, 104

Association Deficit Pathology (as category), 21

Association for Children with Learning Disabilities (ACLD), 9; state offices listed, 255–274

Association for Retarded Citizens, 249

Associative control, lack of, 63

Attention disorders, 86; attention deficit disorder, *see* ADD; excessive attention, 29; medication for, 226; and speech problems, 59

Auditory: abstraction, 27; discrimination, defined, 295; memory, defined, 295 (*see also* Memory disorders); perception and decoding, 26, 29, 30; perceptual disorder, defined, 23; reception, 30; sequencing, 27, 84; tests, 102, 103. *See also* Hearing disabilities; Listening comprehension

Autism, 80

Ayers, Jean, and Ayres Space Test, 218–219

"Baby book," usefulness of, 107

Ball, 244

Barkley, Russ, 61

Barry, 221

Barsch, Leo, 221

Basic skills. *See* Skills

Bayley Scales of Infant Development, 102

BEAM (brain electrical activity mapping), 81

Beery Visual-Motor Integration Test, 103

Behavior: and ADD, 62–64; age-appropriate, 45–47, 86, 190; aggressive or disruptive, 50, 51; antisocial, 52; inconsistent or erratic, 51, 53; lack of control of, 64; LD, what to look for, 50–56, 62–63; learning (remediation and), 210; management of, by LD child, 181, 186–193, 201

Behavioral history of LD child, 110

Behavioral modification, 181, 185–186, 187, 189–193, 200, 210; cognitive (CBM), 191, defined, 295; "reconditioning" and, 212; in teaching reading, 214, 217

Bender Visual Motor tests, 103

Bennison, Anne, 243

Benton Visual Retention Test, 103

Bias, cultural, ethnic, and economic, 100, 129, 239, 244–245. *See also* Blacks; Disadvantaged, the; Minorities

Biofeedback, 231

Biologically oriented remediations. *See* LD: REMEDIATION

Birth complications, 48, 89, 107

Blacks, 169, 215. *See also* Disadvantaged, the; Minorities

Brain, the: asymmetry/imbalance of, 75, 78, 87 (*see also* Hemispheric [cerebral] dominance); and brain waves (delta, alpha), 82, 231; high-technology studies of, 81–82, 240; structure and function of, 72–86

Brain-injured (as category), 21; minimal damage/dysfunction, 21, 22, 24, 138, 243, 297; organic dysfunction/syndrome, 22, 24, 298

Brain injuries, 69–70; endogenous and exogenous, 71–72; and patterning, 223–224; testing for, 103

Brain Research Laboratory of New York Medical College, 240

British Medical Journal (1896), 18

Broca, Paul, 69, 70

Bryans, James and Tanis, 168, 176

Bureau of Special Education (BSEA), 152, 159
Buss, Allan, 243

California Achievement Test, 104
California Test of Personality, 105
Cambridge, Massachusetts, outreach program in, 36
Canada, 17, 60
Carrier, James, 243, 244
Case Western Reserve University, 237
CAT (computerized axial tomography) scans, 81
Cavanaugh, James A., 45
CBM (cognitive behavioral modification), 191. *See also* Behavioral modification
Central nervous system. *See* CNS
Cerebellar-vestibular imbalances. *See* Vestibular system
Cerebral architectonics, 75–76
Cerebral dominance. *See* Hemispheric (cerebral) dominance
Cerebral palsy, 42, 43, 44, 103; minimal (as category), 22
Chall, Jeanne S., 208
Characteristics and symptoms, 38–45, 48–49, 66; ADD and, 61–64; behaviors to look for, 50–56, 62–63; compensatory, *see* Compensatory skills; "profile" of, 56–60. *See also* LD: IDENTIFYING
Cher, 196
Children's Apperception Test, 105
Children's Hospital (Boston), 81, 236
Children's Language Comprehension, Assessment of, 104
Children's Personality Questionnaire, 106
Chromosome, 15, 81, 240. *See also* Heredity (genetics)
Civil rights. *See* Legal rights
Civil Rights, Office for. *See* OCR
Clarke, Louise, 45
Class action, 144–145. *See also* Legal rights

Classroom: regular vs. special, 122, 124–126, 244; resource room, 123, 298; self-contained, 122, 126, 299
Close, Chuck, 196
Closure, defined, 296
CNS (central nervous system): brain structure and, 76, 78; defined, 42, 295; dysfunctions of ("hard" and "soft" signs), 42–44
CNS (central nervous system) Disorder, 21; defined, 23
Cognition, defined, 296
Cognitive approach (to remedial reading), 213
Cognitive behavioral modification (CBM), 191
Cognitive disorders; disabilities defined, 23; integration disability and, 27; problems to watch for, 53–54
Coles, Gerald, 241–242
College facilities and programs, 205; directories of, 293–294
Color phonics, 216. *See also* Reading
Columbia University, 212
Communicative control, lack of, 64
Compensatory skills, 33, 64–65, 86, 196, 234–235, 246–248; creativity, 65, 195, 241; resiliency, 172; and types of intelligence, 130, 195
Comprehension, 84; auditory, test for, 103; language, test for, 104; listening, 29, 30, 42, 220; reading, 42
Concentration, 87. *See also* ADD
Concepts, rigidity concerning, 54
Conceptualization, defined, 296
Conceptually Handicapped (as category), 21
Congenital, defined, 296
Congenital Alexia, Congenital Strephosymbolia (as categories), 21
Connor Scale of Hyperactivity and Conduct Problems, 106
Consent by parents. *See* Parents, intervention by

Consistency: and inconsistent behavior of LD child, 51, 53; in teaching, 183 (*see also* Skills, teaching of)

Contracts, family, 188–189

Control, lack of, 63–64. *See also* Emotional disorders

Converted scores, 115. *See also* Tests

Cooper, Arlene, 117

Coordination, 196; eye-hand, 220, 222, 296; and incoordination, *see* Motor activity disorders; visuomotor, 210, 220, 299

Corpus callosum, 76

Cost: of evaluation, 113, 150–151; of legal fees, 156, 158; of special education, 141, 238; of therapy, 198

Cott, Allan, 230–231

Council for Exceptional Children, Division for Learning Disabilities of, 65

Counseling: for LD child, 197; for parents, 175, 200. *See also* Therapy

Creative learning, 216–217. *See also* Reading

Creativity of LD child, 65, 195, 241

Critchley, William, 79

Crook, William, 230

Cruickshank, William, 128, 129, 221

Cultural bias. *See* Bias

Cultural deprivation. *See* Disadvantaged, the

Cumulative approach (to remedial reading), 213

Cylert, 225

Daydreaming, 51, 53, 63

Deafness. *See* Hearing disabilities

Deaner, 225

Decoding, 214, 215, 216; auditory, 29; defined, 55*n*, 296; kinesthetic, 30

Delacato, Carl, 223, 224

Delinquency, 52, 61, 171, 178, 239

Delta waves, 82

Denmark, 17, 60

Denver Developmental Screening Test, 102

Depletion, fear of, 165

Depression. *See* Emotional disorders

Deprivation. *See* Disadvantaged, the

Detroit Tests of Learning Aptitude, 102

Development: defined, 296; inappropriate, as (chronogenic) cause of LD, 91; "normal," sequences of, 45–50; stages of, in learning to read, 208; tests of, 102–103, 105

Developmental disabilities, defined, 296

Developmental history of LD child, 107–108

Developmental immaturity, 86, 91

Developmental optometry, 222

Development therapies. *See* Therapy

Devereux Rating Scales, 101

Dexedrine, 225

Diagnostic and Statistical Manual for Mental Disorders (APA), 62

Diagnostic Reading Scales, 104

Diet, 210; elimination, for allergies, 230; K-P (Feingold), 228–229, 230. *See also* Nutrition

Differential psychology, 243

Diffuse Brain Damage (as category), 21

Digit Memory Test, 103

Dilantin, 226

Disadvantaged, the, 239; culturally, economically, environmentally deprived, 44, 90, 129; PL 94–142 and, 245; success deprivation, 172. *See also* Minorities

Discrepancy, 38, 59, 101; academic "retardation" as, 41–42; LD child's awareness of, 197; LD defined as, 30–32, 296

Diseases. *See* Illnesses

Disinhibition. *See* Emotional disorders

Disorganization. *See* Organization disability

Disorientation. *See* Spatial disorientation; Temporal orientation

Distractibility, 54, 63; defined, 296

Dolch Basic Sight Word Test, 104

Doman, Robert, 223, 224
Draw-a-Person Test, 105
Drive for perfection, 52
Dropouts, 239
Drugs. *See* Medication
"Drugs in the Management of MBD"
  (Millichap), 225
Duane, Drake, 172
Due process, 142, 143; defined, 296.
  See also Legal rights
Duffy, Frank, 81
Durrell Analysis of Reading Difficulty,
  104
Dyscalculia, 21; defined, 23, 296
Dysfunction, defined, 296
Dysgraphia, 21; defined, 24, 296
Dyslexia, 21, 80, 210, 212, 245;
  defined, 24, 296; "Definitions of"
  (Eisenberg), 69; genetics and, 45,
  79, 81, 213, 239–240; hemispheric
  (cerebral) dominance and, 70–71,
  75, 78, 246; ITPA and, 220; Medical
  Treatment Center for, 88; National
  Advisory Committee on, 238; under
  PL 94–142, 138; "pure," 25. *See also*
  Orton Dyslexia Society; Reading
  disabilities

Early intervention, 36–37, 38, 92, 236–
  239; defined, 296. *See also* Parents,
  intervention by; Protection and
  advocacy services
Ear problems. *See* Auditory; Hearing
  disabilities; Inner ear
Economic deprivation. *See*
  Disadvantaged, the
Education, Departments of. *See*
  Massachusetts; U.S. Department of
  Education
Educational deprivation, 90, 91
Educational history (of LD child), 106,
  109
Educationally Handicapped (as
  category), 21, 57
Education for All Handicapped
  Children Act (1973). *See* PL 94–142
Einstein, Albert, 196, 247

Eisenberg, Leon, 69, 160
Emotional development and
  personality tests, 104–106
Emotional disorders, 28–29, 49, 50; as
  by-product of LD, 98; depression,
  50, 52, 80, 98, 165; disinhibition
  (lack of self-control), 28, 52, 64;
  frustration, 50, 51, 53, 98; inability
  to control behavior, 63–64; mood
  swings, 29, 50, 51, 64; reading
  failure and, 239; social immaturity,
  52; social maladjustment, 28, 52,
  167–172 (*see also* Peer relationships);
  temper outbursts, 29, 51; testing for,
  103; verbal disinhibition, 64
Emotionally sound approach (to
  remedial reading), 213
Emotional stress, 44, 90, 98, 165
Emotions of parents. *See* Parents
Encoding, 215, 216; defined, 55*n*,
  296
Enfield, Mary Lee, 215–216
England, 17, 60
Environment: alteration of, 210; effects
  of, 61, 72, 89–92, 230; least
  restrictive, *see* LRE; for study or
  therapy, 182–183, 185, 220, 221
Epilepsy, 43
Etiology: defined, 68, 296; of LD, *see*
  LD: ETIOLOGY (CAUSES)
Evaluation, 133–134, 145, 147; core,
  99; cost of, 113, 150–151; defined,
  296; dissatisfaction of parent with,
  177 (*see also* independent, *below*);
  independent, 112, 113, 144, 149–
  151; legal right to, 37, 112, 142,
  143–144, 236; length of time for,
  159; need for, 37, 39; parent- or
  guardian-initiated, 96, 127, 143;
  PL 94–142 on, 138; psychological,
  defined, 298; of reading problem,
  213–214; referral for, 143, 145, 146.
  See also Tests
Evaluation meetings, 112, 113–117,
  145, 147–148
Explicitness, 182–183. *See also* Skills,
  teaching of

Expressive language, defined, 296

Expressive One-Word Vocabulary Test, 104

Expressive vocal and expressive motor disorders, 30

Extracurricular activities, 170–171, 181, 196

Eye defects. *See* Vision problems; Visual

Eye-hand coordination, 220, 222; defined, 296

Fagan, Joseph, 237

Failure, fear of, 165

Family, 178; contracts between members of, 188–189; IEP (Individual Family Service Plan) for, 238; interactions of, as LD cause, 176, 242; LD child's function in (as taught skill), 181, 182–185, 186–189; LD child's relationships with, 60, 166–167, 175–176, 184–185, 186–189, 201, 250; and relatives, 177–178. *See also* Parents; Parents, intervention by; Siblings

Family history, 80–81, 106–110. *See also* Heredity (genetics)

Family therapy. *See* Therapy

Farnham-Diggory, Sylvia, 22, 57, 58, 60, 69, 129

Fears (of LD child), 165; discussion of, 193; phobias, 52

Federal Rehabilitation Act (1973). *See* Section 504

Feingold, Benjamin, 228–229, 230

Fernald, Grace, 212

Figure-ground perception, defined, 296

Fine motor skills. *See* Motor skills (fine and gross)

First Grade Screening Test, 102

Focal control, lack of, 63; medication and, 225

Ford, Gerald, 135

Foundation for Children with Learning Disabilities, 9

Fragility (of mood of confidence), 51. *See also* Emotional disorders; Self-image/self-esteem

Frames of Mind (Gardner), 33, 130, 195

France, 17

Franklin, Barry M., 243

Fredericks, Bud, 249

Frostig, Marianne, 103, 217, 220, 221; Visual Perception Test and Training Program of, 103, 220

Frustration. *See* Emotional disorders

Function-deficit approach, 206, 218. *See also* LD: REMEDIATION

Galaburda, Albert M., 75–78 *passim*, 82, 83, 85, 240

Gardner, Howard, 33, 91, 130, 195, 242, 246

Gates-MacGinitie Reading Tests, 104

Genetics. *See* Heredity

Germany, 60

Geschwind, Norman, 76, 78, 79–80, 82, 83

Gesell, Arnold, 222

Gesell Developmental Schedules, 102

Getman, Arnold, 222

Gillingham, Anna, 212

Goldman-Fristoe Test of Articulation, 104

Goldman-Fristoe-Woodcock Test of Auditory Discrimination, 103

Good For Me kit, 183

Gottlieb, Marvin, 21

Grade equivalent: defined, 297; score, 115. *See also* Tests

Graham-Kendall Memory for Designs test, 103

Grandparents, 177–178

Gray Oral Reading Test, 104

Gretsky, Wayne, 196

Grief, parents', 131, 174

Gross-Glenn, Karen, 239, 240

Gross motor skills. *See* Motor skills (fine and gross)

Group therapy. *See* Therapy

Guides and directories, list of, 293–294

Guilt feelings: of LD child, 165, 200; of parent, 166, 172–175, 177, 201; of siblings, 176

Hair: analysis, 229; premature graying of, 45, 80
Hallahan, Daniel P., 25, 26, 28, 41, 42, 44, 45
Hammill, Donald, 243
Handbook for Parents of Children with Learning Disabilities (Schoonover), 145
Handicapped children, 134–135; laws benefiting, 134–140; LD children classified as, 135; physical disabilities, 80, 169. *See also* PL 94–142 (Education for All Handicapped Children Act, 1973); PL 99–457 (1986 Amendments to PL 94–142)
"Hard signs" (of CNS dysfunction), 42–43, 44
Harvard: Graduate School of Education, 208; Medical School, 75
Hawks, Bonnie, 137
Hayes Adaptation of Stanford-Binet test, 102
Headache, 49; migraine, 44, 80
Health. *See* Illnesses; Medication; Nutrition; Physical disabilities; Physical examination
Health, Education and Welfare, U.S. Department of, 238
Health insurance/HMO, 198
Hearing disabilities, 97; tests for, 102, 103. *See also* Auditory
Helping Children Overcome LD: A Handbook for Teachers (Rosner), 206
Helplessness, learned, 165
Hemispheric (cerebral) dominance, 69–70, 73–76, 92; defined, 295; and dyslexia, 70–71, 75, 78, 246; mixed (ambidexterity) or anomalous (AD), 43, 79–80; patterning for, 223–224
Heredity (genetics), 48, 57, 60, 76, 83, 91; and dyslexia, 45, 79, 81, 213, 239–240; "genetic" defined, 297; and

hemispheric dominance, 79–80. *See also* Male-female ratio
Hinshelwood, James, 70, 71
Hiskey-Nebraska Test of Learning Aptitude, 102
Histories, family, educational, and personal, 80–81, 106–110; record-keeping for, 144
Home Is a Learning Place (Weiss and Weiss), 194
Home teaching, 194–195. *See also* LD: REMEDIATION
Homework, 181, 194, 195
Hostility, 50
House-Tree-Person Projective Technique (test), 106
Hygiene of LD child, 171, 181; sample routine, 182–183
Hyperactivity, 21, 71, 80; causes of, 87; defined, 24, 28, 51, 297; diet and, 229; medication and, 224, 225, 226; as subset of ADD, 61; test for, 106
Hyperkinesis, defined, 24, 297
Hyperkinetic Behavior Syndrome (as category), 21
Hypoactivity, 21, 51; defined, 24, 28
Hypoglycemia, 90, 231
Hypokinetic Behavior Syndrome (as category), 21

IEP (Individualized Education Plan), 98, 116–122, 177, 195; annual review of, 127–128, 156; defined, 297; for family (Individual Family Service Plan), 238; and LRE, 123, 125; Massachusetts Guidelines regarding, 158–159; as model for life at home, 164; parental participation in, 116–117, 121–122, 127–128, 144, 145–161, 214; under PL 94–142, 136, 138, 144; sample, illustrated, 118–119; in sample case, 146–156; therapy programs under, 197, 203
IEP Primer, The (School and Cooper), 117

Illinois Test of Psycholinguistic
Abilities. *See* ITPA
Illnesses: causal connection with LD
denied, 80; childhood (medical
history), 107, 108; CNS
dysfunctions and, 42–43, 44; ear
infection, 88; family history of, 109;
maternal, in pregnancy, 89;
metabolic imbalances, 89. *See also*
Allergies; Birth complications;
Headache
Immaturity. *See* Maturity
Immune system disorders, 80
Impulsiveness, impulsivity, defined,
51, 297
Inconsistent or erratic behavior, 51, 53
Incoordination. *See* Motor activity
disorders
Individualized approach (to remedial
reading), 213
Individualized Education Plan,
Individual Family Service Plan. *See*
IEP
Information agencies, list of. *See*
Organizations
Information processing, 83–84, 211
Information-processing disorders, 26–
28, 84–89, 210; defined, 24
Informed consent. *See* Legal rights
Initial Teaching Alphabet (ITA), 216
Inner ear, 88, 222–223. *See also*
Vestibular system
Input disabilities, 26
Institute for the Achievement of
Human Potential (Philadelphia), 223
Instruction-oriented approach. *See* LD:
REMEDIATION
Insurance (covering therapy), 198
Integration: defined, 297; disabilities,
26–27; in processing information,
26, 84. *See also* Cognitive disorders
Intelligence: defined, 297; and IQ, 100,
101, 115, 246; of LD child, 36, 60,
72; seven types of (Gardner's view),
130, 246; and "word blindness," 69.
See also Skills

Intelligence and readiness tests. *See*
Tests
Interpersonal and intrapersonal skills,
130, 189. *See also* Skills (social)
Intervention. *See* Early intervention;
Medical intervention; Parents,
intervention by; Protection and
advocacy services
Introduction to LD (Hallahan and
Kauffman), 25
Inversion, defined, 297
IQ, 57, 100, 101, 115, 246
Irlen, Helen, and Irlen Institute, 88–89,
222
ITA (Initial Teaching Alphabet), 216
ITPA (Illinois Test of Psycholinguistic
Abilities), 102–103, 104, 220

Japan, 60
John, E. Roy, 81–82
Johnson, Doris, 216
Johnson, Stanley, 16
Joint Association of Neurologists and
Pediatricians, 224
Juvenile delinquency ("JD"). *See*
Delinquency

Kaiser-Permanente Clinic (California),
228
Kauffman, James, 25
Kaufman Test of Educational
Achievement, 104
Keogh, Barbara, 65, 66
Kephart, Newell, 222
Kinesthetic, defined, 297
Kinesthetic skills: decoding and
encoding, 30, 216; development of
(and movigenic curriculum), 220,
221; reading programs and, 216; as
type of intelligence, 130. *See also*
Motor skills (fine and gross)
Kinetic Family Drawing test, 105
Kingsbury Laboratory School
(Washington, D.C.), 52
Kinsbourne, Marcel, 245
Kirk, Samuel, 20, 103, 217, 220

Kirk, Winifred, 20, 220
K-P diet. *See* Diet
Kronick, Doreen, 175–176, 233, 242, 247

Labels. *See* LD: DEFINED
Labile emotions (mood swings). *See* Emotional disorders
Language: Black English, 215; defined, 297; developmental sequence of, 47; -experience approach to reading, 208–209, 210; expressive, defined, 296; ITPA and, 103; Japanese, 60; and linguistic skills, 130; native (non-English), and rights of child and parent, 113, 115, 152; reading and, 207; receptive, defined, 298; spontaneous or demand, 27
Language Comprehension, Assessment of Children's, 104
Language deficits, 23, 87; developmental, 49; language deprivation and, 90; output disability and, 28; problems to watch for, 54; tests for, 102, 103, 104; therapy for, 219–220. *See also* Speech problems; Symbolism disorders
Language Disability (as category), 21; defined, 24; specific, 71 (*see also* Dyslexia)
Language Disordered Child (as category), 21
Language therapy, 220
LD: action against, 95–122 (*see also* LD: REMEDIATION; IEP [Individualized Education Plan]; Tests); adults with, 239, 247; age and, 57, 60; alternative theories of, 241–244; causes of, *see* LD: ETIOLOGY (CAUSES); cultural deprivation and, 44, 90, 129; and delta wave activity, 82; economic loss due to, 239; emotional disturbances and, 44, 90, 98, 165; existence of, argued, 15, 241–244;

"good things about," 234–235 (*see also* Compensatory skills); intelligence and, *see* Intelligence; and legal rights, *see* Legal rights; male-female ratio, 56, 57, 58, 60, 61, 77–78, 79; parents and, *see* Parents; Parents, intervention by; as perceptual processing deficit, 85, 86; and physical diseases, 80; population figures, *see* Population afflicted with LD; prediction of, 80, 81, 82, 237; prognosis for, 247; racial bias and, *see* Bias; racial distribution of, 56, 59; research on, 239–241; as social and political issue, 44–45; specific (as category), 22, 24, 71, 137, 138–139, 141; vs. TD ("teaching disability"), 33
LD: DEFINED, 14–16, 18–21, 25–30, 41, 72; definition criticized, 241–245; as discrepancy, 30–32, 296 (*see also* Discrepancy); and labels, 15, 20, 33, 123–124; by PL 94–142, 18, 19, 137, 138–139, 243, 245; and purpose of definition, 65–66; two-years-behind definition, 141–142, 151–152, 232; by U.S. Education Department, 18, 90
LD: ETIOLOGY (CAUSES), 68, 69–92, 97; brain structure and, 73, 75; chronogenic, 91; Cott's vitamin theory of, 230–231; emotional, 98; external, 89–90 (*see also* Environment); family interactions and, 176, 242; genetic, *see* Heredity; organic, 88–89, 92 (*see also* Hemispheric [cerebral] dominance); pediagenic, 91; prenatal, 48, 70, 76–77, 89, 107; and remedial programs, 210–211; sociogenic, 91; unimportance of, 90–91
LD: IDENTIFYING, 35–66, 93–132; age and, 57–58; age-appropriate behavior in, 45–47; behaviors to look for, 50–56, 62–63; characteristics and symptoms, 38–45, 48–66; cultural/ethnic bias in, 239, 244–245; discrepancy and, *see*

Discrepancy; LQ and, 16; methods questioned, 242, 244; parents and, 31, 143; patterns in, 38, 41, 80; screening for, 36–37, 96–116, 141, 145, 146–147, 215 (*see also* Tests)

LD: REMEDIATION, 202–233; alternative plans, 203, 215; behavioral/emotional therapies and, 204 (*see also* Behavioral modification); biologically oriented, 202, 209–210, 224–231; child's contribution to, 113–114, 182–185, 186, 191–193, 248; current efforts criticized, 242–244; defined, 298; developmentally oriented, 202, 209, 217–224; early intervention and, 36–37, 38, 92, 236–239, 296; federal support for, 140–142; function-deficit, 206, 218; goal-oriented, 209, 210, 232; goals of, 204–207; home teaching, 194–195; instruction-oriented, 202, 210–217, 220; and learning style, 86, 87–88, 209, 241; parental participation in, 145–161, 193–201 (*see also* Parents, intervention by); placement levels, 121–122, 123; process-oriented, 209, 210, 232; prognosis for, 247; progress reports, 127–128; reading programs in, *see* Reading; self-image and, 164–165, 202 (*see also* Self-image/self-esteem); special classrooms for, 56, 122, 123–124, 298, 299; teaching of skills as, 181–210 (*see also* Skills, teaching of); therapy and, 196–200 (*see also* Therapy); tutoring as option, 37, 128, 195, 217. *See also* IEP (Individualized Education Plan)

LD children: academic skills of, *see* Academic skills; adolescent, 50, 171–172, 178–179; after school, 163–179 (*see also* extracurricular activities of, *below*); anger of, 98, 165–167, 201 (*see also* feelings/viewpoint of, *below*); and attention problems, *see* Attention disorders; behavior of, *see* Behavior; Behavioral modification;

cerebral dominance and, 75 (*see also* Hemispheric [cerebral] dominance); characteristics of, *see* typical problems of, *below;* Characteristics and symptoms; and child's awareness of problem, 67, 131, 162, 180, 198–200; college or trade school for, 205, 293–294; compensatory skills of, *see* Compensatory skills; defined, 19; and delinquency, *see* Delinquency; different ways of learning by, 86, 87–88, 209, 241; drug use by, 171; emotional problems of, 165 (*see also* Emotional disorders); extracurricular activities of, 170–171, 181, 196; family life of, *see* Family; Parents; Siblings; famous, 196, 247; fears of, 52, 165, 193; feelings/viewpoint of, 13–14, 164–172, 205 (*see also* anger of; fears of, *above*; guilt feelings of, *below;* Self-image/self-esteem); future for, 234–250; goals for, 204–207; guilt feelings of, 165, 200; histories (family, educational, medical) of, 80–81, 106–110, 144; identifying, *see* LD: IDENTIFYING; IEP for, *see* IEP (Individualized Education Plan); intelligence of, 36, 59, 60, 72; legal rights of, *see* Legal rights; mainstreaming/LRE for, 122–127; medication for, *see* Medication; nonrecognition of (before PL 94–142), 135; organizations serving, *see* Organizations; ostracism of, 169; participation/responsibility of, in program, 182–185, 186, 191–193, 248; and peers, 124–125, 167–169, 171, 178, 189–192; in population, *see* Population afflicted with LD: "profile" of, 56–60; reading programs for, 207–217 (*see also* Reading); self-care (hygiene, time management) by, 171, 181, 182, 183–185; self-image of, *see* Self-image/self-esteem; self-reliance of, 247; sense of proportion lacking in,

LD children (*cont.*)
193; social life of, 167–172 (*see also* and peers, *above*); and sports, 196; support systems for, 178, 189 (*see also* Support groups and services); survival strategies for, 181–201; teachers' perceptions of, 169–170; teaching of, *see* LD: REMEDIATION; and telling child what is going on, 113–114; testing, *see* Tests; therapy for, *see* Therapy; typical problems of, 52–56

Lead poisoning, 90, 230

Learned helplessness, 165

Learning disability. *See* LD

Learning Disabilities (Osman), 25

Learning Disabilities: A Psychological Perspective (Farnham-Diggory), 22, 57, 69

Learning Disabilities: The Unrealized Potential (Ross), 14, 32

Learning Disability Quarterly, 126

Learning Disabled Child, The: Ways That Parents Can Help (Stevens), 95, 204

Learning Mystique, The (Coles), 241

Learning Quotient (LQ) equation (Johnson and Morasky), 16

Learning style. *See* LD: REMEDIATION

Least restrictive environment. *See* LRE

Left-handedness, 79–80, 205

Legal rights, 114, 134–161; administrative appeal, 142, 145, 154–155; appeal process, 142–145, 151–155, 157–160; civil rights, 135, 139, 161; Civil Rights, Office for (OCR), 142, 156, 254–255; civil suit, 142, 145, 155–156; class action, 144–145, 156; to complaint, 142, 155; and cost of legal aid, 156, 158; to discussion and mediation, 145, 148–153; due process, 142, 143, 296; hearing process, 142, 153–154, 177; informed consent, 112, 115; to LD testing and evaluation, 37, 112, 142, 143–144, 236; Massachusetts Guidelines to, 158–159; to native

(non-English) language in testing and at meetings, 113, 115, 152; for parents to attend evaluation meetings, 112; for parents to see test work and scores, 113; practical issues concerning, 157–160; to services, 136; to specific instructional method, 215; to therapy, 197–198. *See also* PL 94–142 (Education for All Handicapped Children Act, 1973)

Legal Rights Primer for the Handicapped, The (Roberts and Hawks), 137

Leiter International Performance Scale, 101

Levine, Mel, 61, 62, 63, 64, 240–241

Levinson, Harold, 88, 222–223

Librium, 226

Limbic system (brain formation), 73

Lincoln-Oseretsky Motor Development Scale, 103

Linguistic approach (to remedial reading), 213

Linguistic disability, defined, 297

Listening comprehension, 29, 30, 42, 220. *See also* Auditory

Lithium carbonate, 226

Local education agency (LEA), defined, 297

Logical-mathematical skills, 130. *See also* Academic skills

LQ (learning quotient), 16

LRE (least restrictive environment), 122, 123, 126, 127, 160; defined, 297; and IEP as more restrictive, 150; PL 94–142 and, 125, 136, 142

Lubs, Herbert, 81, 239, 240

Lubs, Marie-Louise, 81

MA (mental age), 101, 116

McCarthy Scales of Children's Abilities, 103

McDonald Deep-Screening Articulation Test, 104

Mainstreaming, 123–127; defined, 297. *See also* Classroom; LRE (least restrictive environment)

Male-female ratio, 56, 57, 58, 60, 61, 77–78, 79
Malnutrition. *See* Nutrition
Marriage problems. *See* Parents
Martin, John, 215, 216
Masland, Richard, 246
Massachusetts: Department of Education, 131; Office for Children, 160; placement levels in, 121, 123; 766 Guidelines, 158–159
Maternal health. *See* Prenatal conditions
Mathematical skills, 42, 130. *See also* Academic skills
Maturity, 84; and developmental immaturity, 86, 91; maturational lag, 24, 212, 297; social, test for, 102; and social immaturity, 52
Mean score, median score, 115. *See also* Tests
Mediation. *See* Legal rights
Medical Dyslexic Treatment Center, 88
Medical history: of family, 80–81, 106, 107, 109; of LD child, 107, 108
Medical intervention, 175, 206. *See also* Medication; Pediatrician
Medication, 210, 223, 224–228
Megavitamins. *See* Vitamins
Mellaril, 226
Memory disorders: auditory or verbal, 27, 29, 102; defined, 29; developmental, 49; long-term, 27, 102; and perceptual development, 102; short-term, 27, 102; tests for, 102–103; visual, 27, 29, 102
Memory span, defined, 297
Mental age. *See* MA
Mental retardation, 72, 139
Mercury, toxicity of, 90, 230
Metabolic imbalances, 89
Metropolitan Achievement Test, 104
Migraine, 44, 80
Millichap, Gordon, 225
Mills vs. *The District of Columbia Board of Education*, 135
Minerals, 229–230

Minimal Brain Damage, Minimal Brain Dysfunction (as categories), 21, 22, 138, 243; defined, 24, 297
Minimal Cerebral Disorder, Minimal Cerebral Palsy (as categories), 22
Minnesota Reading Project, 215–216
Minorities: bias in recognizing LD, 239, 244–245; bias in testing, 100, 129; LD among (racial distribution), 56, 59; and native language (non-English), 113, 115, 152. *See also* Blacks; Disadvantaged, the
Misunderstood Child, The (Silver), 26, 164
Mitchell, Bill, 249
Mixed dominance, 43. *See also* Hemispheric (cerebral) dominance
Mnemonic devices (in spatial orientation), 205
Modality, defined, 298
Model-building (in identifying LD), 50
Mood swings. *See* Emotional disorders
Morasky, Robert, 16
Morton, William Pringle, 18, 22, 69, 70, 71
Motivation, 84
Motor activity disorders, 24, 27, 28; developmental, 48, 49; hyperactivity, *see* Hyperactivity; hyperkinesis, 24, 297; Hyperkinetic, Hypokinetic Behavior Syndromes (as categories), 21; hypoactivity, 21, 24, 28, 51; incoordination, 28, 49, 88, 196, 210; lack of motor control, 64; perseveration, perseverance, 28, 52, 298; poor kinesthetic decoding, 30; symbolism disorders and, 30
Motor agnosia (as "soft sign"), 43
Motor skills (fine and gross), 27; defined, 297; developmental sequence of, 46; instruction methods, 220, 221; testing of, 102–103; visual, 84. *See also* Kinesthetic skills
Movigenic curriculum (Barsch), 221

Multidisciplinary approach (to remedial reading), 213
Multisensory, defined, 298
Multisensory approach, 213, 221. *See also* Therapy
Multisensory Disorders (as category), 22
Musical skill, 130
Myers, Patricia, 243
Myklebust, Helmer, 21

National Advisory Committee on Dyslexia, 238
National Institute of Mental Health, 78
Nausea, 49
Negative attitude, 50, 52
Neocortex (brain formation), 73, 76
Nerve cell migration, 81. *See also* Heredity (genetics)
Neurobiology, neurology, 20, 43, 92; and male-female ratio of LD, 57; research in, 69–71
Neurological, defined, 298
Neurological disorders, 212, 225; defined, 24
Neurological evaluation, 97, 242
Neurological Immaturity (as category), 22
Neurophrenia, Neurophysiological Dyssynchrony (as categories), 22
Neuropsychological tests, 106
Neurotransmitters, 76, 83
New York Institute for Child Development, 28
New York Medical College, 81; Brain Research Laboratory of, 240
No Easy Answers (Smith), 21, 52, 157
No One to Play With: The Social Side of Learning Disabilities (Osman), 189
Norms, 116. *See also* Tests
Northwest Syntax Screening Test, 104
Notification of referral, 145, 146. *See also* Evaluation
Nottebohm, Fernando, 92
Numerical score, 116. *See also* Tests

Nutrition: childhood history of, 110; and malnutrition, 72, 77, 89–90. *See also* Diet

Obstetrical history. *See* Prenatal conditions
Occupational therapy (OT). *See* Therapy
OCR (Office for Civil Rights), 142, 156; list of regional offices, 254–255
Ocular, defined, 298
Ocular therapy, 222
Office for Civil Rights. *See* OCR
Office of Special Education and Rehabilitative Services (OSER), 156
Ojeman, George, 81
Oral expression (as basic skill), 42. *See also* Verbalizing
Organic Brain Dysfunction (as category), 22
Organic brain syndrome, defined, 24, 298
Organicity (as category), 22
Organization: in processing information, 27, 84; teaching LD child skill of, 182–185
Organization disability, 27, 53, 54, 59, 165
Organizations: local, for LD child to join, 189; local education agency (LEA), defined, 297; national (special needs and advocacy), 251–252; state-by-state, 255–274. *See also* Protection and advocacy services; Support groups and services
Orientation, defined, 298. *See also* Spatial disorientation; Temporal orientation
Orthomolecular approaches, 228–230. *See also* Therapy
Orton, Samuel T., 70–71, 72, 74, 81, 212–213, 214, 217, 220
Orton Dyslexia Society, 71, 213, 232; branch offices listed, 255–274
Orton-Gillingham system, 212–214, 215, 216

Index

OSER (Office of Special Education and Rehabilitative Services), 156
Osman, Betty, 25, 26, 28, 189
Osmond, Humphrey, 230
OT (Occupational therapy). *See* Therapy
Output disabilities, 27–28. *See also* Language deficits; Motor activity disorders
Owen, Freya, 56, 57, 58, 59, 60

PACs (parent advisory councils), 131. *See also* Support groups and services
Parents: child's anger toward, 166; and child's self-esteem, 167, 174, 176, 182; counseling for, *see* therapy for, *below;* education and grades of, 58–59, 60; emotions (grief, guilt) of, 35, 131, 162, 166, 172–178, 180–181, 201, 235; and marriage problems, 162, 163, 173–174, 175, 178; medical records of, 106, 107; perspective of, regarding LD, 130–132, 172–179, 235–236; PL 94–142 and, 136, 140, 142–145 (*see also* Legal rights); role of, in creation of LD, 242; self-image, self-esteem of, 173, 174, 237; skills taught by, 181–201; support groups for, *see* Support groups and services; tests given to, 101; therapy for, 175, 200. *See also* Family; Parents, intervention by
Parents, intervention by: in academic and extracurricular areas, 181, 193–196; burden of proof on, 143; in choice of program, 206–207; consent by, 112, 115, 145, 147; as decisive factor, 160, 161, 233; discrepancy recognized by, 31 (*see also* LD: IDENTIFYING); early, 36, 38, 236–239; and evaluation, *see* Evaluation; Evaluation meetings; keeping an eye on things, 95, 127–128, 183, 195, 248 (*see also* Tests); LD child's resentment of, 171; and mainstreaming, 124–127;

notification of, in referral, 145, 146; overcompensation, danger of, 174–175; participation of, in IEP, 116–117, 121–122, 127–128, 144, 145–161, 214; plan of action for, 95–122; record-keeping by, 107–110, 144, 149, 154, 187; responsibility of, 99, 130, 144, 248–250; rights of, 37, 68, 99, 105 (*see also* Legal rights); in social situations, 171, 177, 192; steps to take, 145–161; support groups for, *see* Support groups and services; in teaching social skills, 181–201; and testing of child, 105; and ways to help LD child, 249–250; when to stop, 231–233. *See also* LD: REMEDIATION; Therapy
Parents Anonymous, 237
Patience. *See* Skills, teaching of
Patterning programs, 223–224
Peabody Individual Achievement Test, 104
Peabody Individual Vocabulary Test, 102, 104
Pediatrician, 37, 39, 81, 131, 237, 238; examination by, 97, 108–109; parent relationship with, 175. *See also* Medical intervention
Peer relationships, 124–125, 167–169, 171, 178, 189–192
Pennsylvania Association of Retarded Citizens, The vs. *The Pennsylvania Board of Education,* 135
Percentile, 116. *See also* Tests
Perception: defined, 298; figure-ground, defined, 296; in processing information, 84
Perceptual development tests, 102–103, 219
Perceptual disorders, 24, 26, 29–30; defined, 23, 29, 30
Perceptually Handicapped (as category), 22, 243; defined, 24; under PL 94–142, 138
Perceptual processing deficit, LD as, 85, 86

319

Perceptual Skill Project (Rosner), 221
Perinatal history, 107
Perseveration, perseverance, 52; defined, 28, 298. *See also* Motor activity disorders
Personality tests, 104–106
PET (positron emission tomography) scans, 81
Pharmacological remediations. *See* Medication
Phenobarbital, 225, 226
Phobias, 52. *See also* Fears
Phoneme, defined, 298
Phonics/phonetics. *See* Reading
Physical disabilities. *See* Handicapped children
Physical examination, 97, 108–109. *See also* Medical intervention; Tests
Physical therapy (PT), 219. *See also* Therapy
PL 94–142 (Education for All Handicapped Children Act, 1973), 134–145, 152; Amendments to, *see* PL 99–457; and civil suits, 155–156; criticisms of, 141, 160–161, 245; defined, 298; and evaluation meetings, 114; LD defined under, 18, 19, 137, 138–139, 243, 245; and LRE, 125, 136, 142; major components of, 137–139
PL 99–457 (1986 Amendments to PL 94–142), 139, 142, 158, 238, 239; defined, 298
Placement levels, 121–122, 123. *See also* LD: REMEDIATION
Play Therapy Observation test, 105
Population afflicted with LD, 16–17, 56–58, 60, 140, 141, 142; racial distribution, 56, 59
Porch Index of Communicative Ability in Children, 104
Pregnancy. *See* Prenatal conditions
Prenatal conditions, 48, 70, 76–77, 89; obstetrical history, 107
Primary Reading Retardation (as category), 22
Private schools, directories of, 293–294

Processing deficits, 86–89. *See also* Information-processing disorders
Projective testing, 105; defined, 298
Project Read, 215–216
Protection and advocacy services, 135, 157, 158, 248; and class action suits, 156; national and state organizations listed, 251–252, 255–274
Psycholinguistic Disability (as category), 22
Psychological evaluation, defined, 298. *See also* Evaluation
Psychometric tests. *See* Tests
Psychostimulants, 225
PT (Physical Therapy), 219
Public Law(s) 94–142, 99–457. *See* PL 94–142; PL 99–457
Public school system. *See* School, the
Pugach, N., 244
Purdue Perceptual-Motor Survey, 103

Quantitative Electrophysiological Battery (QB), 81–82, 240

Racial bias. *See* Bias
Racial distribution. *See* Population afflicted with LD
Radiation stress, 90
Raw score, 116
R-complex (brain formation), 73
Readiness tests. *See* Tests
Reading: and comprehension of, as basic skill, 42; definition of, 207; developmental stages in learning, 208; factors involved in, 207–208; goals for, 205; language-experience approach to, 208–209, 210; learning behaviors and, 210; oral, perseveration in, 28; Orton remedial system, 212–215; phonetics and phonics defined, 298; phonics/phonetics approach to, 208, 209, 211, 212, 213, 214, 216; problems with, *see* Reading disabilities; relative importance of, 246; silent, subvocalization in, 30; skills tested, 104; teaching methods/special

projects, 208–217; tinted lenses and, 89, 222; vision problems and, 88, 97, 222; whole-word approach to, 208–209, 210, 212. *See also* Visual

Reading disabilities: consequences of, 239; developmental, 49; input disability and, 26; inversion (defined), 297; as major cause of school failure, 207; Orton's theory regarding, 212–213; problems to watch for, 54–55; reversal (defined), 298; and "right not to read," 244. *See also* Dyslexia

Reading Disability, Reading Disorder (as categories), 22

Reagan, Ronald, 139

Reasoning: disturbances of, *see* Dyscalculia; mathematical, 42; spatial, 130

Receptive auditory and receptive vocal disorders, 30

Receptive language, defined, 298

"Reconditioning," 212. *See also* Behavioral modification

Record-keeping by parents. *See* Parents, intervention by

Referral for evaluation of LD. *See* Evaluation

Rehabilitation Act, Federal (1973). *See* Section 504

Reitan-Indiana Neuropsychological Test Battery, 106

Related services, 136, 137

Remediation, defined, 298. *See also* LD: REMEDIATION

Repetition. *See* Skills, teaching of

Research, new directions for, 239–241

Resource room, 123; defined, 298

Retardation. *See* Academic retardation; Mental retardation

Reversal, defined, 298

Rewards. *See* Skills, teaching of

Rey-Osterreith Figure Copy Test, 103

Right-left ambivalence, persistent, 43

"Right NOT to Read, The" (Snyder), 244

Rights. *See* Legal rights

Ritalin, 225, 226

Roberts, Joseph, 137

Rockefeller, Nelson, 196

Rorschach Inkblot Test, 105, 106

Rosner, Jerome, 206; Perceptual Skill Project of, 221

Ross, Alan, 14, 32, 33, 129, 244

Roswell-Chall Auditory Blending Test, 104

Rumsey, Judith, 78

Sampson, Carlene, 15

Saunders, Roger, 232

Scheibel, Arnold, 78

School, Beverly, 117

School, the: change in school system advocated, 242–243; and medication for LD child, 228; public, inadequacies of (PL 94–142 and), 134–135. *See also* IEP (Individualized Education Plan); Teachers

Schoonover, Robert, 145

Scores (of evaluated tests). *See* Tests

Screening. *See* LD: IDENTIFYING

"Secret code," 191

Section 504 (Federal Rehabilitation Act, 1973), 139–140, 142, 152, 156, 161; defined, 298

Sedatives, 226

Self-contained classroom, 122, 126; defined, 299

Self-control, lack of. *See* Emotional disorders (disinhibition)

Self-image/self-esteem, 52, 98, 167; of adolescent, 50, 172; dependency on parents and, 167; importance of, 164–166, 202; labels and, 15; of LD adult, 239; mainstreaming/LRE and, 125–126, 127; of parents, 173, 174, 237; parents' feelings and, 174, 176, 182; peer relationships and, 169; rebuilding, 181–183, 189, 195–197, 199, 202, 232; teacher expectations and, 170

Sensorimotor, defined, 299

Sensorimotor development, 88

Sensory control, lack of, 63

Sensory deprivation, 90
Sensory Integration International (Los Angeles), 219
Sensory integration therapy, 218–219. *See also* Therapy
Sensory skills, testing of, 102–103, 219
Sensory systems, stimulation of, 219
Sentence Completion Test, 105
Sentence Memory Test, 103
Sequencing, 26; auditory and visual, 27, 84; defined, 299
Sequential approach (to remedial reading), 213
Short attention span. *See* ADD
Siblings, 59; helping LD child, 183, 188, 190, 200; -LD child relationships, 51, 163, 167, 176, 187–189; tests of, 57
Silver, Larry, 26, 28, 30, 61, 164
Skeletal malformations, 80
Skills: academic, *see* Academic skills; basic, steps for acquiring, 182–185; compensatory, *see* Compensatory skills; information-processing, 83–84, 211; linguistic, 130; motor, *see* Kinesthetic skills; Motor skills (fine and gross); organizational, step-by-step strategies for learning, 182–185; sensory, testing of, 102–103; social, 130, 164, 189–193, 200 (*see also* Peer relationships)
Skills, teaching of, 181–201; consistency in, 183; environment and, 182–183; explicitness in, 182–183; patience/repetition in, 183, 188, 192, 214; rewards in, 183–184, 186; social, 164, 189–193. *See also* LD: REMEDIATION
Sleeter, Christine, 244
Slingerland, Beth, 215, 216
Slosson Drawing Coordination Test, 102
Smart Kids with School Problems (Vail), 31, 65
Smith, Sally, 21, 23, 52, 53, 157
Snyder, Russell, 244

Social control, lack of, 63. *See also* Emotional disorders; Peer relationships
Social history of LD child, 109
Social life of LD child, 167–172. *See also* Peer relationships; Skills, teaching of
"Social Life of LD Youngsters, The" (Bryans and Bryans), 176
Social maladjustment. *See* Emotional disorders
Social skills. *See* Skills; Skills, teaching of
Society Pays (Anderson), 172
"Soft signs" (of CNS dysfunction), 43–44
Somatosensory system, stimulation of, 219
Southern California sensory integration tests, 103, 219
Spatial orientation: Ayres Test of, 219; defined, 299; and disorientation, 30, 43, 205; and spatial reasoning, 130
Spaulding, Robert, 216
Special education: cost of, 141, 238; state offices for, 255–274
Specific Dyslexia (as category), 22
Specific language disabilities, 71. *See also* Dyslexia
Specific Learning Disability (SLD; as category), 22, 71, 137, 141; defined, 24, 138–139
Speech: defined, 299; and language tests, 102, 103–104
Speech problems, 59; articulation defects (as "soft sign"), 43; developmental, 48; therapy for, 219–220. *See also* Symbolism disorders
Spelling, 27, 55, 205
Sports, 196
Stanford-Binet Intelligence Scale, 100, 101; Hayes Adaptation of, 102
Stanine (scoring system), 116
Stevens, Suzanne, 95, 122, 204, 205, 232
Strauss, Alfred, 71–72, 74, 81, 83, 243
Strauss syndrome, 22, 72

Strephosymbolia, 21, 22; defined, 71, 299

Stuttering, 80

Success deprivation, 172. *See also* Self-image/self-esteem

Summer camps, 171; directories of, 293, 294

Support groups and services, 9, 175, 178, 189, 200, 237–239, 248–249; lists of, 251–274; PACs, 131–132. *See also* Organizations; Protection and advocacy services

Survival strategies, 181–201

Symbolism disorders, 30. *See also* Strephosymbolia

Symptoms. *See* Characteristics and symptoms

Syndrome, defined, 299

Systematic approach (to remedial reading), 213

Tactile, defined, 299

Tactile perception, 26

Tasks of Emotional Development test, 105

TD ("teaching disability"), 33

Teachers: cooperation of, with home teaching, 195; evaluation initiated by, 96, 99; LD children as perceived by, 169–170; parents' relationships with, 177; test given to, 101

Teaching. *See* Classroom; LD: REMEDIATION; Skills, teaching of; Therapy

Temper tantrums. *See* Emotional disorders

Temporal orientation: defined, 299; and time management by LD child, 184–185

Testosterone, 57, 75, 77–78, 79, 80

Tests, 97–114; achievement, 57, 99, 102, 104; administered to parents and teachers, 101; aptitude, 99, 102; auditory, 102, 103; of brain activity, 81–82, 240; and child-tester relationships, 111–112; criticisms of, 100, 128–130, 242; of development,

102–103, 105; diagnostic, 99; discrepancy of scores on, 31, 59, 101; documentation of, before therapy, 198; emotional development and personality, 104–106; evaluation and, *see* Evaluation; Evaluation meetings; intelligence, predictive, 237; intelligence and readiness, 59, 99, 100–102, 237; of LD siblings, 57; legal rights in, 113, 140; length of time for, 112, 113; native-language (non-English), 113; neurological, 97, 242; neuropsychological, 106; in occupational therapy, 218, 219; and "overtesting," dangers of, 150; perceptual development, 102–103, 219; personality, 104–106; physical examination, 97, 108–109; preschool, 112, 151; private services administering, 112–113, 150–151; projective, 105, 298; psychometric, 56, 59 and remediation, 210–211; scores of, 100, 115–116; spatial orientation, 219; speech and language, 103–104; standardized, 99, 116; visual perception-motor skill integration, 102, 103. *See also specific tests*

Their World (newsletter), 9

Thematic Apperception Test (TAT), 105

Therapy, 196–200, 203–204; allergy, 230; basic principles of, 206; behavioral, *see* Behavioral modification; cost of, 198; development, 202, 209, 217–224; drug, *see* Medication; family/parent, 175, 199, 200, 241; goals of, 199, 204–207; group, 199, 200; language, 220; LD child's feelings about, 198–199; legal right to, 197–198; occupational (OT), 218, 219, 220, 221; ocular, 222; orthomolecular, 228–230; patterning, 223–224; physical (PT), 219; sensory integration, 218–219; speech and

Therapy (*cont.*)
language, 219–220. *See also* LD:
REMEDIATION
Thorazine, 226
Thyroid disorders, 80
Tic, defined, 299
Time management. *See* Temporal
orientation
Tofranil, 226
Toxins, environmental, 90, 230
Toys to Grow On (company), 183
Trace elements, 229–230
Tranquilizers, 225–226
Truss, Orian, 230
Tutoring. *See* LD: REMEDIATION
Twins, dyslexia in, 79

U.S. Department of Education, 238;
LD defined by, 18, 90; Office for
Special Education, 56, 156; regional
offices, 254–255; state Special
Education offices, 255–274
University of Iowa, 212
University of Miami Medical School,
81, 239
University of North Carolina School
of Medicine, 61
University of Pittsburgh, 221
University of Tennessee, 45; Center
for Health and Sciences, 106

Vail, Priscilla, 31, 65, 91, 165, 246
Valium, 226
Velten, Emmett, 15
Verbalizing: symbolism disorders and,
30; verbal disinhibition, 64. *See also*
Speech problems
Verbal memory. *See* Memory
disorders (auditory or verbal)
Vestibular, defined, 299
Vestibular system: disorders of, 88,
222–223; stimulation of, 219
Vigilance Tests, 106
Vineland Social Maturity Scale, 102
Vision problems, 88, 97; ocular

therapy and, 222; tests for, 102, 103;
and tinted lenses, 89, 222
Visual: abstraction, 27; agnosia (as
"soft sign"), 43; discrimination,
defined, 299; memory (long- and
short-term), *see* Memory disorders;
motor skills, 84; perception, 26, 299;
perception, tests and program for,
102, 103, 220; perceptual disorders,
24, 26, 29–30; reception, 30;
sequencing, 27, 84
Visuomotor coordination: defined,
299; problems, 210, 220
Vitamins: deficiencies in, 90, 229; and
megavitamins, 230–231
Vocabulary, defined, 299
Vocabulary tests, 102, 104

Waysider (as category), 22
Wechsler Intelligence Scale for
Children. *See* WISC
Weiss, Helen Ginandes and Martin S.,
194
Wepman Auditory Discrimination
Test, 103, 104
Werner, H., 243, 244
Whole-word approach to reading. *See*
Reading
Wide Range Achievement Test, 102,
104
WISC (Wechsler Intelligence Scale for
Children), 59, 100, 128; WISC-R
(Revised), 31, 101, 129
Wisconsin Card Sort Test, 106
Withdrawal, 50
Woodcock Reading Mastery Tests, 104
"Word blindness," 18, 22, 69, 70, 71
Write-to-Read project, 215
Writing Road to Reading program,
216
Written expression: as basic skill, 42;
expressive motor disorders and, 30;
inversion in, 297; problems to watch
for, 55–56. *See also* Spelling

"Yeast theory," 230